JE   '09

D0010059

WITHDRAWN

DecideBetter!

Improve Your Life Through Better Decisions

For a **Better Life**

Micheal E. McGrath

Mount Laurel Library
100 Walt Whitman Avenue
Mount Laurel, NJ 08054-9539
856-234-7319
www.mtlaurel.lib.nj.us

motivation
PUBLISHING
Addison, Texas

DecideBetter! For a Better Life

Copyright © 2008 by Michael E. McGrath.

All rights reserved.

Printed in the United States of America.

No part of this publication may be reproduced, stored in a retrieval system, or transmitted in any form or by any means — electronic, mechanical, photocopying, recording, or otherwise — except for brief quotations in printed reviews, without the prior written permission of the publisher.

For more information, visit www.MotivationPublishing.com

Library of Congress Control Number: 2008927500

ISBN-13: 978-1-935112-00-6
First Edition

This book is dedicated to all of my family, friends, and business associates who worked with me to make decisions throughout my life and shared the results of those decisions, both good and bad.

Contents

Acknowledgments

In some ways this book and DecideBetter! have been lifelong pursuits. Hundreds, maybe thousands, of people shaped my insights on decisions. About five years ago, I started writing this book to help others make better decisions, but I put it aside a couple of times before completing it and launching Decide-Better! I have many people to thank for completing this book; it has been a real team effort.

First and foremost, I want to acknowledge the collaboration on this book with my son Chris. Once the project became serious, he jumped in to help with the writing, but this evolved to creating great chapter ideas for the book. Chris is responsible for many of the final chapters selected for this book, and is a complete collaborator in its success. His talents are clearly reflected in the final product, and without his help I would still be writing. I've also enjoyed the personal experience of working with him on this project. I learned to appreciate the depth of his skills.

Second, I want to express my heartfelt appreciation to Jennifer Cary for not only her help in marketing and promoting DecideBetter!, but even more importantly, for inspiring me to restart this ambitious project and keep with it when I was unsure. She really saw the vision of DecideBetter!, and her enthusiasm for it was a major motivation for me to complete it. In addition, she applied her creativity and tremendous marketing talent to create DecideBetter!. Without her, this book may never have existed.

Third, I could not have done this without my invaluable assistant Trudi Pevehouse. Once in a while in life you find someone who has so much talent that she seems to be able to do everything needed. Trudi managed my schedule, managed all of the administrative tasks to create and operate DecideBetter!, did valuable editing for the book, and provided exceptional insights and opinions throughout the project. I found that she has many talents and is always there to do what has to be done. I'm not sure where we would be without her.

Several talented people helped to edit the manuscript. My dear friend Vicki Cooper edited much of the early versions of the book. Michael Lecky worked on editing some of the early chapters. Vince Scolero and Candace Hutto used their expert mastery of grammar and writing to provide the final edits.

I'd like to thank the talented people at Brand Mechanix for their creativity and graphics mastery. Others also contributed their talents, including our attorney Evan Fogelman, Allison Ratan, and Peter Cao, of Greg Booth and Associates, who did the photography for the book.

Throughout my life, I had the unique opportunity to work with many wonderful people who shared their experiences and helped me learn about decisions. I'm indebted to my partners at my former consulting firm, PRTM, especially Bob Rabin and Ted Pittiglio who I'll always remember for our experiences together. I'd also like to express my appreciation to my clients at PRTM: more than 1,000 executives and managers with whom I worked on some of the most challenging decisions.

In my leadership roles at i2 Technologies, Thomas Group, IDe, and SOLVation, I'm thankful for the support of the management teams and employees for helping make most decisions successful. My work on corporate boards with some great people at Entrust, SensAble Technologies, Atlantic Ventures, as well as i2 and Thomas Group, and others helped me to understand decision-making from a governance perspective. In my trustee and advisory roles in the non-profit sector at York Hospital, St. Michael's College, Aidmatrix Foundation, Berwick Academy, and Boston College, I collaborated with some wonderful people who added to my experiences in decisions.

As always, I'm deeply indebted to my family, especially Diane and Molly, for their support and tolerance. I'm not always the easiest person to live with when writing a book, and they not only put up with me, but they provided understanding, encouragement, ideas, and suggestions. Diane's different approach to decisions inspired me to explore the variety of ways people make decisions, which is a key theme of this book. Molly's creative ideas and her own writings encouraged me throughout the process. My entire family — Jill and Carmen, Mike and Sarah, Chris and Becca — also helped provide wonderful ideas and input for the book.

Finally, I'd like to thank all of the many people who use our DecideBetter! website to share the decisions they are facing. This always helps keep me grounded in the problems faced by so many people as they decide their way through life!

Michael

Introduction

The decisions that you make shape your life, and inevitably, making better decisions will make your life better. This is the simple principle behind DecideBetter!.

Successful people are where they are because of good decisions. While sometimes they just make lucky decisions, most of the time they're successful because they make better decisions. Other people struggle in life. Sometimes, these people may just have bad luck, but much of the time, they're struggling because they make poor choices.

Think about your life and how you got to where you are today. Think about how your life would be different if you made better decisions. Would you have different relationships? Would you have a different career? Would you be at a different income level? Would you have different interests? Would you live in a different location or in a different house? Would you owe less money or have more? And — most importantly — do you think these different decisions would make you happier?

Like most people, you've probably made both good and bad decisions throughout your life. You realize that you can improve your decisions. What you may or may not know, however, is that by working on your decision skills, you can make more good decisions and fewer bad ones. That's the purpose of Decide Better!: To help you improve your decisions. Everybody can benefit from better decisions. Making better decisions is universal. It's more important than improving your eating habits, exercise, or other skills. It affects all aspects of your life.

Whether you realize it or not, you will make almost a million decisions in your lifetime. Most of them are routine: What time are you going to get up in the morning? What will you wear? What are you going to have for breakfast? Other decisions that you make are not so routine. These include decisions about your professional life: What career do you want to pursue? Where will you work, and when will you decide to change jobs? Will you start your own business? There are also important decisions that you'll make concerning your relationships and family: Whom will you date? Will you break up with someone? Whom will you marry? Will you have children? As a parent, you will make countless decisions for your children. Will you make the right decisions for them?

Throughout your life, you will make numerous purchase decisions: Will you buy or sell a house? Will you buy a new car? What investments will you make? What clothes and gifts will you buy? Where will you go on vacation? While these decisions may not shape your life in a major way, they will have an impact on the quality of your life. There are many decisions you'll make regarding your health. Whether you recognize it or not, you decide — possibly by default — how much you weigh and how much you exercise. You decide if you will smoke and risk the medical consequences. At some point in your life, you'll be confronted with serious medical decisions, and you may need to decide on a course of treatment, including what doctor to see and what medical advice to follow.

There are many types of decisions, and there is no one simple formula for them all. The situations we find ourselves in when we need to make decisions are broad. The circumstances surrounding our decisions vary widely. And people tend to approach decisions differently, depending on their personality and previous experiences. So I don't promote one universal approach to making decisions. *DecideBetter! for a Better Life* offers a series of chapters that cover a wide range of decision situations. Some provide insights into how decisions are made by helping you to better understand how to approach decisions, so you can see your decision-making strengths, weaknesses, and quirks. Others will help you understand why certain people approach decisions differently than you do. The book provides concrete advice and practical tips for making better decisions, and gives you a roadmap — or process — for making the best life-shaping decisions.

You may find some of these lessons immediately useful when you read each chapter. Others you may find useful at some point in the future when you're facing a new decision, and you realize it's just like one of the chapters you read in the book. Yet others you may have wished you'd read before, so you could have avoided bad decisions in your past. You may want to keep it as a handy reference guide for the future and review it again from time to time to see what lessons apply as your life unfolds. As you read the book, you may think that a particular lesson or two may be helpful for your friends, family, or coworkers. Don't hesitate to give the book to others. You could actually be giving them the gift of better decisions and a better life. Isn't that a great gift?

You can read this book in one of two ways: from beginning to end or by randomly reading chapters that look interesting. Although there are a few exceptions, you don't need to read the chapters sequentially. As you may have already noticed, each chapter is only a few pages long, and each one contains an individual lesson, technique, or insight into better decisions. You can read it on the go, as you have time; it's written to fit into your busy lifestyle.

Each chapter is designed to be entertaining as well as educational, using anecdotes, stories, and examples to teach each lesson. History is filled with great stories and examples of exciting and horrible decisions. Except for the historical references, the names and details of examples used in the book are largely based on actual events and situations, but these have been fictionalized to better explain the lessons. Any resemblance to real people or real situations is coincidental. These examples do, however, tend to represent real situations, and many are disguised, modified, or composites of actual situations.

DecideBetter! is more than just a single book. It's a broad set of essential resources to help you make better decisions. The DecideBetter! website (www.DecideBetter.com) is the hub of these resources. Periodically, you will see references in this book to decision sheets, roadmaps, and other tools to help you. These are all available on the website, so feel free to download them when you want to use them.

This book is the first of a series of DecideBetter! books. Some will be focused on specific categories of decisions that you or those you know may face in different aspects of your lives. Some of the next books in the series, for example, will focus on helping college students, and those applying for college, to make better decisions; helping executives, managers, and all people involved in a wide-range of business activities to make better decisions at work; and, helping people make better relationship decisions.

People have asked me what makes me qualified to create DecideBetter!. I'm not sure anyone is really a master decision-maker, but I am an experienced decision-maker, having made more decisions than most others make. I don't want to imply that I've always made great decisions. I've probably made more bad decisions, in fact, than most people make. In my early education, I studied decision-making theory. In business, I've started six companies, some of which have succeeded and some of which have failed. I've consulted for more than 25 years to senior executives of more than 200 companies on strategy and decisions. Together with great business partners, we built one of the most successful management-consulting firms in the world, PRTM. At PRTM, I had the opportunity to create PACE™, which became the standard decision-making process for the best high-technology companies. Later in my career, I lead the successful turnaround of two public companies as CEO and executive chairman. I've also served on the board of directors of more than a dozen companies and non-profit organizations. All of these experiences have helped me to understand decision-making and the techniques that can be used to improve the outcome of important decisions — both in business and in life.

On the personal side, I've made many of the decisions people make in life with relationships, marriage, divorce, and raising four children. I've bought, built, and sold houses and made other major purchase decisions. I've made hundreds of investment decisions (probably more bad ones than good ones). I've faced important health decisions.

I've found that, over the years, people looked to me to help them make their major decisions. This has helped me reflect on what I've learned from my own experiences and how to share those experiences with others.

Perhaps most importantly, decision-making has been a fascination of mine over the last 20 years. I've been an avid observer of decisions, and I've strived to formulate common theories and understandings across decisions.

It is my humble goal to make the world a little better for a lot of people by helping them to make better decisions. I encourage you to look at decision-making as a skill that you can develop, improve, and become more proficient at. I hope the stories, lessons, techniques, tips, and guidelines of *DecideBetter! for a Better Life* help you make better decisions and have a better life.

Michael

Frog in Boiling Water

Y ou've no doubt heard the story of the frog in boiling water. If you drop a frog into boiling water, it immediately jumps out (or so the story goes). However, if you put a frog in a pot of room-temperature water, and then bring the water to a boil very, very slowly, the frog will stay in the water until it dies. It's an odd experiment that I have no intention of testing in my kitchen, but it's an apt metaphor for how people sometimes deal with slowly deteriorating situations.

When we are confronted with an abrupt negative change, we tend to react immediately and decisively. Coming in contact with a flame will cause us to pull away instantly to avoid getting burned. We don't think about it, we just react. Yet we will sit in the sun for hours and get badly burned. We know full well that we're getting burned, but we tend to sit there anyway, because there is no instantaneous sensation to trigger a decision to get out of harm's way.

> **It's the absence of decision triggers that causes people to miss opportunities.**

It's just this absence of decision triggers that causes people to miss opportunities or to get into trouble that could have been avoided. Fortunately, being smarter than frogs, we have the ability to create decision triggers for our own good. If we're sunbathing, for example, we might place an alarm clock deliberately out of reach and set it to go off every half hour. When it goes off, we have to get up, go over to it, and turn it off.

This triggers a decision: "Should I expose myself to another half hour of sun, or have I had enough?" Without the clock, deliberately placed at an inconvenient distance and annoying us every 30 minutes, we are likely to keep telling ourselves, "Just a few minutes more," and then a few minutes more after that, and so on, until it's too late. The time-to-get-out-of-the-sun decision trigger arrives the following morning when we turn over in bed and wince in pain. By then, it's too late to avoid the trouble.

The frog-in-boiling-water syndrome, as I like to call it, can arise in other, more serious, situations throughout our lives where we willfully ignore an increasingly dangerous situation. We tell ourselves that we'll do something about it "soon."

Take putting on weight as an example. Nobody decides to get fat, yet many people will just keep putting on more and more weight without doing anything about it. They keep telling themselves, "I'm going to lose some weight soon." Similarly, people don't make a conscious decision to keep smoking until they get lung cancer. They tell themselves, "I can stop anytime, and I will, but another day, or week, or month won't matter." So they remain like the frog in the pot, slowly burning up their lungs.

The frog-in-boiling-water syndrome doesn't apply just to self-destructive behaviors. It can also trap people facing important career decisions. This is the case for people who stubbornly remain in a job or occupation that isn't satisfying or isn't offering sufficient opportunities. Like the simmering frog, they stay where they are. They tell themselves that things might improve while knowing they won't, instead of changing

Remind yourself that you are too smart to be complacent about a steadily deteriorating situation.

employers or acquiring new professional skills. They may complain about the situation to others, but they never do anything about it. Many times, they find themselves trapped in a miserable, dead-end job, or worse, they lose their job without any updated skills to go forward in a more successful direction.

People stuck in deteriorating or stagnating relationships also fall prey to the frog-in-boiling-water syndrome. They are unhappy, but they just go on being unhappy without deciding to do anything to improve the relationship or to get out of it. Just like the frog, they stay where they are as the water slowly reaches the boiling point.

This syndrome can also trap people who are not in a relationship but would like to be. They do not take any action to help themselves meet someone, and the years pass. Slowly they lose their "window of opportunity" to meet a person who might become a lifetime partner.

Some people even believe that the frog-in-boiling-water syndrome applies to the way a society can ignore critical decisions. For example, we may be gradually depleting our limited resources without making any conscious decisions about replenishing them or slowing the depletion. Instead, we're letting the situation boil away until it becomes too late to preserve a sustainable environment. We may be creating global warming, yet we ignore or reject any solutions until our polar ice caps melt away, and we find our coastlines submerged. Likewise, as the economic gap between the lower and upper classes increases, we do nothing to avert the inevitable ramifications from such a gap. We sit in the water of our own apathy and denial without taking action.

Don't be like our friend, the simmering frog. You are smarter than the frog. Step back from time to time and take stock of situations in your life such as your health, your relationships, your career or job, your business, and your investments. Do this regularly. You might take stock on New Year's Day, your birthday, or quarterly. Set that alarm clock and put it someplace where you'll have to get up and go over to turn it off.

Remind yourself that you are too smart to be complacent about a steadily deteriorating situation.

Moreover, if you think a friend is falling into the boiling-frog syndrome, share this story. It might save a life.

Decision-Maker in Your Pocket

Believe it or not, if you have a coin in your pocket, you're in possession of a powerful decision-making device. Flipping a coin is a vastly underrated method for making decisions. It works well most of the time, but not for the reason that most people would imagine. Let me explain.

Here are some common decisions, ranging from the trivial to the critical, that we can be indecisive about. Should I order the Pinot Noir or the Cabernet? Which dress should I buy? Should I leave my comptroller position at Allied Amalgamated to accept the offer from Federal Fruit and Vegetable? While you may have weighed and reweighed the two choices, you still can't make up your mind. This technique works best when you have done all the analysis you can on a decision or when you don't have enough information to make a more thorough decision. You are at the end of your deliberation and are still having a difficult time choosing one option over the other.

It's time to flip that coin. Heads for one choice, tails for the other. But are you going to let chance determine your decision? You don't have to. The power of the decision-maker in your pocket is that you don't have to accept the result, but you can learn from it.

Watch your reaction the next time you flip a coin. After it lands, you immediately have a sense of having "won" or "lost" the coin toss, even though you had been prepared to accept the results when you decided to flip the coin. Once you've flipped the coin, if you don't like the result, simply throw it out like a dictator declaring null and void the result of his country's first democratic election. Why? For the same reason as the dictator: You don't like the result. Your dissatisfaction with the result of the coin toss points you straight to the decision you actually prefer.

The pocket decision-maker works so well because it forces you to confront your true feelings about the two decision options. The coin gives you an answer and directly confronts you with the decision it made for you. Immediately, you feel either comfortable with the outcome or uncomfortable with it. If you feel comfortable with the coin's decision, then go with it. If you think the coin gave you the wrong decision, and you begin to argue with yourself for the other outcome, then go with that other outcome.

The decision-maker in your pocket works by summoning your intuitive powers in the service of good judgment. Toss a coin, and the decision alternatives are suddenly vivid. On several occasions, tossing a coin put me in touch with what my intuition knew was right for me all along. Because of my propensity for analysis and the pressures of time and circumstance, however, I wasn't willing to accept my first choice without further "testing."

> **The pocket decision-maker works because it forces you to confront your true feelings about the two decision options.**

If we examine this technique analytically (I can't help myself), we see that the decision device (the coin) is programmed statistically to select either alternative with an equal probability. The only thing that I have found — and it is not a statistically valid sample — is that on many occasions people have a tendency to override the coin's selection and go with the alternative not selected by the coin. I'm not sure why, but it may be that they are not yet ready to make the decision. They will, therefore, react by refusing to accept the outcome of the coin toss, or they may learn that they simply have a reverse bias to the coin's selection.

If this happens to you, you might decide to keep flipping the coin until it comes up with the decision you like best. "I think I'll do the best of three flips of the coin . . . or maybe I'll do the best of five." Or maybe you decide that the first flip, or three flips, were really just "practice." These techniques work, because they are part of the learning process about how you really feel about a decision. Remember that the objective is to make the right decision, not to let the coin toss determine your life's path.

Some people like flipping the coin in the presence of others, which forces them to verbalize their reaction to the result. Articulating their reaction seems to help them make a better decision. Other people find that this is best done using a "lucky" coin, one that will always give them the correct decision. This coin has been tested by other decision-making tosses that they agreed with. The point is that the coin toss facilitates a process of finding out how and why we feel the way we do about something important to us. Whatever works.

You can also use the coin flip decision-making technique when someone wants you to make a decision that they don't want to make. By taking out a coin, flipping it, and giving them your decision, you make the point that they could have easily made this decision without you. It may also show them that you are not necessarily able to make the decision any better than they could have.

If you don't like my psychological explanation of why a coin can be a good decision aid, that's fine: Go ahead and accept the result of the toss. The coin has spoken! If it turns out to be the right decision, you now have a "lucky" coin. If not, you can blame the "unlucky" coin and throw it away or slip it into a rival's loose change.

*!*3

At Knifepoint

I n October 1988, I was on my way to Singapore and had a one-night layover in Los Angeles. Before I went to bed for the night, I decided to take a short walk down Century Boulevard between the Marriott and Hilton hotels. Soon after I started my walk, a car pulled up behind me on the sidewalk, and a passenger jumped out and headed for some newspaper boxes in front of me. He then turned and came at me with something that looked like a machete.

Since it was the night before Halloween, at first I thought that he was joking. I soon learned differently. As I turned to run, the driver of the car pulled the car around to block my escape. Before I knew what was happening, I found myself lying on my back on the sidewalk with a knife pointed at my chest. The mugger demanded that I give him my wallet.

Now I had to make a decision at knifepoint: Give the mugger my wallet or not. In that situation, I learned you don't really make a decision; you simply react. A reaction is not a logical response. It's typically driven by a strong emotion such as fear, anger, or love.

In my case, my dominant emotion was anger. I was angry with my assailants, angry with myself for being so stupid as to go for a walk alone, and angry with the people driving by. Century Boulevard is a major road, and dozens — perhaps hundreds — of cars passed me by. Nobody stopped or turned around to help.

In my anger, I responded by refusing to give the two men my wallet. Interestingly, this confused them. They didn't seem to know what to do. I could see the confusion in their eyes. I did try to yell for help once, but one assailant started to push the knife into my chest, so I decided that was not such a good idea.

They kept screaming at me to give them my wallet, and I kept screaming back, "No." (Actually their language and mine were a lot more colorful.) Eventually, I gave them a few dollars from my pocket, and they jumped into their car and sped away. I returned to the hotel, and the hotel clerk called the police. The police told me that these guys had done this more than 20 times over the last three weeks in that vicinity (something I would have appreciated knowing before I went for my innocent walk), and they thought that my refusal to give them my wallet might slow them down a little. That wasn't much comfort.

The lesson I learned from this incident is that when you are confronted by a threat like this that requires an immediate decision, you'll likely make the decision based on emotion and not logic. In hindsight, it would have been better for me to give them my wallet. I could easily have been severely injured or killed by these two guys, who the police told me were likely on drugs.

> When you are confronted by a threat that requires an immediate decision, you make an emotional decision, not a logical one.

A few weeks later, a close friend of mine, who is a Tae Kwon Do master, taught me a move to use the next time I found myself in this position. He said I should twist my body around, reach into my back pocket, and give my wallet to the mugger!

The moral of this story is that all decisions are not made in deliberate states of consciousness. Once a strong emotion takes control, you will react to that emotion. The emotion, not logic, determines the decision. I reacted in anger (and perhaps stubbornness) by refusing to give in. Had I reacted in fear, which was probably a more appropriate emotion, I would have quickly handed over my wallet.

Emotional reactions can take control over rational decisions when you are confronted by fear or other powerful emotional states. Someone may say something that angers you, and you respond in anger without thinking about, and rationally deciding, what to say or do. You can easily say something that you really didn't mean. In most cases, if you had time to decide your reaction, you would decide to do something differently.

Here's my advice if you make an emotional decision that you later regret: Simply apologize. Admit you acted irrationally and stupidly out of emotion and try to reverse your decision. If you are fortunate, you will be able to reverse it.

Next time I'm mugged at knifepoint — "Here's my wallet."

4

Yankee Gift Swap

Have you ever participated in a Yankee Gift Swap? A Yankee Gift Swap usually happens at a party when the host asks everyone to bring a wrapped gift for a gift exchange. The gifts are placed on a table, and each participant is randomly assigned a number that determines when it will be his turn to select one of the gifts. After he unwraps the one he chooses, he shows it to everyone else. He can then choose to keep the gift or swap it for one of the gifts previously opened by another person at the party. The person who opened the first gift has a chance at the end of the selection process to swap his gift for any of the others.

> **People tend to place a higher value on something that belongs to them than they would place on that same item if they had to choose to purchase it.**

I've participated in several of these swaps, and I'm always struck by the oddity that most people refuse to swap the gift they initially chose for one that they would have most likely preferred had all the gifts been displayed unwrapped on the table. It has made me wonder why people hold onto their first selection when better alternatives are available. Why is it that people tend to place a higher value on something that belongs to them than they would place on that same thing if they had to choose to purchase it?

Whatever the reason, people tend to be possessive about their possessions. In economic and psychological theory, this ownership bias is referred to as the "endowment effect." It describes the difference between the maximum price we are willing to pay to acquire something and the minimum price we would be willing to sell it for.

Essentially, the value of something increases when it becomes part of a person's "endowment." Classical economic theory holds that the difference between the two prices should be zero, or nearly zero. The willingness to pay for something should be equal to the willingness to accept an offer to sell it. Yet in situations where the endowment effect applies, the minimum acceptable selling price predictably exceeds the maximum acceptable purchase price. This suggests that the fact of ownership immediately "endows" the possession with extra value.

The endowment effect can make some types of decisions less rational. For example, I tend to become attached to particular stocks in my investment portfolio. I resist selling them even when I think they're overvalued.

Don't let the endowment premium influence you to make non-rational decisions.

In fact, I resist selling them at a price that I think would be ridiculous to pay to buy them. I also tend to place higher performance requirements on stocks I'm considering buying than on the ones I already own. Being too tolerant of one's "own" stocks and too critical and demanding of all the others opens the door to two types of losses: the losses from clinging irrationally to stocks that decline in value and the lost opportunities to acquire stronger or more promising stocks at favorable prices.

I've often had this experience with cars that I've owned over the years. Every time I'm ready to purchase a new car, I look into selling my existing car or trading it in to the dealer for a newer model. Inevitably, when I'm given an offer for my used car, it's much less money than I hoped to get for it. If the shoe was on the other foot, however, and I was the one purchasing a used car, I would not pay as much as I expected to receive as the seller.

In this way, I have had firsthand experience with the influence of "ownership rights" on the determination of value. In legal disputes, the endowment effect creates a gap that is sometimes hard to bridge. The person who is asked to give up something that he thinks he has a legal right to will value it higher than will the person who wants to buy that right.

I've been to four NFL Super Bowls and was fortunate enough to get my tickets at list price. I absolutely would not have paid the going market rate of $2,500 to $7,500 for a ticket similar to mine. Yet when someone asked if I would sell my ticket for this high market price, I wouldn't even consider it. I valued the ticket I already owned much more than I would be willing to pay for it.

Some research suggests that the endowment effect has more influence on people who have a strong aversion to loss than those who do not. For the former, there is a premium for this emotional attachment, and this premium increases the longer they hold onto something. Maybe this accounts for why so many people, when moving into a smaller home, put highly valued items into storage rather than letting them go. The value is an emotional value, not an economic one, and the price is sometimes very high when you consider the cumulative cost of storage over time.

There is also a smaller endowment premium for goods that have become commodities. Stocks are commodity products to a stockbroker. The broker has learned to be dispassionate about the buying and selling of stocks — much more so than the amateur investor. The premium that the broker puts on stocks diminishes as his market discipline and experience grow.

The endowment effect is routinely exploited in commerce. It's part of the rationale behind money-back guarantees. Retailers know that customers are not inclined to return something once they own it, even if they wouldn't buy it again at the same price. Automobile dealers apply this principle by letting potential customers take a test drive. Even the temporary ownership of a test drive can in some cases impart an endowment premium. Realtors have learned that people who put their homes on the market almost invariably expect a higher price than they would consider paying if they were prospective buyers.

The Yankee Gift Swap lesson and the endowment effect provide helpful insight into certain decision situations. Be aware of how this decision bias affects both your decisions and the decisions of others. It can be an important element of negotiations. Understand how various characteristics can create an endowment premium. Don't let the endowment premium influence you to make non-rational decisions — like holding onto stocks you own for too long. I've paid a high premium for this mistake on too many occasions.

5

Decision Deadlines

couple, who are friends of mine (at least until they read this), had great difficulty deciding on names for their three children. That's not usually a problem of any particular consequence, but it is in Austria, where their three children were born. Under Austrian law, parents must name their newborn child by noon of the fifth day following birth. Otherwise, the child is assigned a generic first name, and the parents need to go through a long legal process to change it.

With all three of their children, my friends waited until the fifth day before deciding on a name and filing the necessary legal papers. In the case of one child, they filed the name a few minutes before the stroke of noon. Why did this happen? In each case, my friends knew almost nine months in advance that they were going to have a baby, and in two of

> If deadlines cause you anxieties or mental blocks, it's time to change your relationship with them.

the three cases, they had known the baby's gender for months. Had there been no legal deadline for making a decision, I wonder if my friends might still have three nameless children. On the other hand, it's possible that the deadline contributed to my friends' indecision. Perhaps their anxiety over the deadline distracted them from concentrating on the task at hand.

If decision deadlines cause you anxieties or even lead to mental blocks, it's time to change your relationship with them. Deadlines are not our opponents. They can be good masters, and even better servants. Either way, they're on our side. They're trying to help us to accomplish more and get more out of life. Meeting deadlines with some room to spare is a wonderful way to reduce stress. That is why I think deadlines are friends worth cultivating.

Decision deadlines are often imposed from the external world, as was the case for my Austrian friends. To get the most out of decision deadlines, however, try creating some for yourself. Self-imposed deadlines have served me well in making decisions over the years. Sometimes, I set a deadline for making an important decision or taking an important action, but then I give myself an extension. On rare occasions, I've given myself two or even three extensions, but I've actually come to enjoy meeting my own decision deadlines.

Let's explore how decision deadlines can work for you. First, there's a real sense of satisfaction in controlling externally or internally generated deadlines, rather than always letting them control you. Many of my best decisions over the years have been within self-imposed deadlines. These deadlines have helped me create a mental focus and sense of urgency about the decision at hand.

But what if you fail to meet your own deadline? This failure may indicate that your criteria for the decision are not feasible and that you may need to reassess them. My Austrian friends experienced this when trying to choose the name for their third child. Since the father is American, the mother is Austrian, and they lived in Germany, they wanted a name that sounded good in German/Austrian as well as English. As their externally imposed deadline approached, they realized that accomplishing this task would be impossible for them so they changed their criteria, deciding instead to pick a name from a country that was located somewhere between Austria and the United States. After finding Icelandic names difficult to pronounce, they decided on an Irish name even though neither of them is of Irish descent.

My point is this: If you face an external decision deadline, think of it as your ally. "Act by midnight and get a $100 round-trip flight to Paris!" Do you want to go to Paris? Don't wait until 11:59 p.m. to decide because your watch might be a minute slow. If you face a decision with no specific external deadline, set one for yourself.

> **Deadlines can be good masters, and even better servants.**

The most important decisions of our lives are often of this deadline-specific type. Moreover, these decisions are perishable, which means that the day will come when it's too late to make them. They will have been made for us, slowly but surely, by default.

"What career should I pursue?" "Where do I want to live?" "Do I want to raise a family?" These aren't the kinds of decisions that you must make by noon of the fifth day from today. You won't be assigned a career or a home or a name if you miss the filing deadline. And that's the danger. These big, perishable decisions cry out for internal deadlines.

Where do you want to be in five years? You don't have five years to decide. Set an internal deadline for yourself to make a decision and then begin to execute it.

I've Been Framed

'Ve been framed. You've been framed. We've all been framed. I've even successfully framed others. But why am I bragging about something that sounds reprehensible? What I'm talking about isn't illegal, unethical, or immoral. It's decision-framing.

What does decision-framing mean? Our decisions are framed by the choices offered to us and by how those choices are presented. There are several varieties of framing, and you can often direct someone's decision by how you frame it. But the same can be done to you, so be on the lookout for decision-framing.

Decisions are framed by how choices are presented to us.

I learned long ago from selling management consulting projects that how you frame a project usually determines what the client ends up buying. For example, suppose a client is given a $500,000 project proposal. The client may well think that's an awful lot of money and balk at hiring you. So instead of presenting only one proposal, I found it was more effective to give the client three alternative project proposals at different price points — say, at $250,000, $500,000, and $750,000.

I can tell you from experience that the client will immediately focus on the value of the services each figure represents, rather than on the amount of money you're charging. I can further tell you that the client will choose the $500,000 project and feel good about it.

Why am I so confident about this? I've learned that given three graduated options, people will gravitate toward the middle option, so it's just a matter of placing the option you want the customer to choose between a cheaper and a costlier option. Happily, I can report that the middle option was almost always the best value for both my company and its clients.

Why do people gravitate toward the middle option? Perhaps they don't want to seem cheap by selecting the lowest-cost alternative or that it won't meet their needs. The highest-priced alternative is usually rejected as not being a good value. It may have some nice extras, but the customer reasons that those extras are probably not worth the additional money. Also, there's usually nothing of substance in the top option that isn't provided by the middle option.

It's likely that we were all taught the merits of the "happy medium" as children. Goldilocks continually selected the middle alternative, finding it "just right."

A rule of thumb for framing prices: If you use the highest-priced alternative as 100% of the value, then the lowest-priced alternative should contain 20% to 25% of the value for 33% of the price. The middle alternative should offer 80% of the value for 67% of the price. Again, the middle offers the best value because the alternatives were framed with that objective in mind. A carefully framed range of alternatives is a potent tool for inducing decisions in others. This type of framing doesn't always steer the decision-maker toward the middle, but it usually induces a decision in the framer's favor, one way or the other.

To test this theory, go to a major-chain hardware store and look at the rakes or shovels. You're likely to see three models labeled "Good," "Better," and "Best." You were just looking, but suddenly you're saying to yourself, "Hmm. Which one should

I get? One of them has to be right for me." You've been framed, albeit in a minor way. This "Three Bears" framing technique is used by purveyors of everything from management consulting services to vacation cruises to caskets. I've used it successfully to frame my children into making a decision — on their own — that I thought was best for them.

Another common form of framing is the discount game. People feel infinitely better about buying a piece of furniture that has been marked down by 25% to, let's say, $600, than they do about buying the same item for a list price of $600. The discount shifts the decision-maker's focus from the $600 cost to the $200 "savings." (Stage magicians call this tactic "misdirection.") This framing technique works so well that shoppers often think they're saving money rather than spending it.

Even colleges and universities use this form of framing. They use inflated list prices to frame students, few of whom ever end up paying the list price for a college education. Here's an example: A young man decides to attend College A because it has offered him a $10,000 scholarship — i.e., a $10,000 discount — from the list-price tuition of $30,000.

> **If you're being framed, ignore the frame and focus on the picture.**

College B, which is equal to College A in every educational respect, offered him only a $5,000 scholarship from its list-price tuition of $25,000. Although the net cost of attending both institutions is the same, the student thinks he is getting a better savings at College A.

Another framing technique takes advantage of emotional aversion. People tend to reject decision options that contain an explicitly negative consequence, but will select that same alternative if it is framed in positive terms. This principle has been proven through decision-making exercises such as the following: One hundred people are stranded and at imminent risk of dying. There are two possible plans for saving them. Under Plan A, half of the victims will live, and half will die, with 100% certainty. Under Plan B, there is a 50% chance of saving them all but a 50% chance of saving none. Leaving aside the moral agony intentionally built into this decision exercise, let's focus on how the framing of the two options affects the study subjects' decisions.

Cognitive experiments have repeatedly shown that most people will choose Plan A because of its positive framing (50 will live). The all-or-nothing alternative of Plan B is not so attractive. When Plan A is worded as "under Plan A, 50 will die," however, then most people will select Plan B. The outcome in Plan A is the same either way, but how it is framed profoundly changes the likelihood that it will be selected.

There are two sides to the framing game. Either someone is trying to frame you, or you're trying to frame someone. There are some offensive and defensive techniques that can help you get what you want from either situation. If you're doing the framing, frame the decision in positive terms and present multiple options, even if you have only one option in mind. Hold out a few carrots, or positive benefits of the options — not just the one you want to sell.

If you're the one being framed, ignore the frame and focus on the picture. Take the decision out of the context of the framed alternatives and reframe it around your own objectives. If the framer is offering you A, B, or C, your best choice might well be D, or none of the above. This is a great way to manipulate the outcome so that it meets your objectives.

Last, consider alternative ways to frame a decision before you make it. Sometimes, the best decision is not to make one. When you're being framed, make sure you realize it. For best results, when you're framing someone else, make sure he or she is not aware of being framed. As long as you're offering real value at reasonable prices, you can rest assured that you're playing fair.

7

Experience Counts

A successful businessman was once asked for the reasons behind his success. "Good decisions," he replied quickly. "And what was your secret to making good decisions?" asked the interviewer. The businessman thought about it briefly and then replied, "Experience." The interviewer asked him to be more specific. "What kind of experience?" "Experience from making bad decisions," came the response.

The point is not to make bad decisions intentionally but rather to learn from them. Bad decisions build an invaluable experience base that helps improve future decisions. Of course, good decisions also build an experience base, but we tend to learn more from our bad decisions, probably because they inflict costs — and often very expensive and painful costs. But we can recoup these costs in the future by learning how to make better decisions.

> While it is acceptable to make mistakes, it is unacceptable to make the same mistake twice.

After more than 30 years of business experience, I have a personal philosophy that, while it is acceptable to make mistakes, it is unacceptable to make the same mistake twice. Making the same mistake twice indicates a failure to apply your past experiences to your present decision-making. It's paying twice for the same bad decision.

All too often, when people make bad decisions, they get angry or depressed instead of constructively channeling their energy into learning from the experience. When you make a bad decision, ask yourself not just what you did wrong, but how you will make a similar decision differently in the future.

❶ Did you have the necessary information to make the decision before you made it?
❶ Did you make the decision prematurely or too late?
❶ Did you weigh the pros and cons of the decision appropriately?
❶ Did you learn something about yourself — perhaps your strengths or weaknesses or biases — that you didn't know previously?

These insights are exactly the kind of experience that the businessman in our story was talking about: The experience that helps us to do better the next time. Success is based on good decisions, which come from experience, which often comes from bad decisions. This is why we turn to our elders for decision advice. We instinctively understand the correlation between mistake-making and better decision-making.

Here's a simple example of learning from bad decisions. My friend John bought a new car. His old one had 120,000 miles on it from his long commute back and forth to work every day, and it was becoming costly to repair. When he went car shopping, he started looking at pickup trucks. He thought a truck would be helpful for his weekend furniture-making hobby and that his friends would think that it was cool. Secretly, he had always wanted a truck and thought that maybe this was the right time in his life to have one. He thought he negotiated a good price and good financing, so he reasoned that the truck wasn't too much more expensive than a car.

While John liked his new truck, he soon realized that he had made a bad decision. He commuted 100 miles to work every day and was now spending $150 a week on gas, compared to $85 a week for his car. John was on a tight budget, and he could not afford the additional fuel cost of $3,380 per year. He was furious with himself for not considering the gas mileage difference when he made his decision, but he resolved to learn from his mistake. That meant not just considering the cost of gas and financing when he bought his next car or truck, but also generalizing his experience even further. He now realized that it was important to understand not just the immediate costs, but the total costs over the long run when he made any future decisions that had a financial impact. This lesson was expensive, but John knew that he could look at the truck purchase as an "investment in learning."

You can learn from the bad decisions of others, which is an ideal way to gain experience.

If you are observant, you can also learn from the bad decisions of others, which is an ideal way to gain experience. This way of learning provides pure profit at no expense to you. So to grow wiser, learn from your decisions — especially your bad decisions. Never pay twice for the same mistake. It's a waste of experience.

8

Of Two Minds

ave you ever been of two minds about a decision? You feel so strongly about two alternatives that you are unable to choose between them. Being of two minds on a decision, however, is different from simply being unable to choose between two alternatives. When you are of two minds, you are enthusiastic about both alternatives. You can argue each alternative strongly, and you really do want each of them.

Generally, when you are of two minds, you favor one alternative because of a strongly held belief, and you favor the other because of a different belief that you hold just as strongly. The problem isn't just choosing one; it's rejecting one of your strongly held values or beliefs in order to make a decision in favor of another.

Here's a relatively simple example of being of two minds: Sam and Patty were very close friends with another couple who entered into an ugly divorce. Sam and Patty liked each of their friends equally and didn't want to take sides in the breakup. They were of two minds on whom to support. They wanted to support each of them because they were both very close friends, but they didn't want to turn against the other. As the divorce got uglier, they were increasingly pushed into making a decision on whom to support. When they discussed what to do, they realized that they were in agreement that they were of two minds.

Here's another example: Tom was presented with a great opportunity to become CEO of a company, but to take the job, he'd have to relocate from Dallas to Chicago. He believed that this was the best possible career opportunity he could have and was enthusiastic about it. Yet he also believed in the importance of family, and he would need to uproot his family or leave them behind and commute home to see them. He was drawn to the opportunity and against hurting his family. He was of two minds on taking the job.

In Les Miserables, by Victor Hugo, the main character, Jean Valjean, served many years in prison for stealing a loaf of bread, and after his release, he broke his parole and disappeared. Later, in disguise, he successfully became the owner of a factory and the mayor of a small town but was then confronted with a dilemma. He had promised a woman on her deathbed that he would find and raise her daughter, but at the same time, an innocent man was accused of being the fugitive. Jean Valjean would need to confess to keep the other man from going to prison but then would not be able to keep his promise to the dying woman. He struggled with his decision because he was of two minds. He believed that he had a duty to fulfill his promise to the woman on her deathbed, which he could not do if he were sent back to prison. He also strongly believed that it was unfair for an innocent man to go to prison in his place.

Sometimes, the only way to resolve such a situation is to find a creative alternative to selecting either one or the other. Jean Valjean confessed so the innocent man would go free, but then he escaped to fulfill his promise to the woman. He spent the rest of his life in hiding, giving up his factory and his position as mayor. He found a creative solution to accomplish both contradictory beliefs.

Public policy sometimes puts people in situations of two minds. For instance, some people were of two minds at the initiation of the war in Iraq. While they believed strongly that America should do everything to stop terrorism, they also believed that war should be avoided unless absolutely necessary.

Some people are of two minds about major social issues. For example, on the issue of abortion, they might be pro-life because of a strong belief about the right to human life but pro-choice because of other deeply held principles such as the right of an individual to make decisions about her own life.

> In "of two minds" decisions, we are confronted with a choice between two rights.

In decisions of two minds, we are not confronted with a choice between right and wrong. We are confronted with a choice between two rights.

So, what to do? The first thing you need to do is to recognize that you are of two minds about a decision. This self-awareness gives you a better sense of the decision you face and enables you to approach it in the most appropriate way. In some cases, including issues of social or public policy, you may not need to make a decision. You can just remain of two minds. But your thinking eventually may evolve toward one position over the other.

In the case of the couple whose friends split up, they decided not to choose. They determined it was better not to support either of their friends than to turn on the other. As was the case with Jean Valjean, you might be able to come up with a creative alternative or middle course of action somewhere between your two minds. Otherwise, you will need to choose one strongly held belief over the other.

You should find some comfort in knowing that your choice of one alternative does not mean you are completely rejecting your belief in the other. It's just a situation of conflicting beliefs. Life sometimes confronts us with these "of-two-minds" dilemmas.

!9

Hobson's Choice

ave you ever heard of a "Hobson's choice"? When you are facing a Hobson's choice, you are being asked to either accept what's offered to you or pass it by and not accept anything. In other words, take it or leave it.

The term "Hobson's choice" actually refers to Thomas Hobson, a stable owner from the turn of the 17th century in Cambridge, England, who rented horses out, largely to students from Cambridge University. In an effort to keep the horses in the best possible shape, he set a rotating order for which horse would be rented when, placing the next horse that he was going to rent out nearest to the stable door. When someone came to rent a horse, they were told they could rent one, but it had to be the one closest to the door. While they may have wanted another horse for any of a variety of valid reasons (they needed a stronger horse or a faster horse, for example), Thomas Hobson told them they could either rent the one at the door or go away with no horse. Hence, Hobson's choice — you can either take it or leave it.

> A Hobson's choice is always posed by someone to intentionally create a difficult decision.

Perhaps the most well-known Hobson's choice in somewhat more recent history was Henry Ford's famous Ford Model T car. Henry Ford sold the car by saying that you could buy it in any color you wanted, as long as it was black. In reality, while the car could have been produced in any color, due to the overwhelming number of orders, they all were painted black for production efficiency.

We face Hobson's choices in many areas of our lives, from career decisions to financial decisions to personal decisions. A Hobson's choice is always posed by someone else to intentionally create that difficult decision. These choices are presented in situations where one person holds some type of power over the other person, and they require the other person to accept the one option they are presenting if they want anything.

One common place where Hobson's choices are presented is between parents and children. Parents start setting up their children to face Hobson's choices almost from the time they are born and continue to do this to them throughout their entire childhoods. When children are still young, parents provide them with only one option for a lot of things. What do you want for dinner? Chicken fingers? The child may want macaroni and cheese, but since you don't have time to make this tonight, you simply tell them that they can only have chicken fingers. The only alternative? Go to bed hungry. They take the chicken fingers.

When the child is older, they may ask to borrow the car, and more specifically, the nicer car. You, of course, don't want them driving your brand new car, so you tell them that if they want to borrow the car, they can take the minivan. They may complain, but in the end, if they want to go out with their friends, they will end up taking the one choice you've given them.

We also face this type of decision in our relationships with others, both with our friends and with our significant others, often at a turning point for the relationship. You may be upset with one of your friends, for example, because they have a habit that you don't like or because they've done something that made you very upset with them. When you confront them about it, they may say to you that they refuse to change, so you can either accept them for who they are, or your friendship will be over. It can also happen the other way around, with you demanding they change or apologize to you, and if they don't, you will cease being their friend.

A similar situation may happen with someone who you're dating. I see this quite often with people who ask me for decision-making advice. Emma is a good example of this. She was in her late 30s and had been dating her boyfriend, Phil, for the last five years. She feels like the relationship has come a long way and believes that they are in love, but she's not sure that it's leading up to marriage. She realizes that she's reaching the end of her prime for marrying someone and having a family. So she decides that she is going to tell Phil that she wants to get married and have children within the next few years. She realizes that he may not be ready, but she's presenting him with a Hobson's choice — either move the relationship to the next level or end it. If Phil is not the one she's going to marry and have a family with, then she needs to move on and begin to find the person who she can spend the rest of her life with. Now the decision is Phil's to make.

> Presenting someone else with a Hobson's choice is sometimes the best course of action when you want someone to do something and you're not sure they'll do it.

There are risks in forcing someone into a Hobson's choice decision. Some people resent being presented with an ultimatum and will reject it on that basis alone. For example, Phil could resent the ultimatum and break up with Emma because of it, even though he intended to marry her. Presenting someone with a Hobson's choice can also force him to make a wrong decision. What if Phil gives in to marry Emma even if it's not the right decision, and they would have both seen that had they waited a while longer?

You really have very few options when you face a Hobson's choice requiring you to take it or leave it. Are you going to accept what's being offered to you, or are you going to reject it? So which will it be? You can approach this decision much like you approach other decisions that you face. If you do a cost-benefit analysis, you can begin to understand what the costs and benefits are of accepting your only option, then compare it to the costs and benefits of not taking that option. You can then either select the option presented or no option at all based upon this cost-benefit analysis.

You should also realize that sometimes it's your decision to present someone else with a Hobson's choice, as Emma did to Phil. This is often the best course of action when you want someone to do something, and you're not sure if they'll do it. It can also be a great way for you to use your power when someone wants something from you, but you want to limit the choices you give them, as happens with parents giving one choice to their children.

So the next time you face a Hobson's choice, are you going to take it or leave it?

🖉10

Personality Type

H ave you ever wondered why you and your spouse or
friends or business associates make decisions in such
different ways? People make decisions very differently,
to say the least. It's not that one person approaches a decision
correctly, and the other doesn't. Sometimes two people arrive
at the same decision through almost opposite mental processes.
How does that happen? The reason is that our decision processes reflect our personalities. Different computers, if you will,
have different operating systems. Similarly, personality shapes
decision-making.

The theory of cognitive differences based on personality
type, posited by C.G. Jung in 1923, was expanded into a widely
used diagnostic framework by Katherine Briggs and her daughter, Isabel Myers. The Myers-Briggs Type Indicator (MBTI), as
the framework is now known, is a very useful method for determining personality-based differences in how we process information and make decisions.

The MBTI defines four dimensions of personality characteristics. The first characteristic separates Extroverts (E) from
Introverts (I). Extroverts prefer to reach decisions interactively,
i.e., by talking them through with others. They believe in con-

sensus through discussion, assuming that all involved will express their opinions. When people do not express an opinion, the Extrovert interprets their silence as consent.

Introverts tend to prefer private reflection. Here's an example of how the decision paths of an Extrovert and an Introvert differ in the context of a marriage. The Extrovert partner says, "It might be interesting to spend the weekend in the city," where she's merely thinking out loud about that alternative and is soliciting her husband's opinion. But her Introvert husband interprets this as his wife's unilateral decision to spend the weekend in the city and then gets upset because "she wasn't even willing to discuss it. I wanted to go to the lake and fish, but it didn't matter what I wanted."

As for the second Myers-Briggs characteristic, Sensors (S) prefer to make decisions by looking at detailed facts and are very reluctant to reach a conclusion until they have all of the facts they think they need. Sensors, in other words, are analytical and wary of analytical error. In contrast, Intuitives (N) typically want to consider

> Our differing personalities shape our differing decision-making styles.

alternatives at a less detailed level so they can make decisions within the context of the broader picture. Let's use an example: A couple, S and N, are trying to decide where to go on vacation next year. S begins by gathering details on various destinations, including hotels, costs, weather, and things to do. N becomes resentful of too much detail being kicked in his face and pushes back. "We're getting way ahead of ourselves," he says. "We might want to go skiing, we might want to sit on a beach, and we might want to go on an adventure trip. We haven't even discussed all of the different things we might do, and you're plunging into all kinds of details." To this S responds, "How can we decide where to go or what to do without knowing any facts? If we don't have any information, we're just daydreaming." An S and an N must both be very tolerant in order to make a decision together.

The third major characteristic in the Myers-Briggs Type Indicator involves Thinkers (T) and Feelers (F). Thinkers don't mind making the difficult decisions themselves and can't understand why anyone gets upset about things that aren't relevant to the decision. They tackle decisions in a detached fashion and tend to be objective and logical. They rarely become emotionally involved in a decision, but rather they assume that every problem has a correct answer and that it's their business to figure out what the answer is. In contrast, Feelers believe that a good decision must take into account the feelings of others. They are driven by interpersonal involvement and tend to approach decisions subjectively, trying to incorporate all of the expressed points of view into a decision that will prove acceptable to everyone.

Even though they go about it very differently, Thinkers and Feelers don't always end up in disagreement. Let's look at two parents, T and F, deciding whether to buy a car for their teenage son. T may be against it because of the cost, or he may be in favor of it because it would free him from having to drive his son to activities or from having to share the family car. F may be against it because their other children would feel like their brother is getting preferential treatment, thus stirring up trouble within the family. She may be in favor of it because having his own car would build a sense of independence and self-reliance in her son. Although many of the MBTI personality categories are not related to gender, the Thinking/Feeling personality characteristic tends to be. Thinkers tend to be male, and Feelers female. (This isn't to say that females don't think, and that males don't feel.)

> The more we take our personalities into account, the better we'll be at making good decisions.

The final personality characteristic influences how easy or difficult people find decision-making. Judgers (J) are decisive and deliberate; they reach decisions without much stress. They like everything organized and controlled, and they readily make the decisions necessary to achieve and maintain control. At their extreme, Judgers will sometimes make uninformed and even indefensible decisions just to get them done. Furthermore, they may find it very difficult to change a decision once they've made it — even an obviously bad one. Perceivers (P), on the other hand, don't want to be forced to make a decision. They like to keep their options open. Making decisions causes them anxiety. They prefer to take a wait-and-see approach. At their extreme, Perceivers are virtually incapable of making decisions and make every decision more complicated than it needs to be.

When a J and a P face a joint decision, it's often an exercise in mutual exasperation. Suppose that J and P are considering a new car. J is ready to make a decision after looking at only a few cars or maybe even after seeing just one. J wants to "get it done." P reacts negatively to this, to say the least. "How can you make such a rash decision?" she says. "We've barely looked at any cars at all." J will respond, "We don't need to look at every car on the face of the earth. This is the right car for us." Even if J gets his way for now, the battle may not be over. Tomorrow or the next day, P may insist that they reconsider things. Although J can't tolerate indecision, P dreads making a mistake. In other words, they're paralyzed.

The better we understand our personalities and the more we take them into account, the better we'll be at making good decisions. I've determined that I'm an ENTJ, based on the Myers-Briggs Type Indicator, and I can work to improve my decision-making by understanding this. What about you? Think about yourself and the people you make decisions with in terms of the four personality dimensions. If you do, you may be able to frame the choices in a way that is more agreeable to your companion or colleague. At the very least, you'll be a more tolerant and tolerable decision-making partner.

11

The Two-Step

For important group decisions, I've found that a two-step process works best. In step one, the group meets to become familiar with the decision. What is it that needs to be decided? What is the goal or the desired end result? What factors need to be considered? The purpose of this first meeting, in other words, is for the members of the group to arrive at a set of common understandings about the decision that needs to be made.

You can't make a decision about a problem unless you understand the nature of the decision that needs to be made, and in a group decision, the group needs to come to a common understanding of the decision and the alternatives.

Step two, which should commence with a second meeting, is the time when the decision is actually made. In between these two meetings, group members have time to think about the problem and to talk it over with one another or with anyone else they think might have some insights. Perhaps there have been some disagreements among the group members that also need to be explored and resolved. When the group meets a second time, it will usually make a much better decision than it would have made if it had tried to make the decision at its first meeting.

Let's look at an example from the corporate world. The chairman of the board of a company gets a phone call from the CEO. "We have this huge opportunity, but we don't have the capital to jump on it. Can you get us the money?" If the chairman is any good, several questions immediately occur to him. Is the opportunity really that fantastic? If so, is the cost rational for the business? Is it the right opportunity for this business? Can we raise the money in the necessary timeframe?

The chairman decides to do the two-step. He calls a board meeting, and the CEO's proposal is put on the table. "We need to decide on this," says the chairman, "but not at this meeting. Today, we're here just to look at it and agree on a list of the issues involved. I ask you not to jump to any conclusions." For the next few hours, the board and the management team examine the nature of the opportunity, the potential capital needs, and the different alternatives for raising the money. Again, the objective is to understand and frame the decision, not to make it.

A list of assumptions and alternatives takes shape. The group revises some of the assumptions and changes the alternatives by adding a new one and deleting two that are not attractive. The new alternative is made possible because of a change in the original estimates. The group ends the meeting with agreement on the definition of the capital needs and the feasible alternatives for achieving the end result. It also identifies some additional analysis and information it wants from the management team prior to the second meeting.

> You can't make a decision about a problem unless you understand the nature of the decision.

For the next two weeks, the board members do their homework. They receive and examine the financial estimates they asked for. They do some independent research. They discuss it by phone. They rack their brains. They have a few arguments. When the date for the second meeting arrives, they're ready to make a truly informed decision. Instead of being combative, the decision meeting is quiet and courteous. A common understanding of the issues and a sharing of viewpoints, has led to a consensus or something close to it. The board's decision might prove right or wrong, but it's the highest-quality decision they're capable of making at this time.

The two-step works best with small groups rather than large, deliberative bodies. It can work well for families facing major decisions, such as the medical treatment of a family member or moving the family to a new city to take a new job. I've even used the two-step process myself to make personal decisions. By that I mean properly defining the problem in my head, assigning myself a set period of time for study and analysis, and then making my decision when the time's up.

There are several reasons why a two-step decision-making process is better than a one-step decision-making process. Two-step decisions are better structured. The group making the decision has the opportunity to consider the decision and structure the alternatives. This almost always results in a better definition of the alternatives. Two-step decisions are generally better because they're better understood. Those making them are better prepared. The two-step process prevents people from rushing straight past the question in their desperation for arriving at the answer. It arrests the rush to judgment.

Two-step participants, who thought they knew the answer at the first meeting, often change their minds by the time of the decision meeting. Of course, there isn't always time for the two-step. It tends to be too time consuming for tactical decisions, but it's invaluable for critical, long-term decisions. If time is short, even an hour of group preparation followed by a couple of days of deliberation can make a big difference in decision quality.

Identifying and using the two-step is a leadership responsibility. The leader of the group needs to institute this process for major decisions and to do so early enough for the process to be applied across two meetings. This is the key. The two-step process requires decisions to be addressed earlier rather than at the last minute. You need to anticipate the upcoming need to make a decision and get an early start on making it.

The next time your management team, non-profit board, civic organization — or even your family — faces a big decision, try the two-step. Get your objectives and understanding straight, go think about what you've learned, and then reconvene to make the decision. It couldn't be simpler — or saner.

12

Batting Average

In baseball, batters don't get a hit every time they're at bat and certainly not every time they are thrown a pitch. The percentage of time that they do get a hit based on the number of times they are at bat is called their batting average, and the higher their batting average is, the more often they get a hit when at bat.

The same is true in making decisions. You are not expected to make a good decision every time you're faced with one. The percentage of time that you "get a hit" with the decisions you make is what I like to call your decision "batting average." Better batters have a higher batting average, just as you can be a better "decider" if you have a better decision batting average.

Perhaps even more important, the best batters hit for a higher average when it matters more — when the game is on the line, maybe with two outs in the bottom of the ninth inning with the bases loaded. This can be applied to decision-making in the same way — you should make better decisions when it matters the most.

Batters continually work on increasing their batting averages by understanding their tendencies and mistakes and with continued practice. So, too, can you as a decider continually work to improve your decision average by understanding your tendencies and mistakes and by practicing. How can you practice? By determining how you're going to approach and make the less important decisions before you're faced with the most important ones.

All batters tend to hit certain pitches better than others. Some easily hit a fastball, for example, but can't hit a curveball. You probably also make certain types of decisions better than others. You may make good career decisions but poor relationship decisions.

You should try to measure your decision batting average, at least generally, and then work to improve that average. What percentage of the decisions you make are good decisions? 90%? 70%? 50%? 30%? According to a DecideBetter! poll of more than 1,000 people, 53% believe that they make good decisions more than 80% of the time, while 23% believe that they make good decisions only 65% to 80% of the time, and 18% believe that they make good decisions only 30% to 60% of the

> Would you bench yourself in your personal and professional decision-making? Not if you practice and come to the plate prepared.

time. Interestingly, 6% believe that they make good decisions less than 30% of the time. What do you think your good decision batting average is?

Most people, 74% to be precise, believe that they make better decisions than other people. It is statistically impossible for this entire group to make better decisions than others in the sample. So you probably think that your decision average is better than others. Is it really? Or do you just think it is? How do you do when it really counts — on the most important life-changing decisions that you face? Do you still think you make better decisions than others?

When it comes to your good-decision average in important situations, how do you do? According to this poll, only 10% feel that they've never made a wrong decision in the most important decisions of their lives. So if you regret making a bad decision when it really mattered, you are in a big group with 90% of the population. If that's the case, you need to work on your decision-making, so you can improve your decision average.

Probably the most value in examining your decision batting average comes from understanding how well you do with different types of decisions. Try rating yourself on the following categories of decisions by assigning yourself a good-decision average for each:

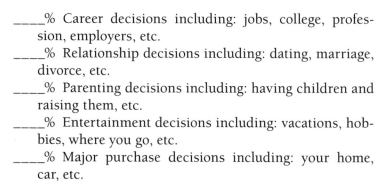

____% Career decisions including: jobs, college, profession, employers, etc.

____% Relationship decisions including: dating, marriage, divorce, etc.

____% Parenting decisions including: having children and raising them, etc.

____% Entertainment decisions including: vacations, hobbies, where you go, etc.

____% Major purchase decisions including: your home, car, etc.

Once you give yourself an average in each of these categories, step back and look at it. How do you feel about each category? Would your life be better if you had a better batting average in some of these categories? What are you going to do about it?

My suggestion is to first look at what decisions you do well on and what decisions you do poorly on and then strive for improvement. Just like a batter in baseball, begin by understanding your decision tendencies and mistakes — how you make your decisions — then practice to make them better.

Facing an important batting situation against a particular pitcher without first practicing your swing to maximize your chances against that pitcher's best pitches would get you benched. If the pitcher you're facing pitches curveballs 75% of the time, wouldn't it make sense to practice hitting curveballs before you face that pitcher? Likewise, if you're facing a curveball decision, practice making that type of decision at batting practice before you face that type of decision on gameday.

Would you bench yourself in your personal and professional decision-making? Not if you practice and come to the plate prepared.

13

Changing Lanes

Don't you hate it when you're late for work, and you come upon someone going slow in the fast lane on the highway? We've all encountered this, probably on both sides of the problem. I know I've been caught going slow in the fast lane, causing the guy behind me to become irate and to ruthlessly flash his headlights at me to move. I've also been the one doing the flashing when someone in front of me was going much too slow, clearly driving in the wrong lane.

While this example applies to driving, it also provides us a metaphor for how we make our decisions and how we live our lives. The lesson that can be learned from this is that you need to live your life in the correct lane — and make your decisions accordingly. You need to decide to live your life in the lane that best suits you at any given point in your life. Sometimes you need to be in the fast lane, and other times you need to be in the slow lane. Most of the time, you probably need to be — or think you need to be — in the middle lane.

> **You don't need to remain in the same decision lane throughout your life. Sometimes you need to change lanes.**

This lesson can apply to many parts of your life and to many of the decisions that you make every day. It can apply to financial decisions, relationship decisions, career decisions, and really, most other decisions in your life.

Do you live your life financially in the correct lane? Many people decide to live in the fast lane or the slow lane financially when they should probably have decided to live in the middle lane. How about your relationships? Did you make a decision to rush into a relationship when you should have taken it slower?

Paul's decisions are an example of regularly making bad decisions on which lane to be in. He has a good job, makes pretty good money, and is generally happy. He is very extravagant in his lifestyle — he eats out at expensive restaurants many nights, he has two very nice cars, and he often travels for pleasure. Though he lives a good life, he constantly makes decisions about spending money at a rate faster than he earns it. He's making decisions that place him in the wrong lane. While Paul was making decisions that put him in the fast lane, he was going faster than he should have. He should have decided to live in the middle lane, at least at this point in his life.

Other people decide to live in the slow lane, not spending any money unnecessarily and saving every single penny they can. While that is not a bad decision to make, if they decide to live their entire lives in the slow lane, they may just let life pass them by.

> The speed at which life approaches you changes, and you need to actively decide when and how to change the speed at which you approach it back.

Ellen provides us with an example of being in the wrong relationship lane. Relationship decisions require both people to be driving in the same lane. Otherwise, there is bound to be an accident. Ellen was dating a guy for several months, and she started to get serious with him. She began to think that maybe he was the one with whom she would marry and settle down.

Ellen couldn't tell if her boyfriend was in the same place as she was in the relationship and couldn't decide whether she should talk to him about it and find out how serious he was. So she spoke with several of her friends about it, and they said to take it slow and not to rush into things. She kept her feelings to herself for a while, taking the advice of her friends, but then she decided that she was tired of waiting to see what her boyfriend thought. She decided it was time to ask him if they could move in together.

The next evening, when they went out to dinner, she brought it up. She wanted to move in with him. From the moment she said the words, she could tell that he wasn't in the same lane. He would no longer look her directly in the eyes. He started to perspire and became red in the face. It was clear what was happening — Ellen had decided to move faster than her boyfriend was ready for. They were in different lanes on the relationship highway, and she was passing him by. They ended up breaking up the next day, and Ellen was very distraught about it. She decided that she would take things more slowly with the next guy she became serious with.

When you're in the fast decision lane, you make decisions quickly, so you can travel fast in that lane. You need to be prepared to make quick decisions, have the resources to back up these decisions, and accept the risks of being in the fast lane. In the slow lane, you don't get as far in the same amount of time, but you have less risk and more time to be deliberate in your decisions.

You don't need to remain in the same decision lane, however, throughout your life. In fact, you may decide that it's necessary to change lanes often, as it suits your needs and your current situation. Changing lanes can be healthy for you, just as it sometimes makes sense to change lanes on the highway. Periodically, you should examine the lane you're in and make a decision as to whether you should stay where you are, move into a slower lane, or move into a faster lane. The speed at which life approaches you changes too, and you need to actively decide when and how to change your speed and lane as a result.

Look at the different decisions in your life — your career, your family, your relationships, your financial situation, etc. Are you in the proper lane and making decisions at the right pace to stay in that lane?

14

Checkmate

When you're in the middle of playing a great game of chess and you've got your opponent on the run, would you trade your knight for his rook? How about for a pawn? Would you trade your queen for his?

A good game of chess is a lot like life in that the decisions we make now have consequences for our futures. If you move your queen in a seemingly meaningless way, how do you know that you won't be in checkmate in three moves? You need to look ahead and predict what your opponent is going to do. If you move one of your pawns up one space and inadvertently open up a way for your opponent's queen to fill the gap and take your knight, you'll feel like quite the fool for not having seen it coming.

> In life, you may feel like quite the fool for not thinking ahead for some of the decisions you make.

Likewise in life, you may feel like quite the fool for not thinking ahead for some of the decisions you make. A good chess player looks five or even six moves ahead, predicting how his opponent is likely to react to his decision and then deciding what he will do in turn to respond to his opponent's move. This requires predicting a very large number of potential moves and countermoves.

How do you anticipate what your adversary is going to do? If you set your opponent up to make a particular move, are you certain he's going to take it? Perhaps you missed something, and he's going to make a move that puts you in a precarious situation? If he has three different moves that he could take, what would you do in each of those circumstances? If he does take one of those three moves and you make your move in response, what will be the options for your opponent at that point? If you can imagine that you have three choices of what move to make, then your opponent has three options in response, and so on. If you plan far enough ahead for four moves, there are 6,561 different possible outcomes.

Anticipating what someone else is going to do is important for successful decision-making in your life, particularly when you're in an adversarial situation with someone else. When I bought my first house, for example, I was very interested in buying it, but I didn't want to simply pay the price the sellers were asking because I thought I could get them to sell it for less. So I was involved in a situation similar to a chess game. If I made an offer of 15% below the asking price, would they just walk away or would they decide to counteroffer by reducing the asking price? I did some research, and the asking price was reasonable, but the sellers were motivated to sell since they were relocating quickly for a new job. I decided to offer 13% less, anticipating that this was close enough for them to counteroffer. They decided to make a counteroffer of 6% less, and then I decided to make an offer at a 10% discount to lessen the gap. At that point it was close enough for us to decide to split the difference, and I bought the house for 8% below the asking price.

> Anticipating what someone else is going to do is important for successful decision-making in your life.

In business, I've applied this technique of anticipating how an adversary was going to react to a decision just as I would in a good game of chess. This happened, for example, in deciding to take legal action against companies for violating patents that my company owned. These companies were clearly violating our patents, and I needed to decide whether or not we would file a lawsuit against them. If I did, what would they decide to do in return? Would they propose to settle it before litigation? Would they fight it with a long and drawn-out court battle that would cost our company millions in legal fees — perhaps even more than we would gain back in penalties assuming we won the suit? Would they counter sue and say that we were violating some of their patents? It became a very interesting game of chess. In fact, it was several games of chess played simultaneously. I had to look at each company as an individual case and make a decision on what to do for each of them.

Ultimately, based on a long look at what the potential reaction of each company would be and what the likely outcome of each action would be, I made decisions for each of my games of chess. In two of them, we proceeded with filing lawsuits, which were ultimately successful without inordinate legal fees. In two others, we decided that because of the enormous legal departments and very large patent holdings of these two companies, we would not go the entire way toward filing a formal lawsuit. We did, however, leave open the option to do so at another point in the future.

Thinking ahead of the potential response to your decisions and how you will then in turn react applies to situations other than those with adversaries. In relationships, for example, you may be considering a decision designed to get a reaction from the other person. Maybe you met someone and want to ask her out for a date. How would she react if you decided to call her right away? What about if you waited a week? How would she react if you sent her flowers before you called?

In a way, relationships are a series of chess moves. You decide to make a move with the expectation that the other person will then make a decision about the next move. You, in turn, will need to decide how to respond to that move. The better you can anticipate the other person's decision, the more likely your relationship decisions will progress in the direction you want them to go. Then you have them in checkmate.

The ability to anticipate the reaction to your decisions applies in many life decisions, just as it does in chess. After all, you don't want to find yourself put into checkmate because you failed to anticipate how someone would react to your decision. To prevent this, think several moves ahead!

15

See If It Fits

"**I** wish I'd known at the time what a bad decision I was making." Have you ever said that to yourself? What if I told you that you could have known? How? It's simple, although it takes a bit of imagination and some mental effort.

When you're facing a major decision, here is a successful technique that I use to avoid making the wrong decision and to be more comfortable with the decision I make. I make a tentative decision and try it on for a while to see if it fits — just as you would test-drive a car before deciding to buy it or try on clothes before deciding to purchase them. Because you are just trying your decision on, keep it to yourself, simulating the results in your mind and watching your reactions to see if you want to keep the decision or toss it out as you would something that does not fit well.

> **When you face a major decision, make a tentative decision and try it for a while to see if it fits.**

If you feel comfortable with your decision, you can metaphorically cut off the tags and throw away the receipt. This means you can "make it official" by announcing it and acting on it. Just as you wouldn't buy expensive clothes from a store with a strict "No Returns" policy without first trying them on, why would you make a decision that is going to have indelible consequences without checking to see if it fits?

If the fit is wrong, the style doesn't become you, or you decide that you just plain don't like the decision you've tried on, then no harm done. You were only imagining it over a few days or weeks. Try on a different decision. You can try on as many as time permits.

What do I mean by imagining it? You can imagine that you have the job or experience or thing you want and then study your feelings about what you have. Here's an example: A friend of mine strongly considered running for governor of his state. He wasn't sure if he would like being governor or if he would be any good at it. So for a month he tried the governorship on for size. Through the media, he closely followed the current governor's schedule, activities, and announcements. At the end of each day, he mentally put himself through the governor's paces: confronting the issues, taking positions on various pieces of legislation, answering in his own mind the questions of reporters, mentally giving speeches to specific groups, and trying to feel what it would be like to make the rounds of public appearances. After a month in the gubernatorial flight simulator of this exercise, my friend realized that he didn't like being governor, and therefore, wouldn't pursue it.

This technique can also be applied on a trial basis. My oldest daughter told her husband that she wanted a convertible, and he thought about buying her one. But first he wisely rented one for the weekend. She loved it and drove it around all weekend, even taking me for a ride. By the end of the weekend, though, she got bored with it and decided that she didn't want a convertible all of the time. By seeing if it fit before making a decision, they saved a lot of money by not buying what would have been a mistake. Instead, they agreed to rent a convertible every once

> **More often than not, bad decisions are made when you fail to try them on before you buy them.**

in a while if they wanted to. This technique can be applied to similar decisions, such as buying a second home or a boat.

The bigger or more life-changing the decision, the more important it is to see if it fits before making it. If you're considering getting married, stop and consider the specific ways in which your life would be different, starting today. What would you be doing today, or not be doing, if you were married? Try on the "marriage" every day for a while, and you'll at least get some idea of whether it fits you or not.

If you're considering having children, start by thinking about how this morning, this evening or this weekend would be different if you were a parent. It may be helpful to observe and listen to parents with children of different ages and mentally put yourself through their paces for a few weeks. How would you have answered that child's question or dealt with that particular problem or misbehavior? What would you do if your child had to stay home sick? Does this dry-run parenthood feel rewarding, or do you feel yourself wanting out?

I've also found that see-if-it-fits method often works well for many business decisions. Suppose, for example, you need to decide whom to promote to an open management position. You have two candidates in mind, both outwardly qualified, but very different. From experience, you have a fairly good sense of both candidates' strengths, weaknesses, and personalities. You understand how they react and operate. Go ahead and make a decision, but keep it to yourself. As you go through the following days or weeks, extrapolate your pick's performance in the context of the situations that arise.

How would the person you've mentally promoted have dealt with these situations? If the person you've privately earmarked for promotion performs well in your mind, announce the promotion. If not, then listen to your misgivings because they're trying to tell you something. You may want to try taking the other candidate for a promotion test drive.

Like all decision techniques, see-if-it-fits has limitations. Obviously, extrapolation won't give you clairvoyance. The technique works only for an individual, or possibly for a very small and trusted group, such as a couple making a decision on having children. Otherwise, it's all but impossible to keep the dry-run decision a secret, and before you know it, it becomes a *fait accompli* — and you'll find you've bought something that you may not have wanted. There's a big difference between a private decision that you changed before anyone knew about it and a decision that people think you changed after you made it.

A tight decision deadline can also limit the technique's usefulness. See-if-it-fits requires some time to simulate, so you may want to begin thinking about upcoming decisions earlier. But insufficient time is rarely a good reason for making bad life-changing decisions. More often than not, the mistake was buying them without trying them on.

Next time you have a major decision to make, see if you have the time for a fitting, and if the shoe fits, wear it.

!16

Against All Odds

I f I asked you to pick a number between one and five and agreed to pay you $25 if you guessed correctly, but you need to pay $1 to play, would you accept? If I agreed to pay you $5 for a correct guess, would you play? How about if I agreed to pay you $2.50? In each case, you can play as many times as you like, at $1 per chance. The $25 payoff is obviously too good to pass up. You'll end up winning an average of $5 each time you play ($25 divided by five, since the chances are one in five that you'll guess the correct number), and it costs you only $1.

At a $5 payoff, there's no advantage either way. You'll end up winning an average of $5 per five tries. Not much of a game. At $2.50 for a correct guess, you'll eventually pay $5 for every $2.50 you win. A law of probability called "regression to the mean" ensures all five outcomes over the long run. It's the law that built Las Vegas.

Gambling is an odd form of decision-making in that there is a statistically precise outcome. In most casino-type games, the odds are that you will lose 1% to 3% over the long run. This average is referred to as the house edge. In games such as black-jack, the house edge is generally less than 1%. For roulette, the house edge is approximately 3%, depending on the rules and the wheel. Over the long run, you can have fun playing the games, and it will cost you 1% to 3% of the amount you play with.

State lotteries give themselves a house edge that leaves casino owners green with envy. Typically, only a little more than 50 cents of every dollar taken in by state lotteries is paid out as prize money (Massachusetts lottery, 69%; Texas lottery, 58%; New York lottery, 57%; British national lottery, 45%).

The odds of guessing six correct numbers out of 36 possible numbers are one in two million. You would need to play a given sequence of numbers two million times to have a rational expectation of winning. And, when you did, you would win back only half of the money you'd paid to play. The chance of picking six correct numbers out of 50 is one in 15 million.

> Too often people make decisions that are against all odds because they don't understand the mathematics of probabilities.

So why do tens of millions of people play the lottery even though the odds are so bad and only half is given back as prize money? There is a saying that mathematicians don't gamble, so could it be that people play because they don't understand the odds? Perhaps, but if this is the reason, then state lotteries must be one of the most immoral gimmicks to raise taxes gained from people who don't understand the underlying odds of the game. At least casinos pay out the majority of the money as winnings.

Gambling, especially state lotteries, illustrates a broader failure of decision-making. Too often, people make decisions that are "against all odds" because they do not understand the mathematics of probabilities.

For example, Sally and Matt thought they could make a "bundle of money" in the stock market in 2000 by investing in hot Internet stocks. So they took their entire life's savings and even took out a second mortgage on their house to invest in several high-risk Internet stocks. Unfortunately, when the market crashed, they lost all of their savings and were then burdened with the second mortgage. They didn't understand the odds of their investment decision before they made it. These were high-risk investments that had a much greater chance of dropping than increasing, but they did not consider this risk in their investment decision.

Most decisions involve unknowns that affect the outcome, but with some, there are probabilities involved. If you are deciding to make an offer to purchase a house, you need to consider the odds that the offer would be accepted. If you are making an offer to hire a new employee, you need to assess the odds that the candidate would accept the terms of the offer. Paying more in either of these cases increases the odds but obviously costs more.

When making a decision where the outcome is dependent on something else — even chance — be sure to understand the probabilities. Calculate the likely outcome mathematically before deciding. You could decide to take a chance or rely on luck, but it is inexcusable not to consider the probabilities of the outcomes.

Even though the results over the long-term are mathematically determined, I cannot deny that luck plays a role. For some reason, I always win a big payoff ($500 to $1,200) at dollar slot machines in the first 15 minutes I play. I have had this experience almost 20 times, including a recent visit to Las Vegas, where I won $1,200, $800 and $1,000 on three consecutive days — each in the first 15 minutes. If I play longer than 15 minutes, I always lose. I've never won after 15 minutes. I guess this is not statistically likely, so it must be luck.

Always consider the results of a risky decision — and be careful about gambling on something where the likelihood of winning is against all odds.

17

Lost at Sea

Decisions made by teams are often better than those made by individuals, simply because the collective experience and brainpower of a team frequently trump the smarts of one person. Some people, however, need to be convinced of this. There's a team-based decision-making exercise called "Lost at Sea" that I have used for many years in teaching project teams the advantages of collective problem-solving.

Here's the scenario: You and five friends are in the middle of the South Pacific on a boat that has caught fire and is beginning to sink. There's a raft on board, equipped with oars, and it's large enough to hold you and the other passengers (your co-partici-pants in the exercise). The wheel-house, however, has gone up in flames along with the ship's com-pass and, sad to say, the captain,

> **Decisions made by teams are often better than those made by individuals.**

who was the only person on board who knew the boat's loca-tion. Beyond some matches and dollar bills that a few people have in their pockets, you have to identify the most important survival items and load them onto the raft before the boat goes down.

Participants are given a list of 15 items they can take and are told to prioritize them. First, each participant prioritizes the list individually. Then the team works together to prioritize the list. At the end of the exercise, the lists prioritized by the individual participants and the list prepared by the team are compared to the U.S. Coast Guard's prioritization of the list. The list prepared by the team invariably comes closer to the Coast Guard's priorities than any of the lists individually created by the participants.

If you'd like to try the exercise alone, here is the list of available items. The Coast Guard's prioritized list is provided in the key at the end of the chapter, but don't read it yet if you want to try it on your own first.

1. Five-gallon container of water
2. Fifteen feet of nylon rope
3. Fishing kit
4. Mosquito net
5. Pacific Ocean map
6. One case of emergency food rations
7. Two boxes of chocolate bars
8. Shark repellent
9. Shaving mirror
10. Sextant (a device used to determine latitude and longitude)
11. Floating seat cushion
12. Two-gallon can of oil-gasoline mixture
13. Transistor radio
14. Twenty square feet of opaque plastic
15. One quart of 160-proof Puerto Rican rum

The Lost-at-Sea exercise demonstrates the advantage of team thinking over individual thinking, but it works for two situational reasons. First, everyone has exactly the same objective: survival. There are no individual agendas. Nobody is worrying about getting individual credit or looking good. Nobody is worried about having to work harder than the others. Nobody is reluctant to speak up, because everyone's life is on the line.

Second, since nobody in the group has any experience in this situation (unless they've survived a shipwreck or have already been through the exercise), no one person is in a position to claim authority. Everyone's ideas and thinking have equal validity, at least initially.

It's interesting to observe a group hammering out its priorities. Often, the group will plunge straight into reordering the listed items, only to pull back when they realize that the first thing to consider is the situation, not the list.

For example, after some discussion, the team will realize that their only hope is to be found by rescuers. Even if they knew where they were, what difference would it make? How far could they row in the middle of the Pacific on five gallons of water? So much for the map and sextant. The immediate danger is death from dehydration and solar exposure, and their only hope is to be found within a few days at most. Hence, all the items that might be useful in the longer term are worthless. It often takes the thinking of several people to put this all together. (To make any of this meaningful, you need to contrast the lists that individuals typically come up with to those that groups come up with.)

This exercise must be used judiciously in team training, because there are circumstances under which group decisions fail. (We'll look at the pitfalls of consensus decision-making in another chapter.) The objectives of the individuals on decision teams are not always aligned, and sometimes some of the team's members have much more experience and should have a greater voice.

Families also make team-based decisions. Parents and their children, for example, may discuss alternatives for vacations, with each expressing their thoughts on the alternatives. The family discussion can identify issues and opportunities that might otherwise have been overlooked. This can be quite effective as long as everyone realizes that he or she may have individual objectives, and that in the end, the parents who are funding the vacation have the final decision based on the cost of the vacation.

If you are ever lost at sea — literally or metaphorically — please remember that team-based decisions can be lifesavers.

Answer Key: 9, 12, 1, 6, 14, 7, 3, 2, 11, 8, 15, 13, 5, 4, 10

18

When Consensus Works

A re consensus decisions superior or inferior to individual decisions? It really depends on two sets of motives: the motives for making a consensus decision in the first place and the individual motives of the participants. If the goal is to bring diverse knowledge, skills, and insights to bear, and if the participants all have the same goal — to arrive at the best possible decision — then consensus can produce excellent decisions.

But when consensus decision-making is an attempt to satisfy everyone involved — or, more accurately, to placate everyone involved — then the process dissolves into a competition, often resulting in a worse decision than the best-informed person would have made alone.

I've seen firsthand how consensus decision-making can lead to a terrible result. A particular company employed consensus decision-making to determine the specifications of a new product it wanted to develop. The Engineering VP wanted to incorporate a hot new technology to make the product "edgy." The Market-

> **Consensus decision-making can prove to be very useful, but it can also be frequently misapplied.**

ing VP wanted to include a long list of features from a major competitor's product. The CFO wanted some changes for the sake of cost reduction. Around and around they went.

In the end, they all got a little of what they wanted, but what they all got was a hopelessly compromised product. It was late to market because of the bug-infested new technology. Its performance was slow because so many features had been stuffed in. The quality was second rate because of the penny-pinching.

We constantly see the downside of consensus decision-making in the realm of politics. Every year, the United States Congress passes a series of spending bills, which collectively comprises the federal budget. Too often, however, Members of Congress support or decline to support a spending bill based on what's in it for them and their districts or states. They cram each one full of spending for special interests, bloating the costs. If these provisions are stripped from it, Members of Congress will oppose the bills. No wonder so many bills are little more than political bone-dispensing machines.

> The dynamics of arriving at a consensus decision enable everyone contributing to the decision to own it.

The problem is not that consensus decision-making is bad. It can, in fact, often prove to be very useful. The problem is that it is frequently misapplied. The goal is not to make everyone happy but to arrive at the best decision based on the experience and talents of those involved. Over my years of consulting, I have found the following principles helpful in making better consensus decisions.

❶ Understand what consensus means. To reach a consensus decision means to reach a general agreement that a majority of the decision-makers believe is the best one for all concerned. A consensus agreement does not mean a uniformity of opinion or a solution that makes everyone happy. The goal is to arrive at the best decision, not one that is acceptable because it satisfies everyone's personal agenda.

❶ Keep the decision group small. Consensus decisions are practical only in a group of approximately four to eight. A smaller group than this may be easier to manage, but it may be missing expertise on some aspect of the problem to be solved. A decision complex enough to warrant a consensus process warrants a complete and well-rounded decision team. Too many participants, however, and the group tends to become a debating society rather than a decision team.

❶ Pick the right people. Skill, experience, and judgment are obviously important to the decision group, but so is compatibility. A disruptive personality or two strongly clashing personalities can poison the process.

❶ Establish guidelines on the scope and process of the decision-making. Groups that make effective consensus decisions usually establish guidelines up front on how they will operate. Agreeing on a few basic rules of the road can prevent accidents and traffic snarls. (The two-step decision process described in an earlier chapter is highly recommended.)

❶ Realize that some opinions are more equal than others are. Everyone's opinion should not be equally valued on every issue. Opinions of those who are more experienced or skilled in some issues should carry more weight. The process is not an exercise in democracy.

❶ Be prepared. Each member of the decision-making group must get up to speed on the issues prior to the final decision meeting. If some members of the team do their homework, while others don't, there is bound to be conflict. Someone with a knowledgeable and carefully considered position will not take kindly to off-the-cuff opinions from ill-prepared participants.

❶ Apply consensus decision-making to the right types of decisions. Consensus decision-making is more appropriate for strategic (what to do) than tactical (how to do it) decisions. It's particularly suited to "go/no go" decisions; for example, where a project team formally proposes a new product to a company's management and asks for permission to commence the design process. Group brainstorming should not be confused with consensus decision-making. They're entirely different in both purpose and process.

The dynamics of arriving at a consensus decision do more than shape better decisions. They enable everyone contributing to the decision to "own it;" to form a commitment to the decision and its implementation. Consensus decision-making is a very adult process. Unlike the political process, it isn't about who gets what. It's about the decision group doing its collective best for the common good. Everyone, in the end, can live with the right decision because they know it has been arrived at after thorough consideration of alternatives, benefits and risks.

19

Indecision Married
with a Lack of Vision

I
n their 1980s hit song "Everybody Wants to Rule the World," the group Tears for Fears sang the lyrics, "I can't stand this indecision married with a lack of vision." They capture what may be the worst combination of decisional deficits: with no goal or plan for the future, there is no basis for deciding what to do next.

Without a set of future goals to guide present decisions, you're making a decision largely at random. If you have no destination in mind, there's no wrong direction to take, right? While this approach may work well when you're on vacation and have the leisure time to explore a new place by wandering around with no agenda or expectation, it is a poor approach to making important decisions that will drastically affect your life.

Some people live their entire lives this way. They often fall into two categories: very unusual people and very unhappy people. The former is exemplified by a man named Heinz Stucke, who has been wandering the world on his bicycle for the past 44 years. He has ridden 335,000 miles at last count and has visited 211 countries. He lives off of donations from his many admirers. But for every person like Heinz, there are innumerable other people living unhappy and unfulfilled lives because they never set any goals, and thus have nothing to guide their decisions.

There's no doubt that goal setting and goal-oriented decision-making come more naturally to some people than to others. The businesses I have been in — management consulting and high-tech software development — attract very goal-oriented and goal-driven people. They have professional objectives, financial objectives, and even domestic objectives, and they can tell you where they intend to be at age 30, age 35 and age 40. They "plan the work, then work the plan," to invoke the business expression.

I'm well aware that not everyone is like that. Some of the most creative, insightful, and interesting people I've known were people who freely admitted that they didn't know what the future would hold for them. They live for today. But it's my experience that the older such people become, the more they regret not having made any plans or more purposeful decisions.

Let me give you a concrete example: Tom and Gail graduated together in the same high school class. Gail had a clear vision of what she wanted from life. She wanted to become a doctor and to have a family. She realized that this meant, first of all, getting into a good college because pre-med programs are very selective. That knowledge drove her to work hard in high school. A high-profile college admitted her, and she applied herself to getting good grades in order to get into the medical school of her choice. And on it went. She worked hard so that she would have options at each decision stage. In medical school, she chose a specialty where she could avoid working around the clock. She joined a medical practice that gave her the flexibility to raise a family. Her life didn't go exactly as she envisioned — she had

> **Some people embrace decisions; some pathologically avoid them.**

an unhappy first marriage — but at age 40 she was very happy with her life.

Tom, on the other hand, was arguably much brighter than Gail. He breezed through high school and got extremely high SAT scores. He was accepted by three prestigious colleges, but he deferred because he wasn't sure what he wanted to do. He worked odd jobs for several years and took a few college classes. But since he had to pay for them out-of-pocket and had rent and car payments to make, he stopped going. Tom became a curio: a startlingly intelligent and well-read guy who never really amounted to anything. He helped a friend write his doctoral dissertation while clerking at a convenience store. He went to his favorite bar a couple of evenings a week and routinely defeated the contestants on the TV show "Jeopardy." Everyone bought him drinks afterward. He liked children but his girlfriend didn't, so they didn't have any.

Tom and Gail both achieved their visions of the future. Some people gleefully embrace decisions. Some pathologically avoid them. Some people are naturally goal-oriented and some are inclined to wander. To tell you the truth, I'd sooner be stuck in an elevator with Tom than with Gail. (I'm certain we would have a more interesting conversation.) But when all is said and done, it's obvious that Gail made her dreams come true. Tom was left to wonder what he might have become had he had a better vision and made better decisions. He clearly didn't realize his own potential. He wasn't as fulfilled or happy as Gail was.

Major life decisions come at us in chronological order, each leading to the next. Each decision opens and closes pathways, and there is no way to soften that fact. We need to consider our choices carefully, but even prior to that, we need to understand what life choices mean — not just for now, but for the future.

Indecision can stem from many reasons, but for future-shaping decisions — whether by individuals or businesses — indecision is truly married with a lack of vision. The corollary is that future-shaping decisions are married to a clear vision. Have you envisioned your future and what you'd like it to hold for you? Once you do, some of those hard-to-make decisions will be easier and will move you closer to making your dreams come true.

!20

Unintended Consequences

I went to dinner with some friends recently, and when I pulled into the restaurant parking lot, it was almost empty. I remarked jokingly, "I wonder what is the safest parking place," and then I actually parked in what I thought was the safest spot. When we came out after dinner, the lot was still empty, but someone had smashed into the back of my car. I then realized that people used the parking lot to turn around in and my car was in their way.

Sometimes you make a decision that has consequences you had not considered. Sometimes you can even make what you think is an insignificant decision that has significant, unexpected consequences. You obviously would have made a different decision if you had any inkling of what might have happened.

On the morning of his inauguration, President William Henry Harrison awoke to a cold, rainy January day. At age 65, he was elected to be the ninth president of the United States after a difficult campaign against the incumbent president, Martin Van Buren. He considered wearing his overcoat and hat as he gave his inauguration speech, but he wanted to create a good first impression and show the American people that he was healthy.

So despite the rain and cold, he removed his hat and coat to deliver one of the longest inaugural speeches on record. This seemed like a good decision at the time, but it had some severe unintended consequences. Harrison immediately became sick and then shortly after came down with pneumonia. One month later, he died. His term in office remains the shortest of any president to date. Had he considered that this unintended consequence was possible, he most likely would have worn his hat and coat and reduced the length of his speech.

Unintended consequences occur all of the time, often with what seems like the smallest decision. You may decide to stop at a store on the way home from work, and you get into a car accident when leaving the store. You could decide to go out with your friends instead of your boyfriend or girlfriend, and then he or she meets someone else and leaves you. You could decide to criticize an employee, and he or she quits shortly thereafter. You could decide to go skiing, and you break your leg. You could decide to drive after drinking too much and cause a fatal accident. The unintended consequences of our decisions are always present.

> Sometimes you can make what you think is an insignificant decision that has significant unexpected consequences.

In his book, *The Five People You Meet in Heaven*, Mitch Albom illustrates the unintended consequences that the main character, Eddie, had on the lives of others — consequences he was unaware of. One by one, Eddie's five people illuminate the unseen connections of his earthly life. His first encounter, for example, was with a man who died in an accident as an unintended consequence of Eddie's insignificant decision to chase after a ball in the road when he was a youngster. He realizes that you can have a life-changing effect on someone else even if you have not met him.

How should we consider, attempt to control, and react to the unintended consequences of our decisions? I divide unintended consequences into two categories: those that the prudent person could consider because they are possible and predictable and those that are virtually impossible to predict. The first category calls for careful consideration before making a decision. The second category is impossible to manage.

Someone who is surprised by an unintended consequence he or she should have considered makes a careless decision. William Henry Harrison should have considered the risk of getting ill from exposure to severe weather. The person who decides to drive after drinking too much should consider the potentially dangerous consequences he could have on others.

If I apply the prudent-person test to a situation, I am able to make a careful, rather than a careless, decision. While I was writing this chapter, for instance, I was supposed to be at church. But there was a New England blizzard outside, and I decided the unintended consequences were too severe to take the risk of driving.

But the unlucky person who had a car accident after stopping at the store on the way home from work could not have prudently considered the unintended consequence of the decision to stop at the store. Neither could I have realized that someone would back into my car in an empty parking lot.

Mitch Albom's young Eddie could not have considered that his decision to chase after a ball in the road would cause someone driving by to have an accident. If you try to consider all of the potential consequences of every decision you make, you may become unable to take any actions at all.

Some people may blame themselves when they may have injured someone else as an unintended consequence of their decisions. They might apply the prudent-person test to themselves. If the prudent person could have anticipated the consequence, then they were careless and must take the blame, but if the prudent person could not possibly have anticipated the outcome, then they cannot blame themselves.

> Someone who is surprised by an unintended consequence he or she should have considered makes a careless decision.

In economics, the concept of unintended consequences suggests that decisions of people and governments always have effects that are unanticipated. It is one of the building blocks of economic theory. Adam Smith's "invisible hand," one of the most famous metaphors in social science, is an example of a positive unintended consequence. Smith maintained that each individual, seeking only his own gain, "is led by an invisible hand to promote an end which was no part of his intention" — that end being the public interest. "It is not from the benevolence of the butcher, or the baker that we expect our dinner, but from regard to their own self interest," wrote Smith.

All wars have unintended consequences. No matter how cautious generals and political leaders are, war sets in motion waves of change that alter the course of history. Generals and political leaders do not always focus on the potential long-term effects of their decisions in war; they are sharply focused on achieving a victory. Yet sometimes, these decisions result in unseen and unintended consequences that overshadow their original objectives.

When it comes to unintended consequences, you should apply the prudent-person criteria and consider the potential consequences and implications of your decisions. Do not be careless by not considering potential consequences; however, do not agonize over unintended consequences that could not have been anticipated. Some things do occur by chance, and there is no way to either anticipate them or prevent them.

21

Good Money After Bad

When I taught MBA students, I used an exercise where I would auction off a $1 bill in order to teach them a lesson on decision-making. The only catch was that the second highest bidder had to pay what he or she bid, but did not get the dollar. The bidding always started out routinely with each student trying to outbid the others, until the bids got close to $1, then everyone generally dropped out except for the two highest bidders.

When these two bidders realized that they had "invested" almost a dollar and might not get it back, they continued the bidding over $1. Their logic was "I've already invested $0.95 or $1.05 or $1.10, so why not pay ten cents more to get the dollar bill?" The bidding continued, typically surpassing $3, and sometimes $5, for that $1. Eventually, one of the bidders realized the forces at work and stopped bidding, paying several dollars and getting nothing in return. The "winning" bidder got the dollar, but he also paid many times what it was worth.

This exercise explains the faulty thinking behind bad investments, bad relationships, and even questionable national policies. Let's look first at an example that most people are familiar with. You may have an old car that requires expensive repairs, and you decide to make them. Then something else breaks and needs to be replaced, but since you just put a lot of money into the previous repairs, it now makes even more sense for you to make these new repairs — or so you think. Then this happens again and before you know it, you've put more money into that old car than it was worth, and you don't have much to show for it. Like the exercise, you have now paid $3 for $1. This is sometimes referred to as throwing good money after bad.

I have seen this same logic applied all too frequently to investment decisions in business. A company invests in developing a new product, but the product is not successful, so it invests more to improve it, but the improvement still doesn't make the product a winner in the marketplace. Now the company has even more at stake, and it needs to salvage its investment — by investing even more. Eventually reason prevails and the incremental investing is halted.

One data communications company spent $80 million over four years trying to develop a new switching device even though they knew that a competitor would be coming out with a better-performing product sooner and at a lower cost. Still, the management team reasoned, "We have spent so much money on it, and we're almost there." Of course, the product never succeeded, and the management team was replaced.

> **When you make decisions on continued investments, be careful of justifying these decisions based solely on what you've invested up to that point.**

People also make decisions to keep investing — despite poor returns — in non-economic areas. Perhaps they have invested so much in a relationship that isn't working or in a job where they're not progressing. Still, they rationalize, "I've invested so much in this, I might as well invest more." As in our MBA exercise, their return on investment is not what was anticipated.

This same decision-making phenomenon is sometimes seen when national policy is set. During the Vietnam War, activist Daniel Ellsberg questioned the reasoning of the U.S. Administration, which was continuing to invest the lives of its soldiers in an effort that was not worth the additional loss of life. He believed that, to some extent, the primary rationale for continued involvement in Vietnam was to show that the lives already lost were not lost in vain. Eventually, many Americans came around to agreeing with Ellsberg's perspective, but only after 58,000 American soldiers were killed and 75,000 severely disabled.

Of course, the decision to keep investing in something is not always the wrong decision. Often, the investments you have already made can put you in a position where an incremental or additional investment will have a big payoff. This can be true for financial investments, relationship investments, and career investments. I know a couple who have been very successful in renovating homes. They buy a home, and then invest incrementally over the next few years in major renovations that move the house into a higher sales bracket. But before making these incremental investments, this couple studies the comparable values in the neighborhood, the mortgage market, and other variables that will affect the value buyers will ascribe to their upgrades. After all, if no mortgages are available at attractive interest rates or if the upgraded house will be out of place in the neighborhood, their additional investments may be in vain and constitute losses instead of gains. They might do just as well to let the house simply appreciate over the course of time. In other words, they pause to think through whether their added investment will have a likely payoff commensurate with their time, trouble, and dollars spent.

When you make decisions on continued investment, whether it is money, time, or something even more precious, be careful not to justify the decision solely on what you have invested up to that point. Look upon your previous investment as a sunk cost and base your new investment on its own merit. Don't just invest blindly, throwing good money after bad, and don't pay $3 for $1.

!22

Nowor Never

The oddest thing used to happen whenever I went shopping for a new car. I would see a car that interested me and begin checking it out. The salesman, who'd been watching me from the moment I'd stepped onto the lot, would approach me. I would honestly and naively explain that I was just shopping, and that I intended to visit other dealers and look at other models before I made any decision. The salesman would then warn me that just before I arrived, or earlier that day, or the previous day, someone else had looked at this very car and was coming back to put a deposit on it. This happened to me every single time I looked for a new car.

It was always just my luck that whatever car I showed any interest in was on the verge of being sold, and that — if I didn't make a deposit then and there — it would undoubtedly be gone when I came back to look at it again. Who was this mysterious person, with my exact taste in cars, who was always one step ahead of me? Why was he always in the process of buying the exact car that attracted me? Who was this uncanny nemesis?

Nowor Never is a sales trick designed to force us into making rash decisions.

This phenomenon didn't just happen with cars. When I was shopping for my first house, the same thing happened. While I was touring a likely property, the real-estate agent told me that my rival had been there the previous day with his wife, and they were expected to make an offer later in the day. Whoever made the first offer would most likely get the house.

When I came to realize that my competition did not really exist, I decided to give him a name: Nowor Never. He's not a person, but a sales trick; a pressure tactic. Nowor Never is summoned from the ether by car salesmen and real-estate agents and purveyors of an infinite number of other goods and services to force us into making rash decisions.

Nowor Never makes his appearance in various guises. Retail stores use temporary discounts or "one day only" sales to get people to buy now. Sales reps pushing industrial products, such as manufacturing equipment and software, use time-based discounts to pressure customers into snap decisions. Some people will buy things they never even wanted just so they won't end up having to pay more for them later (should they ever decide to buy them). It makes no sense, which is precisely the point.

As soon as you realize that Nowor Never is a figment of the consumer's anxious imagination, you can put him to work for you. Once, when I was interested in purchasing an expensive bracelet, I noticed the store manager was transparently anxious to make the sale. At that point, I turned the tables on him and introduced him to my associate, Nowor Never. I told him that I was interested in a certain piece, but if it cost more than 40% of the listed price, I would have to think about it. I'd check out some other stores and maybe get back to him. He stared at his shoes for a moment and then said that for such a large discount, he'd need approval from the owner. He excused himself and went to the back room. He probably just sat and sipped coffee for a few minutes, but

> When a salesman mentions a recent visit by one Mr. Nowor Never, walk away.

when he reemerged, he said that he could give me the price I wanted. Thank you, Nowor Never.

When someone selling something mentions a coincidental recent visit by one Mr. Nowor Never, walk away. Resist the urge to be fooled by this decision-forcing ploy. Don't compete with Nowor Never — now or ever. He doesn't exist. There is no Nowor Never. Take your time, comparison-shop, and don't be pressured.

Of course, there is always the possibility that a real competitor does exist. Once someone else really did buy a car that I wanted, and I could have had it at a very good price had I made a deposit on the spot. Instead, I had to wait three months to order another one, and it cost me more money. So be careful that there really may be a Nowor Never — No. No. No. Don't ever worry about Nowor Never. Walk away whenever someone attempts to use him against you. In the long run, you'll come out ahead because you'll have made decisions that were right for you, not the salesman.

!23

Ucant Havit

People want things that they can't have, and this phenomenon is often used by salespeople to make you buy things. You may be undecided as to whether you want something, but when they tell you that you can't have it, you will certainly decide that you want it. I learned this when I worked my way through college by selling encyclopedias. It was part of the sales program, and we were all trained in the technique. Families were selected to "demonstrate" new encyclopedias for free — well, almost free; they ended up paying over $1,000 for the set by the time the deal was closed.

The sales technique was to show families the encyclopedia set and then interview them to see if they "qualified" for the special deal: a free set. Here's how the sales pitch often went: when you told them that you weren't sure that they qualified for the deal, they decided they wanted it. They signed the purchase agreement, purchased all of the options in the program to prove that they were qualified, and in the process signed a sales agreement for $1,000 or more. It worked one time out

> **Don't be forced into making rash decisions by Ucant Havit. In most cases, it's the wrong decision.**

of every three, even if the people had no reason to buy an encyclopedia.

I call this sales technique Ucant Havit, a close cousin to Nowor Never (introduced in the previous chapter). People deciding to buy were initially happy because they got what they couldn't have. I was happy because I got a commission. The encyclopedia company was happy because it made a sale. Many — possibly most — customers, however, ended up regretting their decisions to purchase the encyclopedias. For most of them it really wasn't a wise decision. They had much better things to do with their money but were tricked into making the decision by Ucant Havit.

Ucant Havit is also used to force other types of sales decisions. Imagine that a potential customer is considering buying one of a company's products or hiring it to do a project for them. While discussing what the company has to offer, it includes a discount. Unfortunately, the discount expires, says the company, if the customer delays its decision to buy. Furniture sales people use this argument with discount expiration dates all of the time.

The Ucant Havit approach can be turned to good advantage, however, in a win/win situation. It worked well for me when I was selling management consulting projects. In this environment, it was always important to get the client to decide on buying the project as soon as possible, so we could assign staff and maintain our cash flow. When I would introduce clients to the consultants who would work on their projects, they were generally thrilled with them but did not immediately close the deal. A few days later, I would call them to tell them that another client wanted to hire us for a project using the same consultants. I would ask the client to hasten their decision process if they did not want to lose this staff. Not surprisingly, the potential clients would always decide within a couple of days. One even called me late at night to confirm a contract because he was so worried about losing the staff he wanted.

Playing hard-to-get is a version of this technique that is used in relationships. One person who is interested in another person will play hard-to-get by making the other person think that he or she is not interested. The reasoning may go like this: "You'll decide you want me more if you think that you can't have me." Or, "I want to increase your desire for me by stimulating your need to get what you can't have."

Ucant Havit also shows itself in different forms in the business world. For example, a company may be recruiting a new employee and may be undecided between two candidates. When one of them tells the company that he or she has another offer, possibly at a competitor, that candidate suddenly becomes the first choice. The company is ready to make the offer and maybe even increase it to "win" the candidate.

The decision-making lesson here is: Don't be forced into making rash decisions by Ucant Havit. While the attraction to something you can't have is strong, don't succumb to it! Realize what's happening and walk away if you wouldn't purchase the product without the deadline.

On the other hand, you can also put Ucant Havit to work for yourself and try to influence the decision you want. But soon after, you may realize that it might not have been the best decision, and now you need to live with the consequences.

As for my encyclopedia sales career, after two months I realized that what I was doing was wrong, and I quit. I didn't like tricking people with Ucant Havit. My conscience caused me to leave the company, and I started doing construction work instead to pay my way through college. The encyclopedia company, one of the largest, was later indicted on multiple counts of misrepresentation. Ucant Havit was called to testify against the company.

24

Executing Socrates

By the time he was 70, the now-famous philosopher Socrates had angered many people in ancient Athens with his outspoken manner of constantly challenging their thinking. We now refer to his approach as the Socratic method of thinking — constantly asking questions and challenging the answers of others in an effort to establish a particular proposition. Athenians claimed that Socrates was strange and evil, and they accused him of corruption. They thought he should be silenced and maybe even executed.

Sometimes the social makeup of the group charged with making a decision affects the outcome of the decision.

At that time Athens used a jury system to decide such matters. Two or three times each month, all male citizens (approximately 30,000) were invited to gather and make decisions on important issues by a show of hands. The opinion of those who showed up was believed to represent the opinion of the majority.

According to legend, approximately 500 Athenian men showed up on the day of Socrates' trial. The prosecution made its case that he was dishonest because he used shifty rhetorical devices to make his weaker arguments defeat stronger ones, and that he had intentionally corrupted the thinking of Athenian youth. According to Alain de Botton in his book *The Consolations of Philosophy*, Socrates defended himself by claiming that he was only trying to improve the lives of Athenians: "I tried to persuade each of you not to think more of practical advantages than of his mental and moral well-being."

But Socrates refused to change his ways, and with a vote of 280 to 220, he was declared guilty. When Socrates sarcastically observed that he was surprised the vote was so close and then challenged the jury again, 360 of the 500 voted to put him to death. A short time and a little hemlock later, he died.

What can we learn from the trial of Socrates beyond the risk of being outspoken in a society where the whim of a majority can vote to have you executed? It provides us some insight into the early traditions of decision-making.

Was this group of 500 Athenians representative of the 30,000 male citizens? Most likely it was not. Quite possibly, the group was recruited for that day by those who accused Socrates. In that case the "deck was stacked against him," and the group's decision couldn't be said to represent the opinion of Athenian society as a whole. Sometimes, the social makeup of the group charged with making the decision affects the outcome of the decision, and this isn't limited to ancient Athens.

> **Make sure the deck is not stacked against you when your head is on the chopping block.**

Here's a modern example. In August 2006, 2,400 astronomers registered for the International Astronomical Union Congress meeting in Prague to decide on redefining the number of planets in the solar system. This had been a heated discussion for years. By August 24, as the conference was wrapping up, only 400 to 500 of the members remained at the meeting, most of the others having left early to catch their flights home. Then those remaining decided to hold a vote to eliminate Pluto as a planet, demoting it to a "dwarf planet." It's not clear that this would have been the majority decision if others had stayed until the end of the conference.

The United States Congress uses similar decision-making tactics, calling for a vote on a motion when key opponents are out of town and unable to vote. This enables a minority, or something less than a simple majority, to pass legislation that otherwise would not have been approved. This "he who shows up votes" model is also a principle of most election processes. Frequently, elections are decided by a small percentage of eligible voters — those who actually show up — and getting the "right" voters to the polls on Election Day is critical to winning an election. This strategy, known as "getting out the vote," is one of the most important factors in winning elections. Campaigns routinely spend large sums of money to hire an army of people to get as many of their supporters to the polls on Election Day as possible.

You have to wonder if decisions made this way are good decisions, as the cases of Socrates and the now "less than a planet" Pluto have shown us.

These examples indicate the pitfalls that can come from group decision-making. (We discuss consensus decision-making in another chapter.) But the primary lesson is to beware the group opinion. It very well may not be representative of what the majority might have decided if given a chance to participate.

!25

Community Decisions

With only 60 year-round residents, Monhegan Island in Maine restricts lobster fishing until after December 1st every year, even though catching lobsters would be much easier in the summertime. Is this community decision a good one? The reason for it is that by catching lobsters in the winter rather than the summer, residents can use the summer for other jobs, such as working at inns and stores that support the tourist business or doing construction to build new homes. In the wintertime such work would not be so abundant, so the lobstering fills a gap.

The start date for catching lobsters, called Trap Day, occasionally is further delayed by inclement weather. Because they have not been harvested for many months, the lobsters are in abundance at this time, and the fishermen catch the greatest number in the first few weeks. As anxious as individual lobstermen are to get started, they have a 100-year tradition of waiting until everyone is ready before they start. If someone is unable to start, or if the weather per-

> **Just because decisions are made by an entire community does not necessarily mean they are always good decisions.**

mits only the larger boats to go out in the water, then everyone waits. The community has reckoned that this gives everyone a fair advantage, and in an environment where fishing may be the only means of survival through a harsh winter, this seems to be a good policy.

When should the decisions of a community — a town, a state, a country, or a company — trump the decisions of the individuals that make up that community? Community decisions are obviously necessary in some cases (establishing laws for crimes, traffic regulations, etc.), but it's less obvious how useful they are in other cases.

On Monhegan Island, the best interests of the community prevail. Instead of each lobsterman trying to get an advantage over the others, the decisions of the community prevail over the interests of the individual. While this may affect the gains of some individual lobstermen, it preserves a community that otherwise might not survive. It's an example of good community decision-making.

But just because certain decisions are made by an entire community doesn't necessarily mean they're always good decisions.

Another town in Maine restricts construction so tightly that it takes 42 months to get a building permit. The goal of this policy is to restrict growth. It's not a matter of community survival, such as the rules about fishing on Monhegan Island; rather, it's a matter of preference by enough of the population to support the growth restrictions. Certainly, it is not of benefit to people who make a living in construction or real estate, those who want to move into the town and can't find accommodations, or those who need to wait those 42 months to build, despite the attendant increases in material and labor costs. It benefits those who already live in the town by inflating property values.

Community decisions are a complex form of decision-making because they raise the questions of who has the authority to make these decisions and how their impact can be measured. Some decisions are the result of traditions. There is one particular group of towns in Maine that celebrates Halloween on the night before the official date. They have been doing so for as long as anyone can remember, and nobody remembers why it was done that way in the first place. But they all agree that the practice works out to everyone's satisfaction, and so they continue the tradition.

Community decisions are most frequently set by enacting new laws or regulations, some of which are difficult to rationalize. Decisions on new laws that protect the public good, such as fire regulations, are obvious and easy for the leaders of the community to justify, since they protect everyone. There tends to be a consensus — or near-consensus — around these decisions.

> It's important to discern whether a group makes a decision for the benefit of the entire community or for the benefit of one segment of the community to the detriment of another.

But laws and regulations that benefit one group in the community over others are much more difficult to justify. In the town with growth restrictions, for example, some citizens benefit because they want to live in a small town or have property that will appreciate in value faster, but other people who cannot afford to live in the town are forced out. Decisions that set one group of community members against another group are not good decisions because the gains for one group come at the price of another's losses.

When listening to arguments in favor of community decisions, be sure to discern whether the decisions being made are for the benefit of the entire community or whether they are actually decisions that will benefit one segment of the community to the detriment of another. Then act accordingly.

!26

Don't Listen

On October 16, 2003, the Boston Red Sox held a three-run lead over the New York Yankees with just five outs needed in the seventh and deciding game of the American League Championship Series. Pedro Martinez, Boston's ace pitcher, was still on the mound after more than seven innings, but he had clearly lost his edge. Red Sox Manager Grady Little went to the mound and asked Pedro if he wanted to keep pitching. Of course he said he did. What else would you expect?

The coach let Pedro make the decision, and the rest is history. Pedro gave up the tying run and the Yankees won the game in the 11th inning. The Yankees went to the World Series, and the Red Sox ended their season prematurely, yet again. (The following year, the Red Sox won the World Series for the first time in 86 years.)

Grady Little made the mistake of letting someone else make a decision for him that he should have made himself. Everyone — apparently except for Grady — knew that Pedro Martinez's opinion was biased. Like any good athlete, he didn't want to give up. He wanted to continue pitching. That's why the manager is supposed to make these decisions and not the players.

Grady Little got fired by the owners of the Red Sox because

of that poor judgment. I bet if they asked him for his opinion on whether he should be fired or not, he would have said no. But unlike Grady Little, the owners knew the decision was theirs to make, not their employee's.

For his part, Grady Little said, "A guy in my position makes 1,000 decisions a week. Sometimes the results are good; sometimes they're not. A lot of friends have said to me, 'Would you have done it differently?' Well, sure, if I knew the results ahead of time." But it's not about one decision of 1,000 or knowing the result ahead of time. There is a lesson to be learned from this example: Don't listen to someone's opinion on a decision when that opinion is obviously colored by his or her unique position.

If you think about this from a personal perspective, it becomes even clearer how biased others can be. If you asked your mother if you should get married and have children, what do you think she would say? If you asked your teacher if you should go to college at his alma mater, he'll likely say yes, whether that school would be the best choice for you or not. How about if you ask your boss whether you should stay or take another job? Most likely — if you have been a productive employee — he will say you should stay. If you ask your real-estate agent if you should buy a house that she will receive a commission on, what do you think the answer will be? Beware the opinions of those who have a bias toward their own benefit.

> **Never listen to someone's opinion on a decision when their opinion is obviously colored by their unique position.**

Sometimes this opinion bias takes different forms. Spouses, for example, sometimes can give poor advice on career moves. Jonathan was offered a new job that he was very interested in accepting. When he discussed it with his wife, she said, "You are worth more than that; tell them they need to pay you 20% more." He based his decision on her advice, demanding 20% more, and they gave the job he wanted to someone else.

As this example shows, while there's no doubt that support from spouses is essential to lifetime success, it can also reinforce inflated self-opinions. Spouses and friends may not understand the context of the situation in which the decision is being made. I won't go as far as to say you shouldn't listen to your spouse or friends, but you should look at their advice as helpful reasoning and not alwaysas a recommendation for a specific decision.

So when you ask for someone's advice on making a decision, first understand where he or she may be coming from. What are their personal interests in your decision? What are their biases? If they're going to be affected in some way by your decision, their opinions are most likely shaped by these biases. In many cases, you don't even want to ask their opinions, since you might ignore them anyway. And if you ignore them, they'll be upset with you for not listening to them.

Sometimes, however, they may give you advice that is counter to their own personal interests and truly based on what is best for you. When this happens, usually it's good advice. Either that, or maybe they have other personal interests that you don't understand. But in general, if you ask for their advice on your decision and then you ignore it, they are more likely to get upset with you for not listening to them.

When you anticipate that someone will give you a biased opinion, but they give the opinion opposite to what you would have expected, it should carry more weight. Once I was diagnosed with a particular issue by a cardiologist in Dallas, where I was working, and he recommended surgery. He said that although he knew a number of good surgeons in the area who did the procedure I needed, he recommended that I go to one of the top hospitals in the country that specialized in the procedure. I took his advice and got the care I needed.

Also remember that the same bias may hold true for advice you are asked to give to a friend, a coworker, or a loved one. When you are asked for advice, you should try to determine whether you have a personal stake in the matter or are somehow biased. Will you gain or lose something depending upon what your friend or spouse decides? If so, be sure you take that into consideration before you attempt to influence the decisions of those around you.

My (unbiased) advice here is: Don't ask for help on a decision from someone who has a personal interest in your decision, and if you get it, don't listen.

!27

Throwing Caution to the Wind

Some people throw caution to the wind when they make a decision. They make risky decisions — or even worse — they make decisions too quickly and without regard to likely outcomes. People who are continually getting themselves into trouble tend to regularly make reckless decisions, throwing caution to the wind. Friends may ask them after they see the consequences of their decision, "What were you thinking?" The answer usually is simple: They weren't thinking! And unless they give a lot more thought to their decisions in the future, they will continue to make bad decisions that have bad results.

Surprisingly, some people may spend their entire lives making calm, calculated decisions, and then all of the sudden abruptly change their decision-making styles and throw caution to the wind. These are people who are normally very cautious in their decision-making, but begin to make a series of risky decisions that they haven't carefully thought through. Often they experience the risks inherent in throwing caution to the wind firsthand, usually with severe outcomes.

> While it's not smart to never take risks, it's important to be careful not to make reckless decisions.

A conservative and prudent investor throughout his life, Thomas set aside a little money every week to build a nest egg for his retirement. He invested his money cautiously, mostly in government and high-quality bonds. While he missed some of the gains when the stock market increased, he was always comfortable that his nest egg was safe, even when the stock market dropped. When he retired, he had enough money to live comfortably.

But when the Internet bubble came on the scene, Thomas decided to put a large amount of money into some "hot" Internet stocks. After losing most of it when the Internet bubble burst, he was forced to borrow money by mortgaging his home. But he didn't stop there. Now desperate to make his money back, he decided to use that mortgage money to buy futures contracts — an even riskier investment — and ended up losing it all. At age 65, he had lost everything.

Sometimes it's not a tempting investment climate that makes people throw caution to the wind. It could be a turn for the worse in personal or job-related circumstances that pushes people over the edge. A woman named Terry was one of the most cautious people I have known. Although she was in an unhappy marriage, she didn't want to take any risks, so she remained in it.

But when her husband unexpectedly divorced her, she was forced to change. At that point, she, too, threw caution to the wind by moving to a new town without giving it much thought. She realized she had made a mistake when she discovered that she didn't like the new town. To comfort herself, she bought a van that she didn't really need. She continued spending money on other things she didn't need and quickly built up too much credit-card debt. She started dating anyone who asked her out and had a string of failed relationships. All of this caused her to have troubles at work, and she eventually lost her job. While it's not always good to never take any chances or to not make any decisions that will lead to change in your life, it is still important to be careful not to throw caution to the wind.

People like Terry and Thomas oddly shift from being cautious to reckless in their decision-making. It's like they just snap and go from one extreme to another. They throw caution to the wind and immediately start getting in trouble. It's not easy to predict what causes this abrupt change. It may be forced upon them from the external world: the divorce in Terry's case and his retirement in Thomas'. Or it may be something in their psychological makeup.

It's hard to give advice on how to avoid these situations, because I suspect that the person doesn't even recognize what's happening until it's too late. But their friends may see it as it's happening, and they can step in and give some strong advice. So if you have a friend who all of a sudden begins to throw caution to the wind, point this out. Maybe it will help him or her pause to consider it. At any rate, you will know that you tried your best to be a good friend.

28

Crossing My Path

You may have heard others talk about unexpected opportunities that crossed their path and how happy they were that they recognized them for what they were. Do you recognize unexpected opportunities as they arise? I think it's easier to do so when you are prepared for them.

I use a mental technique I call "crossing my path" to prepare for the unexpected. Here's how it works: It applies when there is something in the future that you want to do. You've identified it and are determined to watch out for opportunities that might help you realize the vision you've had. You don't want to miss opportunities that cross your path and you certainly don't want to neglect such opportunities. So you keep your vision and goals firmly in mind and remain vigilant in order to recognize opportunities as they cross your path. When I've identified such opportunities, I go after them aggressively.

Here are two business examples of how I used this technique to build a management consulting firm: The firm did extensive work in operations consulting in the 1980s, helping U.S. and European companies catch up with their Japanese counterparts. But I wanted to identify another opportunity for growing the business. After doing research and talking with clients, I realized that companies needed help with their product development processes. Most companies were not able to create enough new products fast enough for market demands.

It was a recognized problem, but nobody seemed to have a solution. One day, we received a request for a competitive proposal from a company that wanted to improve its product development process, and I jumped on it. My colleagues and I worked night and day to learn as much as possible about improving product development in order to win that contract. We put an extraordinary amount of time into it because we recognized that this was an important opportunity. Why? Because it had crossed our strategic path and would enable us to grow our business by expanding our service offerings.

Because we put in this extraordinary effort, we won the contract, beating 10 other consulting firms who probably viewed it as just an average consulting project. We then went on to develop a methodology that became the industry standard for product development management and provided more than $1 billion in consulting as we worked with more than 1,000 companies over the next 25 years.

Another strategic opportunity happened our way when we were looking to expand in Europe. We had an office in the U.K. but were not on "The Continent" yet when we learned of a project in France. Our normal response would have been to ignore this opportunity because we didn't even have an office in France. But we decided to seize the opportunity. We learned more about the request and won the project. It became the platform for us to build a business in France.

While successful in business, I've found that this technique also can be successful in everyday personal situations. Let's say that you want to get married. That is the path you want to take when the opportunity presents itself. But you need to make yourself open to see the opportunity when it crosses your path and aggressively seize it when it presents itself. Don't fret or think it's impossible. Keep looking for the opportunity that might cross your path. It will. But beware that you can easily miss it if you are not looking down that path. You also need to be active in working to create the possibility for more opportunities to arise.

Similarly, you may want to change your profession but don't know when or how to change. Get an understanding of what profession or professions you are interested in and then seize an opportunity when it crosses your path — to learn more, to network at a conference, or to solicit information-gathering sessions with people in the field of your interest.

So how do you prepare to take advantage of opportunities that are in sync with your aspirations? First, you

> It's easy for something to cross your path while you're not looking.

need to look far enough ahead. This technique takes time and patience, so the further ahead you look, the better. But be sure to set timelines. You want to find your marriage partner within two years. You want to change careers in the next 2 to 4 years. You want to expand your business in the next 2 to 3 years.

Your first decision is determining what major paths you want to look down. Focus on one or two of them – not more – since you really can't be exploring too many paths at any given time. Not successfully, anyway.

Then you need to be on the lookout for opportunities that cross that path. It's easy for something to cross your path while you're not looking, but then you'll miss it. You might have met your future husband or wife at a party, but you weren't looking, so you didn't notice. You might even have decided to stay home and missed the opportunity altogether.

Most likely, the opportunity you are looking for will cross your path when you are busy or distracted. The two business opportunities I described both occurred when my company was very busy and would have been likely to miss them. But they came to my attention, and seeing that they were the opportunities we needed to pursue our business path, I dropped everything to pursue them.

Did I mention aggressiveness? You have to pursue these special opportunities that cross your strategic path aggressively. It's not just another thing to do; it's *the* opportunity to do something that is very important to you. Give it the highest priority.

Not all opportunities that cross your path actually end up getting you down the path you want. You may very well find out that the man you thought could be your future husband is really a jerk. You may not get the contract you wanted to expand your business, even after trying very aggressively. In that case, keep looking down that path — another opportunity will eventually cross it.

!29

When You Get to a Fork in the Road, Take It!

all of Fame baseball catcher Yogi Berra was noted for his unconventional wisdom. On the face of it his remarks seemed trite, but on second glance you realized the simplicity and beauty of the hidden messages. One of these was: "When you get to a fork in the road, take it." What did Yogi mean by this? Everyone knows that you can't take a fork in the road; you need to pick one of the two roads it presents to you. But the deeper meaning is that you need to decide, not just stop dead in your tracks because you can't decide which road to take.

Throughout life we constantly come to our own forks in the road when we are confronted by the many decisions we need to make. Unfortunately, some people reach a fork in the road and can't decide which way to go. They are paralyzed by the choices. They may be afraid of making the wrong choice, or they may not know how to go about deciding what path to take.

We need to realize that a fork in the road is a decision point. It demarks a choice between two alternatives. You may not know which one will be better or even where each will eventually lead you, but you do know that each one is likely to lead you in a very different direction. But you have to commit to one of them.

John had a decision to make as he was approaching graduation from college. As he put it, "I needed to decide what I would be doing with the rest of my life." He had applied to graduate school and was accepted, but wasn't sure he wanted to invest another 2 to 3 years in school. He was also offered a job for a company that he had previously interned with. He thought about the decision for months but was paralyzed by having to choose between graduate school and working for the company. After graduation, he ended up deciding to go to graduate school, but since he had missed the application deadline, the school could not enroll him for the current year. When he called the company back about the job, he learned that they had already filled the position with one of his classmates. His inability to make a decision at the fork in the road hurt him more than he had anticipated.

Another major fork in the road for most people is the opportunity to get married. You know that being married is a very different life from being single. You could rationalize that if you continue down the road of being single you might someday hit another fork in the road that gives you another choice of going down the married road. Maybe you can defer the decision.

In business, a company that has just emerged from a difficult period might have the opportunity to begin growing again as an independent company, but it's also presented with a separate opportunity to merge with another company. These are very different roads. At this fork in the road, the company can choose to go in either direction but cannot pursue them both. The CEO and board of directors need to carefully evaluate these two roads and choose one before it's too late.

Fork-in-the-road decisions have several characteristics. First, there is an opportunity to make a choice to take one of two very different, life-changing, or business-changing roads. This is different from stepping back periodically to evaluate how you could change. Here, you are confronted with a specific opportunity to choose a direction.

Second, the fork in the road can sometimes be missed. You can proceed with your life or career with your head down and not even notice that you're at a fork in the road. For example, a couple may be in a relationship that's approaching the decision point for marraige. They may start living together and act like a married couple but never acknowledge the union with a ceremony and the legalities. Or, although they may want to be married, they feel the opportunity to take that path with their current partner has passed and then start looking for someone else. In actuality, the opportunity didn't pass on its own; the couple missed it because they didn't recognize it when it appeared.

It's crucial to recognize when you're at a fork in the road. Often these decisions have specific time limits, so you're forced to make a decision by a certain day. In other cases, there is no clear deadline, but over time you drift down one road without realizing it, or worse, stay at the fork and miss the opportunities.

> **Fork-in-the-road decisions should not paralyze you into sitting at the fork forever.**

Fork-in-the-road decisions are very important and deserve a lot of attention. They should not be made on impulse. But neither should they paralyze you into sitting at the fork forever. Give a priority to evaluating the two different roads. Seek advice from others who may have traveled these roads before you. Do your research to understand as much about these two roads as you can. Clearly identify your expectations of each road and do a reality check on each one.

Then choose the road you intend to travel and never look back. Travel that road with all of your energy and passion and don't harbor any regrets. You may never know where the other road would have lead you, so don't imagine that it would have been better. This is the lesson in Yogi's message, "When you get to a fork in the road, take it."

30

Decision-Proof

ome people — and even some companies — seem to be decision-proof. They simply cannot make decisions.

Management at one company that I provided consulting for actually referred to its executive management team as being decision-proof. No matter how hard anyone tried to get them to make a decision, these senior executives resisted. Mid-level management couldn't make headway on their projects. The way this seemed to work was interesting. Since the CEO preferred a consensus on the executive team, he wouldn't make a decision unless all of the members of the executive team concurred. The members of the executive team, however, avoided taking the lead on any decision until the CEO made up his mind, thus ensuring that nothing would be done — at least not quickly.

As a consultant to this company, I was responsible for getting the executive team to approve the implementation of some sweeping changes that were necessary for the company to stop

> The best way to combat "decision-proof" is to recognize the problems inherent in the decision-making structure and work to make it more viable.

losing money and be successful again. After pondering how to get them to make a decision, I tried reversing the approval process. I presented the plan to the executive team and then asked them if they wanted to make a decision to cancel the program I proposed. I did not give them the choice of proceeding with the program. They all looked around the table at each other, and the CEO said that he didn't see the need for a decision to stop. So I said, "OK, if there is no decision to stop, then we'll go ahead," and they agreed, although rather lackadaisically: "I guess so."

The company implemented the major changes necessary, and the managers were impressed that the executive team could actually make an important decision so quickly. While I didn't solve their decision-proof dilemma (I didn't set out to do that), I was able to work around their ineffectual process by exploiting it.

This decision-proof problem occurs most often in situations where multiple people need to make a decision, but nobody wants to take the lead in making or proposing it.

This is not limited to companies, of course. It happens in teams and families as well. In some marriages, there is a dynamic between husband and wife where neither wants to take the lead in proposing a decision. Both people stall for different reasons. Maybe one feels their spouse will always argue for the other alternative, or maybe one spouse feels he or she will be blamed if the decision does not have a good outcome.

How do you solve this problem? One way is to recognize the problem and discuss it. If one proposes a decision and the other argues against it, then the first person can give in and say, "OK, you're right." Another way is to take out the coin and toss it. If you're trying to actually solve the problem inherent in a decision-proof process, you'll have to analyze the components that are keeping the process from yielding a decision. You'll then have to alter the process to make it more viable and effective.

In the case of our executive management team, if members fear that they will be marginalized for making suggestions or "voting" a particular way on a decision at hand, you could consider having the votes submitted anonymously in writing. When it comes to suggestions or alternatives, for example, you could require each member of the team to submit a short list of suggestions, parameters, alternatives, problems, and benefits of all potential directions. This would allow you to ensure not only that the particular decision you are looking to make right now is done correctly, but that you end the current blockade created by the decision-proof process.

Decision-proof styles of decision-making are lethal. You have to be alert to an ineffectual process and try to either restructure it or work around it. If you restructure your process, you'll find that, instead of a decision-proof process, you'll institute a decision-enabling process. Who knows what you could accomplish with that in place?

31

Que Sera Sera

"Que sera sera, whatever will be will be" are the lyrics from the famous Doris Day song (written for Alfred Hitchcock's 1956 film *The Man Who Knew Too Much*). The song received an Academy Award for best song, but to many people, it acknowledges a fatalistic belief about the results of decisions they make.

These individuals believe that decisions don't really matter because the results are subject to "fate" or inevitable predetermination. To an extreme, these individuals feel that they can't control the outcome of major decisions; for example, choosing a spouse or selecting a course of treatment for a medical condition, because the outcome is predetermined anyway. This outlook can be extremely hazardous for successful decision-making and for a successful, healthy life.

> You can influence your future by making better decisions.

The lyrics in the song include "Since I am just a boy in school, I asked my teacher what should I try?" (for a career). And the reply was, "Que Sera Sera. Whatever will be will be." The song implies that there are no conscious decisions that affect how your future will look. I don't subscribe to this belief.

I believe that you can influence your future by making better decisions. Believing that the outcome of some particular part of your life is predetermined only makes your decisions sloppy. Not making decisions based on the reality of a given situation and believing the outcomes are already determined become self-fulfilling prophesies, since you will inevitably end up with random outcomes.

Even if you believe there is a greater force, such as God, who influences and structures the path your life goes down, and you believe that you are in His hands in some way, this doesn't preclude you from developing your own decision-making abilities. You might look at it this way: Even if God is providing you with the options, you need to make the decisions yourself about which of the options you choose.

Many people use the que sera sera philosophy to go through life without addressing their problems. They may be single and would like to be married but leave it up to fate. Rather than actively looking for the right person, they simply believe that if the right person doesn't somehow magically appear to them, then it's predetermined that they shouldn't be married. Or worse, they could find the wrong person but marry them anyway because they believe it's fate. Why else would they have met this person.

This outlook of que sera sera also causes some people to ignore their health, believing that fate will determine what happens. But when they get diabetes from being overweight, for example, they may realize that they could have prevented it by losing weight and being more careful with their diet.

> **When you are confronted with a decision, it may be fate that you have been put in the position to make that decision, but the outcome is not predetermined.**

An old friend of mine, Mary, was a perfect example of this belief that fate determines everything in one's life. She seemed to just drift through life saying, "que sera sera, whatever will be will be" to everything that happened. And then, when something — or nothing — happened, she would use that as proof of her belief. Whatever the outcome of a given situation was — positive or negative — Mary always believed that it must have been fate that got her there and that there was nothing she could have done or should have done to achieve a different outcome.

Mary worked at a low-paying job because she never went to college. When someone recommended to her that she should work toward a degree that would help her get a promotion at her company, she applied to a school. But when she wasn't accepted to that school, she gave up, never applying to another school. She figured it must be fate that she not receive a degree.

Mary got married to the first person who asked her, then got a divorce only a few years later because her husband wasn't happy in the marriage. Instead of believing that she should look for another person to spend her life with, she said to herself, "que sera sera" and resigned herself to being alone for the rest of her life. Maybe she was right, since she never found anyone else to partner with and lived the remainder of her days alone. Because of her fatalism, Mary will never know whether she could have been accepted by another school if she had applied, or whether she would have found a loving second husband, had a family, and lived a different life than the one she lived.

A better way to look at the question of fate might be to try to use que sera sera to your own advantage. While it may be fate that you are put in a position to make a certain decision, it certainly is not predetermined what the outcome of that decision will be. That outcome is the result of your active participation in making choices — in making decisions once options are presented.

You have the ability to shape your own life, and you need to actively make the decisions that will shape your future. Don't leave it up to fate.

!32

Closed-Minded People

Sometimes I feel sorry for closed-minded people, but sometimes I envy them. They can make decisions much more easily than others by simply refusing to consider certain alternatives. Sometimes they even refuse to consider making new decisions. Some closed-minded people, for example, might not be open to moving from the town in which they were raised.

While this simplifies the decisions they face in their lives, it keeps them from pursuing much of what life has to offer. They may, for example, not consider some job opportunities that require relocation. They won't consider marrying someone who wouldn't move to the town they currently live in. They limit themselves to a restricted set of opportunities.

They do, however, have some advantages over open-minded people. For one thing, they simplify their lives. They don't create the complexity that others do. They aren't bothered (some would say tortured) by the questions many of us ask: Where should I live? Where should I go to school? Where should I work? Whom should I marry? When should I retire?

When I do a national search to recruit a new executive, I sometimes find great candidates, but often they don't want to move. They are closed-minded on the subject. I tell them they are missing a great opportunity — maybe a once-in-a-lifetime opportunity — and they agree, but they still won't take it. While this is understandable if they have children in school and the move would disrupt their family and their spouses' opportunities, it remains baffling. But their closed-mindedness obviously gives them some comfort. It provides a decision framework on what is important and what is not up for consideration in their lives.

People can be closed-minded about many more issues than these. They can and do form habits in their daily lives and refuse to budge from those routines. They can be closed-minded, for example, about the type of clothes they wear, the type of food they eat, where they go for vacation, their religion, the pets they want or don't want, the type of friends they have, what they read, and what kind of movies they will watch and won't watch.

> **While being closed-minded may simplify the decisions in your life, it also may keep you from pursuing much of what life has to offer.**

Tanya was closed-minded in that she had a set of predetermined rules she followed for relationships. She refused to become intimate, for instance, with a man until they had dated for six months. This rule removed all of her anxiety over when to become intimate. It simplified her life and established a threshold she was comfortable with. While this may have caused her to lose some men she dated, she figured the comfort level was more important than the lost opportunities.

A larger problem occurs when people are closed-minded about more significant decisions or about decisions affecting other people. A parent may decide, for example, that his daughter can't go to college anywhere but at the local university. His daughter wants to be an attorney and wants to attend a university that has a better pre-law program, but it's in another state. The father's closed-mindedness about what would be best for his daughter will inhibit her ability to achieve her goals.

This is not as easy as it sounds. Most people are unaware when and how they are being closed-minded. One of the biggest clues is if you're unable to consider alternative ways of looking at an issue or making a decision. Another red flag is when you find your closed-mindedness hindering either your own or someone else's opportunities to enrich their lives.

Being closed-minded isn't always the wrong way to be.

People don't usually recognize that they're closed-minded. If someone you know is closed-minded, watch them during their decision-making and determine whether you think this closed-mindedness is inhibiting their lives. In other words, is it the small decisions or the big ones that they are closed-minded about, or both? If you think that their inability to consider alternative ways of making decisions is causing problems for them or those around them, you may want to help them begin to be a little more open-minded. Be careful, though. You may be closed-minded yourself, so you may want to think about that before talking to others about their potentially flawed decision-making processes.

Being closed-minded can severely inhibit your life or the lives of those around you, but it's not always the wrong way to be in every situation. Probably some hybrid of being closed-minded on some things and open-minded on others is the best advice. When trying to understand the approach that will yield the best outcome, try to think of the advantages and disadvantages of closed-minded thinking.

I give this advice, but I'm not so good at following it — I tend to be too open-minded to actually apply this advice in my own life. When dealing with other people or with your own decisions, figure out if you should or shouldn't be closed-minded.

!33

Finding a Labradoodle

The Internet has revolutionized many things, but a little-observed benefit of it is that it improves our ability to make decisions. How so? It offers information that we can sift through and use in our research before making a decision — information we never would have access to without it.

My family used the Internet, for instance, to help us to decide whether or not to get a dog. I'll explain how. When we decided we wanted to get a dog, we had no idea what type would be best for us and our lifestyle. We found a questionnaire online that recommended several breeds of dogs based on family preferences and circumstances. This questionnaire helped us to narrow our search to five breeds, and we were able to research these breeds on other websites as well.

The Internet has greatly expanded the quality of decision-making by providing more information.

We finally decided that the best dog for our family would be a Labradoodle — a cross between a poodle and a Labrador. The next job was to locate one. Again, the Internet was invaluable, since the breed was rare at the time, and we had to search the world for breeders. There were a few in the United States, but they had long waiting lists. We eventually found our dog in Australia. My youngest daughter named her Nala (from *The Lion King* story), and Nala has become a dear member of our family.

The use of the Internet in decision-making extends way beyond finding a new dog, product, or service. It can be very useful in helping people facing major decisions in their lives, such as career choices or medical decisions. I used it recently before surgery to better understand the alternatives available and their consequences. (Of course, this assessment should be conducted in collaboration with your doctor's advice and guidance.)

People can make career decisions with the help of the Internet by researching potential employers and better understanding the opportunities for a new profession. The Internet can be used to provide critical information on a city or town to which you are considering relocating.

On the lighter side, the Internet can be invaluable in making vacation decisions by providing information on travel, activities, accommodations, and climate. You can use it to find the perfect hotel, both by seeing what the hotel offers through its own website and by searching out what others who have stayed there have to say about it.

While the Internet can be useful in making almost any decision, there are some cautions in using it. Not all of the information on the Internet is accurate and unbiased. This means that you need to assess the information you get from the Internet more carefully than you would some other sources. For example, getting information from an Internet bulletin board on buying or selling a stock may seem like getting "inside information," but it's frequently wrong. People post opinions that have little or no basis in solid research and frequently try to use postings to influence stock prices. In the stock market, for example, there are individuals known as short sellers who have an interest in the stock price going down and, therefore, may post unfounded negative comments about a company. I have encountered this on more than a few occasions in my business career.

You often encounter information that is subjective, too. Restaurant reviews are a good example. Fortunately, many websites containing reviews of restaurants have multiple reviews posted by different people, enabling you to get a range of opinions, both positive and negative.

Overall, the Internet has greatly expanded the quality of decision-making by providing more alternatives and more information. More information almost always leads to better decisions.

In the last decade, the Internet has done more to improve decisions than anything else (with the possible exception of this book!). So when you need to make a major or minor decision, don't neglect to obtain as much information as possible through the Internet. You may just end up with your own perfect Nala.

34

Does Your Vote Count as Much as Others?

Every four years Americans decide whom they want for president. Or do they? If we look carefully at the Electoral College system set up by our founders, we may be left to wonder if it is a fair and representative decision-making system after all. The system certainly is not direct; in fact, it's intricate and complex. It was set up as a result of political compromise. Let's examine its intricacies. I'll leave you to decide whether it's a good decision-making system or whether it should be overhauled.

Why does a person in California get only .85 of a vote for President of the United States? And why does a person in Alaska get 2½ votes? Is this a fair and proper decision-making system for what is perhaps the most important decision made in the United States?

Under this system, different numbers of electoral votes are assigned to states depending, in part, on each state's population. The actual number of electoral votes that a particular state gets is equal to the number of U.S. Senators in that state (every state has two, regardless of its population), plus the number of U.S. Members of Congress in that state. States have varying numbers of Members of Congress, determined by the population of the state. These figures are adjusted every 10 years when the U.S. Census takes into account population shifts over the previous 10 years.

This means that California, the most populous state in the nation, has two electoral votes for its two Senators, and 53 electoral votes for its 53 Members of Congress, for a total of 55 electoral votes. Alaska, on the other hand, has two electoral votes for its two Senators, and one electoral vote for its one Member of Congress, for a total of 3 electoral votes. Since the population of Alaska is only large enough for one Member of Congress, each vote cast by a voter in Alaska is worth more than each vote cast by a voter in California.

Moreover, all of the states — except Nebraska and Maine, which will be discussed later — require that all electoral votes be allocated to a full slate, meaning all 3 electoral votes in Alaska or all 55 electoral votes in California will go to the candidate who wins the most votes statewide. This means that if the Democratic candidate gets the most votes in California — even if he wins only by a single vote — he gets all 55 of the electoral votes.

That being the case, this also means that the votes of all of the voters in California — and every state — who voted for the candidate that didn't win the most votes in the state don't count. In the 2004 election, for example, voters in each of the 50 states and the District of Columbia who did not cast their vote for the candidate who won the electoral votes in their state accounted for an enormous percentage of voters. These voters, whose votes did not make any impact nationally, accounted for 44.73% of all voters. That is an enormous amount of the overall electorate whose votes were ignored — a full 54,697,135 voters!

> Each American gets disproportional votes depending upon what state they live in.

In Maine and Nebraska, the electoral votes are not won as a slate, but are actually divided up in a different way. In these two states, the candidate who wins the most votes in the state will receive the two electoral votes allocated for the two U.S. Senators the state has, while the candidate who wins in each congressional district will receive the one electoral vote for that particular district. While these two states have had this system in place for some time, there has yet to be a case when the districts have been split on which candidate to vote for.

The structure of the Electoral College system also means that the candidate who gets the most votes cast in the United States may actually lose the election. This situation has actually occurred several times in the country's history, most recently in 2000, when Al Gore received more votes than George Bush, but fewer electoral votes. This means that George Bush won the election even though he received fewer votes than Al Gore from the American voters. Gore received 50,996,116 votes, while Bush received 50,456,169, meaning that Gore was voted for by 539,947 more people than Bush. Yet he lost the election.

When there are third-party candidates, it is often the case that no candidate receives more than half of the popular vote, and still there's a winner. This situation has also occurred a number of times throughout American history.

So is the American presidential election decision process a good process? As was mentioned, there have been several cases in American history where the one with the most votes loses, and each American gets disproportional votes depending on the state they live in. In addition, the votes of those in a minority in their state don't even count.

So when you go to the polls to vote for President, how much will your vote count? It may be more than your neighbor living in the state next to you — or even than the house next to you. Or it may be less. In fact, it may not count at all.

35

The Grass Isn't Greener

Everyone has heard the old adage, "The grass is greener on the other side of the fence." What it means, of course, is not that the grass actually is greener, but that it appears greener from a distance. Just as when you see a meadow from a distance it might look like mown grass, but when you get up close you see the brambles, the thistles, the wild flowers, and the bare patches that make up the meadow. So, too, other people's lives and livelihoods might look like smooth lawns, rather than the bumpy hills and valleys that you know your life to be. You can't be aware of the anxieties and quandaries that other people face, so don't jump to conclusions too quickly when considering following their paths instead of your own.

> If you think the grass is greener, or life is better, or others are happier, keep your energy and attention focused on yourself.

Maria learned a lot about this adage when she changed jobs. She liked the job she was in, but didn't think she was paid enough. The positives were that the people she worked with were great, she had a lot of responsibility, and she really liked her boss. The problem was that the company she worked for had a low pay scale, and she thought she should be paid more for her level of responsibility. So she looked around for a company that would pay her what she thought she was worth.

It didn't take long before she got a good offer from another company. She concluded that they valued her talents more than the company she was with, so she took the job. But Maria soon realized that the grass wasn't greener. Her responsibilities in her new position were much below her capabilities, and she was frequently asked to do administrative tasks instead of the more substantive work she expected. The work was boring, and she didn't like the people she worked with, especially her boss. When it was too late, she realized that she had made a mistake. The grass appeared to be greener, but it wasn't. She tried to get her old job back, but it was taken. Maria left her new job after only six month, but still didn't find anything as good as her previous job.

The grass-is-always-greener syndrome is frequently an illusion that induces people to make the wrong decision. In many cases, it only appears to be greener because you don't see everything that is there. You may see only what you are missing in your current situation, such as Maria did with her compensation. Because you are so close to your own situation, you see all of the weeds within it. But when you look afar, you can't see all of the weeds in that situation.

The grass-is-always-greener can also be about jealousy and how we always wish we had what someone else has. It's when we think that other people have things better or easier; when we think that others have more money, or a nicer car, a better job, a better life. But this thinking is a trap that can ensnare us in giving up an acceptable situation for an unacceptable one.

A friend of mine, Bill, works long hours as a teacher. He feels very emotionally rewarded for his good work in an inner-city public school teaching fourth-grade math. But, since this job doesn't pay very well, he spends his evenings tutoring math to high-school students studying to take the SATs. Although he has the summers off from his regular teaching job, he needs to spend this time teaching summer courses to supplement his income. After seven years of teaching in three different schools, Bill keeps looking at all of his friends, many of whom have similar backgrounds in math or economics, who have taken different routes in life. He constantly wonders if they are happier than he is.

Some make more money. Others have more time off from work. But what Bill doesn't realize is that he's really the envy of many of his friends. While the accountant makes more money, he isn't fulfilled with what he accomplishes every day. He thinks that all he does is help companies save a dollar here or a dollar there. He doesn't really think that he's contributing to the betterment of society, as he wishes he were doing. Equally well-off financially, the banker has similarly unfulfilled dreams and aspirations.

People make very different decisions in life and pursue different paths in their careers. Some make these decisions based upon how happy they want to be, how fulfilling of a life they want to live, what types of jobs they are interested in, whether they want to be a family man or stay single, and so on. They have different criteria.

You need to live with both the negative and positive ramifications of your decisions, and there will be many times throughout your life when you will question the decisions that you've made. You will wonder if you would have been better off financially or emotionally, less stressed or happier if you had made different decisions. But this is a futile exercise. I have found the best approach — rather than bemoaning past decisions — is to learn from them.

The one preventive thing you can do when making life-changing decisions is to pause and consider alternatives and likely outcomes. Never make a decision because the grass looks greener. Remember, it just looks greener from where you're standing.

!36

Deceptively Simple

When you don't know much about something, it can appear to be deceptively simple. Of course, it isn't. You just don't know what you don't know. This is a common malady.

Tom and Alice made this mistake when they decided to open a gift shop. Both had just retired and saved enough money to do something new in their lives. A gift shop had a lot of appeal to them and seemed like a very exciting challenge. Alice had spent a lot of time (and money, Tom joked) visiting gift shops wherever they traveled. Tom always wanted to run his own small business, which he thought would be easy after working at large corporations for most of his career.

Something is deceptively simple when you think it's easy because you don't know much about it, and you look at it superficially.

So they invested their savings in a gift shop, Seaside Treasures, in a resort town on the waterfront. They figured it couldn't be that hard to manage, and they would have fun doing it. When one of Tom's friends asked him if he knew anything about running a gift shop, Tom laughed and replied, "No, but really, how hard could it be?"

He soon found out. The couple had to delay the opening of their shop in order to get the necessary permits and insurance and to create a legal business entity. To open the store, they had to invest in a lot of inventory and had to borrow money from a local bank to finance it. They struggled with pricing and never seemed to make enough to pay the bills. They had a hard time hiring competent help, requiring them to work harder and more hours than they ever had before. Rather than being the leisurely, part-time business they had hoped to have in retirement, it became an enormously burdensome full-time effort. The business, financial, and emotional strains eventually started to affect their personal relationship.

After two years, Tom and Alice sold Seaside Treasures at a substantial loss. They lost most of their savings in trying to keep it afloat. They learned an expensive lesson: Sometimes people make major decisions about something they don't know much about because it looks deceptively simple to them.

Something is deceptively simple when you think it's easy because you don't know much about it. You look at it superficially and figure that you know a lot about it when you really don't. Then you make a major decision on this erroneous assumption that it's simple. Like Tom and Alice, you learn that it's a lot more difficult than you thought only when you actually get into it.

Even successful corporations make bad decisions based upon faulty assumptions like this one. A major automotive electronics company I consulted for wanted to expand to another market and identified marine electronics as a great opportunity for expansion. Even though they had no experience in this market, they told me ,"It has to be a lot easier than the automotive market, and it seems to be somewhat similar."

I tried to caution them that there were probably things about this market that they didn't know, but they didn't listen. They lost more than $20 million over the next two years selling less than $1 million of marine products. After investing so heavily in the expansion, they realized that they couldn't make waterproof devices or break into the channels of distribution to sell marine electronics. They had completely underestimated the demand in the market. Soon after, the CEO was fired, and I had the opportunity to have lunch with him. He admitted that this market looked deceptively simple and that he should have listened to my advice.

I had another good friend who made $7 million from selling a software company that he had founded and grown into a very successful company. He decided that he would start a new career in real-estate development. After all, he reasoned, it had to be a lot easier than the software industry. Unfortunately, it just looked deceptively simple, and he lost much of his savings while trying to make real estate pay off for him.

> **Make bold decisions to do something new and different, but do it with your eyes fully open to the challenges it will involve.**

Decisions on major undertakings are most vulnerable to the deceptively simple syndrome. These include decisions on starting a business ("how hard could it be?"), having children ("anybody can do it"), going into a new profession or career ("that looks easier than what I'm doing now"), building or refurbishing a house ("I'll hire professionals to do the things I don't know how to do"), starting a new hobby ("golf looks so easy"), etc. But major undertakings are not to be done lightly. So, before deciding to enter into a new endeavor, do your research. Talk with others who have experience. Think about how you would overcome the challenges you're likely to face.

I don't want to advocate that you avoid major, new undertakings. After all, these provide some of the biggest rewards and joys in life. Make bold decisions to do something new and different, but do it with your eyes fully open to the challenges you'll face. Then assess your ability to take on such challenges. Do you have the emotional, financial, and material assets to take the risk? What is your exit strategy if the venture doesn't pan out?

Remember the words of a wise friend of mine who counsels, "If something looks too good to be true, it probably is." So make sure you find out before you get too deep into it. Don't fall victim to the deceptively simple syndrome.

37

Stand or Sit

People usually think of decision-making as a mental activity, but I've found that it can be a physical activity as well. Maybe you've noticed, for example, that you make better decisions standing rather than sitting, or walking or running, lying on the floor or doing yoga.

Rodin must have believed that placing his chin on his hand helped. I once tried sitting with my hand under my chin like Rodin's "The Thinker," but it wasn't comfortable and didn't work for me. Aristotle became famous for his walkabouts with his students as he delivered his philosophical lectures. This approach became known as the peripatetic method. I can see why he liked to do it; it helped him think.

I make most decisions sitting down, but to get into my very best decision-making position, I need to put my feet up on my desk. Don't ask me why. Maybe this position gets the blood flowing better, or maybe it's just plain comfortable, enabling me to focus on the decision at hand. I've also taken the peripatetic approach, though. Once I had to make a very difficult decision about whether to take my consulting firm public, and I spent the entire day with my cofounder walking the streets of San Francisco. We walked for five hours without stopping, the whole time discussing the merits and drawbacks and implications of going public. We walked until we had made our decision. (After five hours, we were many miles from our hotel, so we hailed a taxi to get back.)

Anyway, we announced our decision not to take the firm public at the worldwide partners' meeting the next day. It was one of the best decisions we ever made. The stock market crashed later in 2000, and the economy declined. Being a publicly held company during that period would have been a disaster for us.

Did all that walking help us think clearly at a critical time? It certainly didn't hurt, and it gave us plenty of exercise. Peripatetic decision-making has other real advantages. Unless you turn it into a backpacking trip, it gives you an implied decision deadline of a few hours. No one can drop in on you with papers for you to sign or to ask your advice about something, so you are completely focused.

Walking is a great shared activity, too, although holding a discussion while walking with more than two people can be difficult. (Aristotle undoubtedly did all the talking on his walks with his students.) So the next time you need to reach a decision with someone, try saying, "Let's take a walk to discuss this."

I've also found that making decisions is easier when I am out running to get exercise — although some people claim that there is no distinction between the pace at which I run and the pace at which others walk. I think running — OK, jogging — gets my adrenalin flowing and helps me to think more clearly.

But there's also the shower, where I've done some of my best thinking and decision-making. If I knew the reason for this, I'd share it, but I have no idea why. Some people have theorized that the flow of water, and the stimulation of your skin relaxes you, thereby putting you in the perfect environment for clear thinking. I'm not sure about that.

Sometimes people think they make better decisions while driving a car, but I don't recommend it for safety reasons. Others like to go to a special place to make important decisions. This approach doesn't work for me. Sitting outside in a beautiful setting is too distracting. I find myself daydreaming instead of decision-making.

Do you believe lying in bed at night is a good time and place to make decisions? I don't, because I've realized that at this time of day, when I'm tired, I tend to worry rather than to think constructively. Still, I have made some important decisions during sleepless nights because I was running out of time. I find airplanes too distracting for decision-making, although in-flight time is good for writing, as I am doing while writing these words.

Business decisions are traditionally made in conference rooms by a group of people sitting around a table. The conference room is probably the best environment for a small group to reach a decision. They can all look at each other while exchanging views and get a sense — both verbally and through body language — of how the decision-making process is progressing.

I find that group decision-making via conference calls, while often more convenient, doesn't work as well. The body language component is missing, and the conversation isn't as dynamic. Of course, conference calls are sometimes necessary, due to the difficulty of getting the right people together and the urgency of making a decision. But I've found sometimes that a conference call will result in a decision inferior to what would have been made by the same group meeting in person. A neuroscientist I know says this may be the result of aural fatigue: Our brains are wired for visual stimulation, and the lack of it on conference calls probably makes us impatient and ready to get off the phone rather than think clearly and comprehensively about an issue at hand. Who knows?

> When you need to make an important decision, do it while walking, running, sitting, or whatever you find works best for you.

It's interesting to watch the chosen decision-making positions of coaches in different sports. Baseball managers and coaches tend to sit quietly on the bench, ruminating. Football, soccer, and basketball coaches stand or pace up and down, gesticulating wildly. Leo Mazzone, the longtime Major League Baseball pitching coach, was famous for rocking back and forth. The worse his pitcher did, the harder and faster Leo rocked. It must have helped him think, or maybe it calmed his nerves.

Assistant football coaches typically sit up in a box above the field and relay their observations and suggestions to the coaches on the sidelines. Basketball coaches have chairs, but they all seem to stand or run back and forth in front of the bench. (Occasionally, they throw their chairs, but probably not while making a decision.) I often wonder if it is difficult for football coaches to make decisions in the pouring rain or sleet, or when it is very cold. I wouldn't want to make a business decision in those conditions. (Business people usually stew in air-conditioned comfort.)

I also think that the clothes you wear when you make a decision can make a difference. Most people make better decisions in more comfortable clothes. Bill Belichick, the head coach of the New England Patriots, wears a comfortable hoodie (a grey sweatshirt with a hood and usually cut-off sleeves) when he makes his decisions during a football game, and it works great for him. I think I'll try out the "hoodie decision-making" method myself.

So think about what position and location are best for you to make decisions. Try alternative positions and locations and evaluate them. Then, when you need to make an important decision, get into the position or place that makes you happiest. We need all of the help we can get when making critical decisions.

!38

Split-Second Decisions

Tom Brady, the future Hall of Fame quarterback for the New England Patriots, is a master of split-second decisions. He quickly sees when a receiver will be open and knows instinctively exactly when and where to throw the ball, a decision that needs to be made in less than a second.

Other quarterbacks in the NFL are stronger and more accurate, but arguably none are quicker at making these split-second decisions than Brady. In 2001, when he was still just a backup quarterback, I watched him play a practice game and predicted that he would be a great quarterback because he made such quick decisions. By the time the season ended, Tom Brady was the Super Bowl MVP.

Split-second decisions are just what the term states; they aren't made over a one- to 20-second time span, but rather in less than a second. In fact, they're so fast that I call them reactive decisions. You need to instantly recognize your situation and immediately react to something that you don't have time to think about. This means that your decisions are based mostly on instinct

> **Split-second decisions are reactive decisions that are based mostly on instinct and training.**

and training — the instincts that you innately have or have gained as a result of experiences that have trained you to recognize the need for action and react quickly.

Many situations in life require split-second decisions, so I think it's worthwhile to understand how they're made. We'll use Tom Brady as an example to explore split-second decision-making and what it takes.

First, to be really good at it, you need to be mentally quick. While this may be an inborn capability, you can improve the speed with which you process information with mental exercises. Brady is obviously mentally quick.

Second, split-second decisions involve pattern recognition. Since you don't have the time to analyze alternatives, you need to react to the patterns you recognize because of continual exposure to similar situations. Brady has an exceptional ability to recognize patterns on the football field. He spends many hours prior to each game analyzing the defensive patterns of his opponent.

Third, you need to instinctively react to these patterns. Each pattern will lead to a range of outcomes, and while there is a statistical probability of particular outcomes, in football there is no time to process these statistics before a reaction is called for. Think about batters in baseball. They must decide in a split second whether to swing at a pitch coming at them at 90 mph.

Fourth, you might say split-second decisions are possible because the decision-maker is "front-loaded" with information. Tom Brady and the New England Patriots prepare extensively to understand the tendencies of their competitors as well as those of their own players. This helps Brady anticipate the next step his receiver will make and how the defender opposing his player is likely to react. He is, therefore, prepared — or preconditioned — to recognize the patterns he can then react to so quickly.

A few people become heroes by making split-second decisions and saving the lives of others. Typically, they do this without thinking; they just act. On January 4, 2007, for example, Wesley Autrey was standing with his two children in a New York City subway station when a stranger had a medical episode and collapsed onto a subway track. In a split second, Autrey jumped onto the track, in spite of an oncoming train, and rolled the stranger into a drainage trough, where the train soon passed over them with only inches to spare. Autrey didn't have time to think. He just acted bravely, risking his life to save another. This requires a special instinct — one that not everybody has. Most would have stood and watched, completely frozen in their position, unable to make that split-second decision.

Autrey knew he had to act, and he instinctively realized what to do. I believe he also instinctively knew that he had a good chance of doing it successfully. It's likely that heroes who make split-second decisions, such as that made by Autrey, have previously decided in the back of their minds that they would risk their lives to save another. When the situation then presents itself, they act in a split-second.

Police officers sometimes need to make split-second decisions on using deadly force. They need to decide in a split second whether to pull the trigger or not. While most of the time they're right, sometimes they're wrong. Recognizing the importance of these split-second decisions, police officers are well trained before they take to the streets — to think quickly, understand patterns, and prepare to make a decision, then to act on them.

Ordinary people also make split-second decisions periodically during the course of their lives. Driving a car, for instance, often presents you with the need for split-second decisions. These decisions might be routine or, less occasionally, life-changing. You may be driving down a highway when the driver in front of you slams on the brakes and stops suddenly. When this happens, you need to decide immediately whether to slam on

Fortunately, you can prepare in anticipation of a potential split-second decision, just as police officers do.

your brakes or swerve into another lane. Either decision could have a bad outcome, as happened with a friend of mine who swerved into an oncoming lane to avoid hitting a stalled car one icy, snowy New Year's day in Massachusetts. Unfortunately, my friend had not noticed the oncoming truck that was plowing that lane. Fortunately, the large blade on the front of the plow blunted the impact. My friend, his pregnant wife, and their dog all survived without a bruise.

Pattern recognition, preparation, and the ability to think quickly come into play here, too. You need to use your intuition to swerve if you don't think there is a car in the other lane, but you need to realize this with some probability before you act instantly. The fact that you have likely confronted this same situation many times in the past helps you to recognize the pattern of responses.

We also make split-second decisions when we are talking or arguing with someone. We decide what we want to say and how to say it in a split second and then have to deal with the impact and consequences of what we said.

Parents need to make split-second decisions when telling children what to do or reprimanding them for something they did wrong. There have been times when I've told my children something in a split second and, even before I finished speaking, realized how stupid it was.

This leads us to one of the unfortunate characteristics of split-second decisions: They're frequently wrong. You can easily make a mistake in a split second and say something that you wouldn't have said if you had actually thought about what you were saying first. NFL quarterbacks — even Tom Brady — miss a lot of passes. Baseball players miss more pitches than they hit. Even some heroes try and fail, often giving up their own lives in the process.

Split-second decisions are unique. You don't use them often — or at least for major, non-routine, life-affecting decisions. They're decisions that you are forced to make in reaction to something. They're instinctive decisions where you don't have time to think before you decide. But you can prepare ahead to make them better. You can practice them to develop more skill in making them, as police officers and quarterbacks do. But in many cases, it's just best to avoid them if you can — unless, of course, you're destined to be a hero.

39

Stuck in a Rut

F ar too many people create a big mess in their lives. I see this continually in the e-mails I receive on the DecideBetter! website from people who are desperately looking for help. They're unhappy because they're in bad relationships, bad financial straits, dead-end jobs, or are generally overwhelmed by their responsibilities. My heart goes out to them and their unhappiness. Much of my concern is related to their condition, but a larger part of it is actually related to the problems they have with making decisions. I struggle to guide them to get their lives back on track.

> **Most of the people who have made their lives a mess get there by a series of bad choices.**

Most of the people who have made their lives a mess get there through a series of bad choices — something that can be solved with better decision-making. Unfortunately, each bad choice, seems to set up the next bad choice and before they know it, they've linked together a series of bad choices that make their life a mess.

Angie is a typical example of someone who made a mess of her life through a series of bad choices. When she graduated from high school, she wanted to be a nurse, so she went to nursing school. During her first year in school, she struggled a little, but with extra effort, she passed all of her courses. In her second year, she moved off campus and made a whole new group of friends — friends who enjoyed life and liked to party and have fun. "You're only young once," one of her new friends kept telling her. So she joined them, started missing classes, and stopped working so hard. Enjoying life is, of course, desired by everyone, especially when you're still in school, but Angie was lacking in moderation.

As a result of missing classes and falling behind in her studies, she didn't do as well in school and began to fail some of her classes. Angie decided that it was necessary to take a year or two off from her schooling. She got a job as a waitress. Soon after, she met up with Tim and within a month, she moved in with him. Her lease was up, and it seemed like a good idea at the time. Tim was 12 years older than Angie and although he didn't have a steady job, he was a promising musician.

Angie worked extra shifts at the restaurant to support both of them. Before she knew it, they had been living together for 18 months, and she became pregnant. They decided to keep the baby. Unfortunately, Tim left her a few months later to go out on his own and fulfill his dream of being a successful musician. After all, how could he be successful as a musician and support a baby at the same time?

Throughout all of this, Angie had lost contact with her family. She said that they had been interfering in her life and trying to tell her what to do, even though she was grown up and could handle whatever life threw at her. After giving birth to her son, Angie struggled to support herself and her new child. She had to work a second waitressing job that required her to be there very late at night, while a neighbor watched her son for her. Tim failed to provide any financial or moral support for her and their son, Evan, and soon moved far away without ever meeting his son.

Angie would occasionally date other men, but those relationships never lasted very long. The men she met weren't interested in taking on the obligations of her and her child. By the
time she was 26, Angie had made a mess of her life. While she
loved her son more than anything in the world, she was now
stuck in a rut that she couldn't work herself out of.

Angie didn't intend to make a mess of her life; she started
out with high aspirations. But each bad choice led to another
bad choice and then another and another. Once someone starts
down a bad path, it's easy to make it worse by continuing down
that path. Angie's first bad choice was to get too involved with
friends who had different intentions than she did. One could
argue that even before that, she made a bad choice by moving
off campus, which opened the possibility of more distractions
from her studies, which she needed to work hard at to succeed.
She could have decided to correct her previous bad choices by
moving back on campus and resuming her hard work, studying
to become a nurse. Instead, however, she opted for the easier
and more attractive choice to take a year or two off. She ratio-
nalized this as only a temporary break in her career plans.

Rationalizing a bad choice that is considered to be an easier
path to take in life is typical of people who keep making a mess
of their lives. Angie's bad choices of getting involved with Tim,
moving in with him hastily, and finally, getting pregnant, continued a string of bad decisions, but once she was this far down
the wrong path, she had only more bad options to choose from.
Angie's example is far from unique. Unfortunately, while helping to steer people to better decision-making, I see too many
people like this. The facts are different, but the pattern is exactly the same. Once someone starts down a bad path with bad
choices, they tend to keep making it worse by making more
bad choices.

It's not that people in this position are stupid. I've seen this
happen to some of the brightest people I've met. They are often
terrific people who get swayed on to the wrong paths at key

points in their lives. They don't realize that they're on the wrong path until they're well along it. As a result, they tend to make choices from a pool of other, less promising options. They don't step back and look at their overall situations. Inevitably, they face a bad set of choices.

My advice is that once you suspect you may be going down the wrong path of life, turn around and go back — as soon as you can. Angie could have done that at several points in her life. Sure, she would have wasted a couple of years that she couldn't get back, but she wouldn't have ended up in the mess she was in.

So what can you do once you have created a mess of your life, as Angie did? You need to step back, realize you're in a mess, identify potential alternatives to get out of it completely, take a deep breath, and start again. In the end, that's exactly what Angie did. She acknowledged that she was in a mess and needed to make some big changes. After so much time being out of touch, she reached out to her family for help and admitted the mistakes she had made. She moved home with her parents, who helped her to take care of her son for four years while she completed nursing school. This time, she kept her focus both on her son and on her studies, putting any social life on hold.

> **If you suspect you may be going down the wrong path of life, turn around and go back.**

By the time she was 30, she moved into her own apartment, put her son in first grade and started the next phase in her life. She even started dating again and had a promising relationship that she was taking slowly this time. Sure, Angie was 30 instead of 26, but she finally had a stable and rewarding life.

I admire Angie and others who have gotten themselves out of the ruts they've gotten into. If you find that you've made a series of bad choices that have created a mess of your life, stop right now and realize what's happened. Stop making any more bad choices, even if they seem attractive right now or if you perceive them to provide quick fixes for your problems. Back-track down the path you've come down by undoing what you've done, or make a drastic change like Angie did, to start all over the best you can. It's *never* too late to clean up your mess and create a happy life instead.

!40

Long and Hard

You've no doubt heard the expression that someone thought "long and hard" about a particular decision before making it. Believe me, that's great advice.

The opposite of this is "quick and easy," and unfortunately that's how too many people approach difficult decisions. Then, when they make a mistake, they seem surprised. If something is important, you need to work at it, and decisions are no exception to this rule.

When I was recruited to come out of early retirement to work as the CEO of a publicly held company, it was a major decision for me, and I thought long and hard about it before making my decision. I had only recently retired and had been looking forward to some time off, but this was a good offer. On the other hand, the company was more than 1,500 miles from my home in Maine.

It turned out that my decision was a good one. It benefited the company and its customers, employees, and investors. The company had previously had a series of unprofitable years and seemed to no longer have the pulse of the market, but I was able to turn it around, reigniting its growth and making it profitable for the first time in many years.

It was also a rewarding experience for me personally. But this decision didn't come quickly or easily. Before making it, I thought long and hard about it. I worked on the decision for many hours each day for two weeks before reaching a conclusion. I consulted with my family and friends for advice. I wrote down the alternative outcomes and evaluated the pros and cons of the move. I did an extensive evaluation of the company and what I would need to do if I took the position.

As a rule, you should think long and hard about all major decisions. This takes a lot of time but is usually worth the investment. Here's a way to calculate the value of your time to make a decision. Let's say that your time is worth $25 per hour to you (this is the equivalent of making $50,000 per year). You're facing a major decision, let's say to change your career, get divorced, relocate to a new city, have major surgery, etc. If you invested 100 hours thinking long and hard about your decision, then your opportunity cost would be $2,500 (100 hours times $25 per hour). Do you value a good decision at $2,500? If someone offered to sell you a certificate good for "one better decision," would you pay $2,500 for it?

When it comes to major life decisions, long and hard is the rule, not quick and easy.

Granted, allocating 100 hours to work long and hard on a decision is a lot. It's 4 hours per day for 25 days. In most cases, you may have less time than that, but give yourself a budget of time for working long and hard on your decision. Give it a priority over other things. Don't procrastinate by letting other things get in the way.

What does working hard on a decision entail besides devoting time to it? I think it's important to write down your thoughts. You need to keep notes on specific facts and tentative conclusions. You must clarify your objectives. You should list the pros and cons of different alternatives, as well as their potential outcomes.

Also, seek out the advice of others. In many cases it's OK to share with others that you're evaluating a particular decision so you can get their advice, although with some decisions, you may need to be more discreet about whom you share your thoughts with. Be sure you weigh the advice of others with your thoughts about the decision. Do your parents think you should make one decision, but your best friend thinks you should make another? How much would you weigh your parents' advice against that of your best friend?

What does working long on a decision mean? It means starting the decision process well in advance of the date needed for the decision. You can't afford to put off a decision until the last minute and then expect to think long and hard about it. As soon as you realize you'll be facing a decision, set up a time schedule for that decision. For example, if you're deciding on quitting your job to start a new career, give yourself 2 to 3 months to work on that decision.

> **The harder you work on making a decision, the higher quality the outcome of that decision will be.**

In some cases, major decisions arise from unanticipated opportunities or challenges. You get a great job offer you weren't considering, but you'll need to move. Maybe you have a deadline that's not too far down the road for making this decision. In these cases, drop everything else you're doing, so you can still work long and hard on the decision. Don't make a poor decision because you had to go to dinner with friends, or you needed to clean the garage instead. When it comes to making major life decisions, long and hard is the rule, not quick and easy. The harder you work on making a decision, the higher quality the outcome of that decision will be.

41

Procrastination

I've been putting off writing this chapter for a long time. Just kidding. Many people procrastinate. They continually put off things they need to do, and this includes procrastinating on making decisions. For example, some people keep putting off major decisions regarding where they will live or changing jobs or careers, or decisions affecting their health or relationships. People also put off smaller decisions, such as where to go on vacation or how to invest their money.

An old acquaintance of mine, Lisa, was a serial procrastinator. One time, she knew she needed to move, since the lease on her apartment was ending, and her roommate was getting married and moving out. But she kept putting off the decision on where to move. It was an uncomfortable decision for her to make. She wasn't sure what she could afford. She didn't know where she wanted to live. As you might guess, she put off making this decision until all of the best apartments were taken, and she ended up living in a run-down apartment with a new roommate whom she didn't like.

Some people are procrastinators by nature. They put off almost everything, including decisions, until the last possible moment. It's not that they are lazy or stupid; I think maybe it's some kind of gene deficiency. But even if it were possible to correct this deficiency with surgery, the vast majority of procrastinators would never get around to making the decision to undergo the surgery.

According to several studies, as many as 1 out of 5 people believe that they are continual procrastinators. With decisions, waiting too long can diminish the quality of your decisions, which, in turn, can reduce the overall quality of your life. You need to make your decisions in less time — or as we saw with Lisa — the available options are reduced to the point where your decisions must be made from among fewer and less attractive options.

People procrastinate on making decisions for a wide variety of reasons, and there are different procrastination-avoidance techniques that you can employ for each type of procrastination problem:

PROBLEM #1: Some people procrastinate with decisions because they are disorganized. They know they need to make a decision, but they put it off for a while and then forget about it. If the decision isn't right in front of them all of the time, they lose sight of the urgency of making it.

SOLUTION #1: The solution to this type of procrastination is to be more organized. Keep a list of decisions you need to make and when you need to make them, and then look at the list regularly (every weekend, every day, etc.) and make your decisions.

PROBLEM #2: Some people procrastinate by putting off a decision because they think it will be easier to make at some point in the future or perhaps that it will even go away if they delay.

SOLUTION #2: While in some cases it may prove to be true that delaying a decision will make it easier or make it go away, most of the time this is not the case. Don't deceive yourself by rationalizing that it's better to wait — it almost never is. Realize that the decisions won't go away and may actually get harder to make as time goes on. Make your decisions without any further delay.

PROBLEM #3: Some people procrastinate on making decisions because they're afraid. They have a fear of making the wrong decision, so they wait. Some constant procrastinators are perfectionists — or think that they are — who keep waiting for the "right" time to make the "perfect" decision. They think that they will be able to "find" more perfect information for the decision or will be able to come up with a new alternative if they wait.

> If you are facing a decision and find yourself procrastinating, try to understand why and apply the appropriate procrastination-avoidance technique.

Sometimes, fear of making a decision is justified. Some decisions have a high risk, so people put them off. Deciding to move, change jobs, get married, get divorced, or have children are typical decisions where people procrastinate. But that certainly doesn't mean you won't have to make them.

SOLUTION #3: You need to realize that at some point you will have the best and most information that you will ever have and that waiting for additional information has diminishing returns. When that is the case, don't hesitate any longer — make the decision.

PROBLEM #4: Some people procrastinate on decisions that involve conflict. Either the process of making the decision or the result of the decision will create conflict with others — a spouse, friends, family, coworkers or others. Because this conflict is unpleasant, it's tempting to procrastinate to avoid the conflict.

SOLUTION #4: You need to recognize that the conflict is likely to be inevitable and will occur sooner or later. Since this is the case, make your decision and then you will be able to get the conflict out of the way and proceed with your life.

PROBLEM #5: Some people procrastinate because they make decisions overly complicated. They lump multiple, related decisions together. They don't know how to get started, since there are so many components to the decision, and it seems the longer they wait, the more complex the decision becomes.

SOLUTION #5: The solution here is to break down complex decisions into several smaller ones. In some cases, you can make these smaller decisions individually and get them out of the way so that you can focus on the genuine thrust of the complex decision.

Procrastination is different from indecision. Procrastination is putting off attempting to make a decision, while indecision is attempting to make a decision but being unable to reach a conclusion. Some people have both problems, making it almost impossible for them ever to make a decision.

Assess yourself to see if you tend to procrastinate on making decisions, and if you do, realize that this may be reducing the quality of your decisions and the quality of your life. If you are facing a decision and find yourself procrastinating, try to understand why you are procrastinating and apply the appropriate procrastination-avoidance technique discussed in this chapter.

Don't wait. Do it today.

!42

Indecision

Indecision may or may not be my problem! This statement, attributed to singer Jimmy Buffet, is a tongue-in-cheek expression about indecision. Indecision is the inability to decide or tendency to vacillate between choices, and many people suffer from this problem. You see it frequently.

Have you ever been to dinner with someone who seems to take forever to make up his or her mind on what to order? By the time they decide what to have for dinner, it's practically time for dessert.

While indecision affects many people when they make both small and large decisions, it tends to be a much more serious problem when people are unable to make major decisions in their lives. Frequently, they go back and forth on their decisions, second-guessing themselves before they make up their minds, not only while they are making the decision but even after.

> It's frequently better to make a good decision that is timely than a better decision that is too late.

Shakespeare's Hamlet is an indecisive character who was unable to make any decisions at all. He was a great orator who took pleasure in his own words. Jean-Louis Barrault referred to Hamlet as "the hero of unparalleled hesitation" because of his inability to make a decision in a timely manner. The most significant example of Hamlet's indecision is evident in the first time he went to kill the King, who he knew had killed Hamlet's father. Although he had an easy opportunity to kill him while the King was praying, he couldn't decide to do it, reasoning that the King might go to heaven if he was murdered while praying. But in reality, this was just a rationalization of his indecision. Hamlet's indecision was also demonstrated in his "To be or not to be" speech at the beginning of Act Three, when he was contemplating life or death. He didn't want to be wrong in his decisions, so he wavered. In the end, he did avenge his father's death. Unfortunately, before getting around to doing it, he also met his own demise and caused the demise of many others unnecessarily.

Indecision can be particularly debilitating in business leaders when others are relying on them. I receive many e-mails from people who are frustrated with the indecision of their bosses. "I wish he would just make any decision. I don't even care anymore if he makes good decisions. I just want to see a decision."

If you think you're indecisive, decide today to work on preventing it in the future decisions you face.

Adam was this kind of indecisive manager. He took so long to make any decision that he frustrated everyone. He kept asking for more information, even if it was only indirectly related to the decision at hand and really didn't affect the outcome of the decision. He always thought he needed to find out everything before he decided. In a trait that is typical of those who suffer from indecision, the smaller and less important the decision, the more indecisive Adam seemed to be.

This was manifested when the walls of Adam's office had to be repainted. He drove everyone crazy with his hesitation. He looked at color samples over and over again. He hired one interior decorator and then another, and then he still couldn't decide. When it seemed like he had finally chosen the color and the painting had started, he made the painters stop for days so he could reevaluate the color choice. By then, all work in the office had ground to a halt; everyone was preoccupied with getting the walls painted — and talking about why Adam couldn't make this simple decision.

The decision still wasn't made when Adam went on vacation, so while he was gone, his assistant, Yvonne, made the decision for him and had the walls painted. When he returned, she told Adam that the landlord made the painters finish the painting, which of course wasn't true, but Adam was pleased with the color, and everyone went back to work.

Indecision is different from procrastination, discussed in the previous chapter. Indecision is the inability to make a decision once you have attempted to make it, while procrastination is putting off attempting to make a decision. They do share some of the same characteristics and some similar corrective techniques.

PROBLEM #1: Some indecisive people are indecisive because they want to make the perfect decision or are afraid to make the less-than-completely-correct decision, so they keep struggling with what to do.

SOLUTION #1: It's important to realize that it's frequently better to make a good decision that is timely than a better decision that is too late or takes an inordinate amount of time to make. As Theodore Roosevelt once said, "In any moment of decision, the best thing you can do is the right thing, the next best thing is the wrong thing, and the worst thing you can do is nothing."

PROBLEM #2: Some indecisive people need to gather more and more information before making a decision. Do they know everything they need to know to make the perfect decision? Maybe not, but how about knowing enough to make an informed decision?

SOLUTION #2: Frequently, people who are indecisive because they keep seeking out more information get to the point of diminishing returns — the additional information they are gathering is less and less significant to making the decision. Realize how much information you have and decide whether you would get better results making a decision based on less-than-perfect information or whether you would be better served obtaining more information. Then simply decide.

PROBLEM #3: Some indecisive people just cannot process all of the information they have at hand to make a decision. This is the opposite of the previous problem, where people think they don't have enough information to make their decision. It's not that these people aren't smart enough — it's that they can't seem to separate the important information from the tertiary information. This is sometimes referred to as "analysis paralysis."

SOLUTION #3: To prevent analysis paralysis from becoming a hindrance to your decision-making process, you need to get perspective on what information is important to making your decision. If the information is not likely to affect the decision, then don't worry about it. One thing that can often work is making a simple list containing all available information and then place each piece of information in order of most important to least important. This should help you to sort out what information you should be basing your decision on.

If you work, live, or do things with indecisive people, you need to develop techniques to deal with them. Whenever possible, avoid getting them involved in decisions — especially ones that are minor decisions. Just make the decision and tell them the outcome. If they object strongly and want to change what you've done, then go along with their decision — at least you got them to decide. If they get stuck, you can help them along by explaining that some information isn't relevant to the decision. Just sort it out for them.

My favorite technique to get someone to make a decision is to create a forcing mechanism. Tell them they need to make a particular decision by a specific time because of some given reason. It's OK even if you just make it up, although it's better if there is some real rationale for it. People who are indecisive tend not to question these forcing mechanisms, perhaps because they are indecisive about the importance of these deadlines.

Finally, you sometimes just need to let your indecisive friend or coworker do their thing. Go away and leave them to work on it but set your expectations appropriately.

If you think you're indecisive, decide today to work on preventing it in the future decisions you face.

43

Deal or No Deal

Have you ever watched the TV show "Deal or No Deal"? It's an interesting laboratory for understanding decision-making. In this show, contestants are presented with 26 briefcases. Each briefcase contains money that ranges from one penny to one million dollars. First, the contestants are required to select one of the briefcases presented to them and claim it as their own, but they have no idea how much money is in the one they've chosen and can't open it to find out how much money it contains until the end of the show. The contestant could win the amount of money inside of the one they choose, but it gets more complicated than that.

The contestants then select from among the remaining brief-cases, which are eliminated as they are opened one at a time. Every time they choose a briefcase, they find out how much money was in that briefcase, and it is eliminated from the group. As the contestants find out what amounts of money are in the briefcases they are eliminating, peri-

Most people don't really understand the expected value of their decisions.

odically someone called "The Banker" makes the contestants an offer to buy the unopened briefcase from them, ending the game.

The potential amount of money in the briefcase they have selected changes as briefcases of other values are opened and eliminated. The contestants can decide to take the offer from The Banker (Deal) or continue eliminating other briefcases (No Deal).

This popular TV show illustrates several interesting lessons of decision-making. First, the contestants seem to have little sense of the mathematically expected value of the outcome. For instance, since the contestants know the values of the money in the briefcases, but not which case each amount of money is in, it is possible to add up the value of the remaining unopened briefcases, including the one the contestant selected but hasn't been able to open. By taking the total amount in the remaining briefcases and dividing it by the number of briefcases left, you get the expected — or average — value.

For example, in one episode of this show that I watched, there were five briefcases remaining to be opened, including the one the contestant had selected at the beginning of the show — worth $10, $100, $300, $500,000 and $750,000. If you calculate the expected value, it would be $250,082 (the total divided by 5). This means that if the game was played enough times, the average would be $250,082 for each time it's played, but of course the contestant plays it only once, so he would win only one of these amounts. The chances are 20% that the contestant would end up with any of the amounts of $10, $100, $300, $500,000 or $750,000.

Most of the time, The Banker offers something less than the expected value, such as $119,000 in this example, and the contestants seem to be oblivious of how this compares to the expected value. From the decisions they make when offered the money by The Banker, they clearly haven't calculated the expected value. Many contestants take the offer of $119,000 (or whatever the value of their offer is).

Sometimes, though not very often from the little I've seen of this show, The Banker offers more than the expected value and the contestant doesn't take it. Watching this show has made me realize that most people don't really understand the expected value of their decisions — monetary or otherwise. (The mathematicians behind this show must have some fun with this.)

I've never seen anyone on this show actually calculate or estimate the expected value, even though you can come up with an approximation very quickly. In the example provided above, if you ignored the first three smaller amounts ($10, $100 and $300) and just added the $500,000 and $750,000, you get $1.25 million, which is $250,000 when divided by the number of cases remaining (5). This is much more than the $119,000 offered by The Banker. This means that accepting the deal is likely to end with the contestant getting less money than if they had turned it down.

In case you are wondering, the expected value before any briefcase is opened is $131,477.54, meaning that this is what the average contestant should win, but of course they don't offer that much at the beginning.

The next decision-making lesson we can learn from Deal or No Deal is related to the endowment effect, which I discuss more in an earlier chapter. Once The Banker offers money to the contestant in exchange for ending the game, then the contestant has something to lose by giving up the offered amount of money to continue. The contestant now doesn't want to "lose" the $119,000 (or whatever the amount they are offered by The Banker) that would be theirs if they stop selecting briefcases and give up.

Almost all of the contestants are willing to sell out for less than the expected value. In the above example, many contestants will take $119,000 for something that has an expected value of $250,082. When they now "own" $119,000, they don't want to lose it by continuing to choose briefcases. If they open another briefcase with a higher amount, The Banker will reduce his offer from $119,000 to some lesser amount. If they open another briefcase with an amount lower than $119,000, however, The Banker may increase his offer.

In addition, Deal or No Deal illustrates an important lesson on how people in different financial situations value money differently and, therefore, make their financial decisions differently. To a contestant who makes $25,000 per year, for example, $75,000 is a lot of money, and they may be more willing to settle early in the game. Another contestant who makes more money in their regular job may be willing to risk more early in the game in hopes of winning big. This is to be expected. In any decision involving money, the value placed on it depends on those making the decision.

> Understand how the decisions you face are structured and what the value of your options are. Only then make your decision.

Finally, a contestant's decision varies by personality. Some people seem to be natural gamblers, while others are more financially conservative. The producers of the show seem to choose contestants who are gamblers. They probably do this because these contestants are more entertaining to watch. They will usually cost the producers less money, because they either gamble and lose or will spend the entire time of the show picking briefcases.

Most of us will never be contestants on this show, but that doesn't mean there aren't decision-making lessons that we can learn from it. Deal or No Deal and similar game shows can help you to improve the outcomes of the decisions you make when you face similar circumstances. You can observe the way others make the decisions they face on the show, and you can analyze these decisions and learn from how the contestants make them. Most important, you can learn from their mistakes so you won't be doomed to repeat them.

In the real-life decisions we face, there are many situations similar to those faced by the contestants in this show, sometimes related to money and sometimes not. For example, you may be looking at changing careers, and you've been offered a great position at a new company that would begin in 6 months. It's a start-up company with a lot of potential but no guaranteed end result. Many start-ups go out of business within the first year or two after starting, and you know that is a possibility. Others make it big, and those who became involved from the beginning become very wealthy.

After being offered the job, however, you were offered another position at a company that is better established, but you need to make the decision to accept or reject the offer within 1 month, before the deadline for deciding to join the start-up. The new offer is stable and provides a substantial raise from your current job, but there's no real opportunity for the type of major financial gain that may be possible in the start-up. So what are you going to do? Will you accept the offer from The Banker and take the job that is a big raise and more stable, or will you keep opening briefcases and gamble by taking the job that has the possibility of huge financial success but also the possibility of going out of business?

When you're in a situation where you could settle for less or gamble it all on the possibility of more, will you calculate your odds and the expected value of your decisions? Or will you forget about the expected value and base your opinion on emotion or the endowment effect? My advice is this: Understand how the decisions you face are structured and what the value of the options are. Only then make your decision in a very calculated manner.

44

Frontal Lobes

n his book *The Executive Brain*, Dr. Elkhonon Goldberg, a Russian neuropsychologist, explains the role the frontal lobes of our brains play in decision-making. The frontal lobes are the only parts of the human brain where internal and external inputs converge. This is where ambiguity is dealt with. Dr. Goldberg argues that whether you are decisive or wishy-washy depends on how the frontal lobes of your brain work. Frontal lobes play a major role in how we approach and process adaptive decisions — those that deal with uncertain, complex, and ambiguous circumstances.

For example, Mortimer knows that he should get up and go to his job in the morning because if he doesn't, there will be negative consequences. He'll annoy his boss, use up a sick day, and have to work that much harder tomorrow to catch up on his assignments. But he doesn't know whether or not he should leave his job to start his own business. He's thought about it carefully, and he's pretty sure he could make it work, but what if he's wrong? What if he's overlooked something? There are so many factors to consider. Mortimer is wrestling with an adaptive decision: uncertain, complex, and ambiguous.

People tend to approach adaptive decisions in either a context-independent or context-dependent way. In the context-independent style, the person applies some hard and fast rule to the decision, regardless of how poorly it may fit the situation at hand. "I never spend more than $25 on a bottle of wine," or "Our country should never negotiate with terrorists." People with this context-independent style of judgment typically base their decision rules on some negative past experience or on childhood indoctrination. Context-independent decision-making can fail badly when the decision at hand doesn't fit the rule into which it's being shoehorned. That said, however, a context-independent decision can be a rational and expedient response to a very new and unfamiliar situation. How should one behave if kidnapped in the mountains of Peru? "It always pays to be polite" might be a good place to start.

By contrast, the context-dependent style of decision-making tries to grasp the particular or unique properties of the situation at hand. A context-dependent person would adjust their wine-spending guidelines to the situation. "I don't normally spend more than $25 on a bottle of wine, but we're in Paris for our anniversary, and this is a five-star restaurant." The problem is that the context or situation constantly changes, leaving the person with an uncomfortable decision-making style — particularly a decision in a situation with insufficient information or a new context. Such decision-makers can appear to be wishy-washy as they grope to find sufficient context.

The optimum approach to making adaptive decisions is probably a balance of the context-independent and context-dependent styles. But, according to Dr. Goldberg, our brain physiology makes that balance difficult to achieve. Dr. Goldberg's experiments showed that frontal lobes are critical in a free-choice situation when it is up to the individual to decide how to interpret

Frontal lobes play a major role in how we approach decisions with unknown consequences.

— and act in response to — an ambiguous scenario. He found that females tend to be context-independent, while males tend to be the opposite. Is the difference biological, cultural, or a combination? Dr. Goldberg found that gender differences in decision-making styles depend on the frontal lobes of the brain. The protrusion of the right frontal pole of the lobe over the left frontal pole is conspicuous in males and less pronounced in females. The idea that male and female brains are physically different in this regard is interesting.

Males appear to derive the tendency for context-dependent decision-making from their left frontal lobe. The two frontal lobes coexist in a balanced way but one of the lobes takes the lead in making a decision, depending on the situation. If the right frontal lobe is damaged, the male appears to become even more context-dependent in his decision-making, and if the left frontal lobe is damaged, there is an increased tendency to make decisions in a context-independent manner.

Yet the case appears to be very different in females. Damage to either the left or right frontal lobe tends to shift the decision-making style from the more prevalent context-independent style toward the context-dependent style more typical in males.

So what are you to do, as a decision-maker, with Dr. Goldberg's observations? A frontal lobotomy to change your decision-making style is an alternative, but not one I would recommend. More practically, his observations provide insight on why you might approach decisions the way you do.

In particular, they can help you focus on the difference between context-independent and context-dependent decision-making styles, along with the possibility that a preference in these styles may explain some of the differences in decision-making styles frequently perceived between men and women. Understanding how your frontal lobes are involved in your decision-making process can help you better understand how you make decisions and how you should approach these decisions.

Prisoner's Dilemma

Have you ever been faced with a prisoner's dilemma? This is essentially a circumstance in which you are required to decide between a penalty for your loyalty to a friend and a lesser penalty for condemning them.

When Charlie and Bruno were arrested for a bank robbery, for example, they were placed in different holding areas for questioning. The police were not sure they had enough evidence to convict them, so they offered each of them the following deal. If one of them were to provide evidence against the other, he would be freed and the other would be convicted with a full sentence of 10 years in prison. If both of them were to provide evidence against each other, they would each be prosecuted but receive a smaller sentence — probably five years — in exchange for their cooperation. If they were both to remain silent, they would still be prosecuted, but on reduced charges and probably sentenced to less than one year in jail. Each had to make the decision on his own.

> When each person puts themselves first, the result can be less favorable than if the group had worked together.

The best outcome for both of them would clearly be to cooperate — not with the police but with each other and remain silent. But since they were being held in different cells, they couldn't communicate this with each other, so they were required to make a decision about whether to condemn the other or not based on their own interests and their expectation of what the other would do.

Charlie thought about what would happen if Bruno decided to cooperate with the police, or if he didn't. If Bruno cooperated and Charlie didn't, then he would get 10 years in jail. If he cooperated at the same time that Bruno did, he would get only five years in jail. Since he was unsure what Bruno would do, he thought he would be better off cooperating.

If Bruno decided not to cooperate and Charlie decided the same thing, he would have received less than a year in jail. If Bruno didn't cooperate but Charlie did, Charlie would go free, but his friend would be condemned to 10 years in jail. So what decision should Charlie have made under those circumstances? Aha, he realized that he would be better off cooperating and providing evidence no matter what Bruno has decided. What did he say? "Jailer, I'm ready to cooperate!"

It's frequently better for two (or more) people to work together for their own mutual benefit rather than try to get the best deal they can on their own. When each person puts himself first, the result can be less favorable than if the group had worked together.

The outcome of a prisoner's dilemma is largely based upon the trust and loyalty that each participant has for each other. If the participants don't trust each other or have no reason to help the other one, then they will make the decision to help themselves at the expense of the other. Even if they merely perceive that the other person has no loyalty or trust, then they may make the same decision.

Prisoner's dilemmas affect us all in many different situations. Here is an example in office politics. Tim and Rob are coworkers and also friends. Their manager is retiring at the end of the year, and they're both candidates to replace him. They each need to decide how to compete for the position, and even though they are friends, they still both want the job. So what do they do? Do they praise each other or disparage each other? Tim realizes that if he praises Rob, but Rob disparages him, then Rob will get the job. Rob realizes the same thing. So they each disparage the other behind his back. In the end, because those responsible for the hiring process see what's going on, they decide to bring in someone from outside the company, and Tim and Rob both end up being forced out of the company for not being team players.

The prisoner's dilemma decision-making theory can also explain a number of public policy decisions faced by governmental leaders. For example, the nuclear weapons buildup during the Cold War was a prisoner's dilemma. During the Cold War, neither the United States nor the Soviet Union could risk cooperation with the other. If one said they would cooperate but didn't while the other thought it was a mutual agreement and disarmed itself, the one cooperating would be vulnerable to attack. Cooperation and disarmament would have clearly been best for both countries, both in terms of security and the economy. Instead of spending the hundreds of billions of dollars on nuclear weapons, they could have spent that money on improving the lives of their people. This example demonstrates one of the major factors determining the outcome of a prisoner's dilemma: Do both parties trust one another?

The prisoner's dilemma can also occur with a series of decisions made by two or more people in relation to each other. This happens often in relationships. Both people would like to have a mutually sustaining relationship where each person puts the other first. They may realize that a bad relationship results from one person taking advantage of the other. So they progressively make decisions based on the decisions made by the other. If one does something supportive, then the other follows. If one does something selfish, then the other follows accordingly. This back-and-forth series of decision-making between two or more people is known as a prisoner's dilemma iteration.

Alice and Tom played out the prisoner's dilemma iteration in their relationship. At first, both of them were happy, but it soon disintegrated. Instead of trying to make Alice happy, Tom started drinking and getting angry. Alice tried to humor him by making Tom his favorite meals and by being extra nice to him, but then she realized that he just took even more advantage of her. So she decided she would stop cooperating. She ignored him and stopped making dinner. He got angrier, and she continued escalating the defection by going out with her friends and buying things they couldn't afford. As you can imagine, the iterated prisoner's dilemma continued to escalate with both Tom and Alice determined that they wouldn't let the other take advantage of them, and they eventually got divorced.

Be aware of the impact the prisoner's dilemma has on decisions. Even though it's usually best for two parties to cooperate in their decisions for their collective best interests, unless they can trust each other sufficiently to make decisions with that objective, then this reasoning has them both acting to protect themselves.

!46

Don't Count Your Chickens

on't count your chickens before they hatch. You may have heard this saying before, but you may not know that it's also a good lesson about being cautious when approaching some decisions.

The saying originates from an ancient fable titled "The Milk-maid and her Pail," written by Aesop. As the story goes, a milk-maid was carrying a pail of milk on her head on her way into town while dreaming about what she could do with the milk. She surmises that she can take the milk and make it into cream, then use the cream to make butter. Once she has the butter, she can sell it in the market and buy a dozen eggs with the money from the butter. She will wait until the eggs hatch into chickens, and then she will breed them to have more chickens. These new chickens will have more and more chickens. Once she has enough chickens, she will sell some of them and buy a new gown to wear to the town fair. Inevitably, the young men at the fair will try to court her, and being as wealthy

> While it's one thing to dream of the benefits you may achieve, it's another to make decisions that assume benefits before they are achieved.

as she will be, she can simply turn her head away from them. When this thought goes through her mind as she was daydreaming, she turned her head as if to make the motion of turning away from the gentlemen suitors. At that point, the pail of milk fell off of her head, and it all spilled. So much for her dreams of becoming a rich chicken breeder. In response to the lost milk, the milkmaid's mother said to her, "Don't count your chickens before they hatch."

In real life, Aesop's fable provides us with a lesson about getting ahead of ourselves when approaching decisions. This can happen in all types of decisions, from relationship and personal decisions to professional and career decisions.

Jack was graduating with an MBA and had a great job offer as a consultant with a $25,000 signing bonus. Even though he had a lot of student loans, he decided to reward himself by purchasing a new Hummer. But two days after he started driving it, he got a call from the consulting firm telling him that they needed to rescind the offer. They lost a major customer contract and needed to cut employees, and they thought it was fairer to rescind offers to people who hadn't started yet than to lay off current employees. Jack was devastated by losing the job and was put into severe financial difficulties because he had "counted his chickens before they hatched." He got another job, but it didn't have a signing bonus, and it didn't pay as much as the one he lost. He couldn't afford the payments on the Hummer and was forced to sell it at a big loss.

Just as you wouldn't spend your lottery winnings before even buying a lottery ticket, why would you make other assumptions in your life before you are sure that the circumstances are in place for achieving those results? Counting your chickens too early can also happen in business situations. In many of the consulting jobs I've done, I've seen company leaders who appear to be doing the victory dance before the end of the first half of the game. One start-up company I consulted for had just landed its first big contract to sell its software, and they were ecstatic about it. They threw a major party for all of their employees, gave raises to all of the developers, and borrowed money to hire more developers to grow the company faster.

Just after the start-up had prepared to deliver the product, the customer unexpectedly went out of business and couldn't make good on the payments listed in the contract for the software. Since the start-up company had already spent a large amount of the profit they believed was forthcoming on raises and the new hires, they now lost money and were in a worse situation than they had been in prior to signing the major contract. They made some bad decisions because they had begun to count their chickens before they hatched, just like the milkmaid.

While it's one thing to dream of the benefits you may achieve, it's another to make decisions that assume benefits before they are achieved. That was the decision mistake that both Jack and the software company made. Many of us will make this mistake and learn this decision lesson the hard way. If you haven't, then hopefully you will learn it from these examples.

When it comes to decisions, remember the milkmaid and don't count your chickens before they hatch.

!47

Conundrum

A conundrum is a confusing or complex situation where, no matter what decision is made, there may not be a satisfactory outcome. In fact, it may sometimes be a completely insolvable problem.

Conundrum decisions are very difficult and often unsatisfactory. They tend to have many interlocking factors dependent to some degree on each other, and there doesn't seem to be any clear outcome. Frequently, each potential outcome has unknown factors, increasing the difficulty in making a good, well-informed decision. Here are a couple of conundrum decisions and some guidelines for addressing them.

Thomas works for a good company and likes his job, but he hates his boss. Not only do they not get along, but his boss is incompetent and treats Thomas as his inferior. It's increasingly difficult for Thomas to get up in the morning and go to work, and this is beginning to reflect on his relationship with his family. He is always fighting with his wife, and she wants him to stop it, but she fails to recognize that his job is the root of the problem. She claims that his problems at work are the result of his anger, too.

On top of this, they have financial problems and can't seem to keep up with their bills. His son is mad because Thomas won't let him buy a car. Thomas is facing a conundrum decision in his career that has significant effects on his personal life. If he confronts his boss, he knows that he will most likely be fired. He can continue with the job and hope that his boss will eventually change jobs or leave the company, and then Thomas can continue with the company. He would like his job without his current boss, but being miserable indefinitely with no indication as to whether his boss would be leaving in the future is not attractive.

If Thomas quits, he can find another job in town, but it won't pay as much, and his two children are reaching college age, so financial stability is important to him. If he moves to another state where there are better job opportunities, then he would need to uproot his family — something that his wife and high school-aged children would certainly be unhappy with. This is Thomas' conundrum.

> You can't solve all of the interrelated problems in your life with a single decision.

Mary faces a similar conundrum decision in her personal life. Her marriage has fallen apart. She no longer wants to be with her husband, and she doubts he wants to be with her. She really wants to get on with her life before she gets too old. But she's afraid to get divorced for a number of reasons. First, she hasn't worked for 10 years and doesn't know how she would support herself. Mary and her husband had decided when they got married that she would stay at home with the kids, and he would keep working. She also worries about the impact a divorce would have on the children. She currently really enjoys her neighbors and where she lives, but she knows they would need to sell the house, and she would need to move to an apartment if they got divorced. Mary frets over this conundrum all of the time, especially since it has so many interrelated components and unknown outcomes.

We all have to face conundrum decisions similar to the ones Thomas and Mary are wrestling with. The alternative options we need to choose from are complex; there are unknown outcomes, and usually you can't solve all of your problems with a single decision. While there is no simple formula for how to approach conundrum decisions, I can offer a few guidelines.

First, realize the characteristics of this type of decision; it's a complex decision with several interconnected components and largely unknown outcomes. Give yourself a break and don't expect to find a clear and simple solution. In part, Thomas and Mary are distraught because they're looking for easy solutions. Difficult situations require some challenging decisions, so you need to try to identify possible alternatives. Most likely there won't be one solution that will solve all of the interrelated components of your problem. In fact, the best solution may even create new, unforeseen problems that you will subsequently have to face.

Second, don't rush into the decision. Take some time to make it carefully and properly. But make sure that you work on it regularly — don't ignore it, because it won't go away. Thomas can begin his process of getting out of the conundrum he faces by having candid discussions with his family to get their opinions and prepare them for a potential change — be it changing jobs or changing states. He can visit other states and explore the possibilities for a new job. He can have discreet discussions with the director of human resources at his company and get her advice about whether he could possibly move to another division or to see if she has any insights on his boss possibly changing positions. None of these will necessarily solve the problem, but it will give him more clarity on the unknowns of his conundrum and provide him with more reliable information to use in making his decision.

Mary can begin to look for a job while she's still married to facilitate the transition back into the workforce should she decide to get divorced. She can try one more time to address the root of the problem by seeking marriage counseling with her husband, and she can also seek advice from friends or professionals about how to proceed.

Third, consider solving this conundrum as a journey rather than an event — usually it is not one simple decision that needs to be made and then you can go on with your life. By working on the decision early, you are preparing for your journey. You are identifying options for which way to go and how to make it work. When you make your decision, you are starting off on your journey toward realizing the outcomes you had hoped for when you began considering your alternatives. Do your best to make it work with the decision that you have made and don't look back on what might have been. With conundrum decisions, you really can't anticipate what would have happened had you decided differently. The journey may actually continue forever, since the decision you've made may have been a completely life-altering one. But you need to make the decision and then proceed full-steam in implementing it.

Finally, realize that you can't solve all of the interrelated problems in your life with a single decision. Usually, you can solve only some of them, and as I said before, some things may even get worse because of the tough decisions you need to make. So when preparing to solve your conundrum, you need to decide on your priorities — what components of the outcome are most important to you?

We all face conundrum decisions at some point in our lives. They seem overwhelming at times. If you are realistic, you can work toward making the best decision possible given the situation.

48

Buyer's Remorse

We have all experienced buyer's remorse. Maybe you bought a new car but then had second thoughts about it when you drove it home. Maybe you bought a new dress, but when you got home and tried it on again, it didn't look as attractive as it did in the store. Or perhaps you bought a new house but began to question your decision as soon as you moved in. Did you pay too much? Was it in the right neighborhood? Was it the right house? Does it need more work than you thought it did?

Or maybe you made an investment, but then a few days later, when your investment looked like it might lose money, you began to think you had made a mistake. These are all examples of buyer's remorse: an emotional reaction that occurs when you feel regret or doubt soon after making a purchase, large or small. You doubt that you made the best decision. You begin to think that you paid too much or that you could have purchased something better had you looked around more. Or maybe the salesman pressured you into making the decision to buy something when you couldn't afford it. Generally, this is a normal emotional reaction and doesn't necessarily mean that you made a bad decision or that you have some type of psychological disorder. Everyone experiences some type of buyer's remorse at one time or another.

While occasionally occurring with small items, buyer's remorse usually occurs with expensive purchases, such as a new home or new car.

An old acquaintance of mine, Jared, is a case in point. After shopping around for a short period of time, he purchased a brand new truck with many of the latest features. Initially, he was excited about his new truck, but when he drove it home from the car dealership, he began to have doubts almost immediately.

He noticed a truck that was on sale online for the same price he paid, but it had additional features that weren't included in his new truck. A couple of his friends told him he should have bought another model that would be more suitable for his purposes. Soon after that, he was disappointed in the mileage he was getting and realized that he would need to pay a lot more for gas than he had expected. Finally, when he looked closely at his monthly lease payments for the new truck, he realized that he would need to make some difficult sacrifices to pay for it.

> **Buyer's remorse doesn't occur only when you make a bad purchase decision. Sometimes, it occurs even though you have made the best decision.**

Jared suffered from his buyer's remorse for more than a month. In his mind, he made some mistakes in his decision to buy the new truck, and this really bothered him. Maybe he should have bought a different model? Maybe, if he had tried to negotiate better, he could have gotten some additional features or a better price? At this point, there was nothing he could do to rewind the decision, since he couldn't return the truck, and he would lose too much money if he tried to sell it.

If I were advising Jared at this point, I would suggest that he enjoy his new truck and stop agonizing over his decision. But I would also counsel him to take more time to research different options and prices in his next major purchase.

Buyer's remorse doesn't occur only in cases where you didn't make a good purchase decision. Sometimes, it actually occurs even though you may have made the best decision you could have at the time. When you begin to second-guess your decision, it's sometimes hard to distinguish between the two scenarios. Are you overreacting, or did you indeed make a poor decision? You need to realize that when making a purchase decision, you never have perfect information. You don't know if the price would have been lower, for instance, if you had waited. How many times have you purchased something and then seen it go on sale the next week?

According to recent accounts in the press, buyer's remorse was experienced by several people who purchased the Apple iPhone when it first came out. It was an amazing device (I actually purchased the first model), but soon after, the price went down significantly. One person went so far as to file a lawsuit against Apple for reducing the price so quickly after so many people had purchased it for a much higher price.

Inevitably, you won't see some of the shortcomings of what you purchase until you begin to use it. You often won't know the opinions and advice of your friends — who may have more information about the products than you do — until after you've purchased something. So give yourself a break and don't fret over your purchase decision. Like Jared, you should enjoy it and stop agonizing, but be sure to learn from it. And do as much research as possible into major purchase decisions before buying.

In some cases when you have buyer's remorse, you might be able to reverse the decision by returning the item or exchanging it for something more appropriate. John and his wife, Alicia, made an offer on a new home, for example, and after several rounds of negotiation, they agreed to a term sheet that required an inspection and a satisfactory mortgage. Initially, they were very excited, but then they started to have buyer's remorse. They drove around the neighborhood and realized that it was mostly families with children older than theirs, while they had been hoping there would be younger children around for their kids to play with. They drove to the new home during rush hour one day and were surprised by the traffic delays. They found some unexpected items in the inspection, and while they were able to get a mortgage, it was for a little more than they had anticipated.

For this couple, buyer's remorse was beneficial. They still had time to reverse their decision. After canceling the purchase, they found a more suitable home in a better location for them. While they had been swayed by certain features of the first house, they learned that other factors were more meaningful in the long run — factors like the number of children in the neighborhood and the commuting time to work. They learned that they should have used a more rigorous decision process for buying their new home. If they had listed all of the factors important to them and then formally evaluated these factors before making the decision, they wouldn't have had to endure buyer's remorse.

The general concept of buyer's remorse also occurs with other decisions you regret soon after making them. This can happen in relationship decisions, decisions on changing jobs, or other things you may decide to do.

When you feel buyer's remorse, the first thing to realize is that it's perfectly normal, so don't let it bother you too much. Enjoy what you purchased, but learn from your decision process. In those cases where you can still reverse your decision, re-evaluate your decision and reverse it if you think it's best. In all major purchase decisions, to avoid buyer's remorse as often as possible, do the best research you can beforehand. You won't regret it.

49

Hedging Your Bet

Unlike with a Hobson's choice (described in a previous chapter), the choice of one alternative instead of another is not always so cut and dry. You may be facing a decision where you have two options and are likely to either lose something or gain something, regardless of which one you choose. Or you may be facing a decision where you can't tell if you're going to win or lose. So what do you do? You hedge your bet.

The classic example of a decision you may face where you can hedge your bet is, obviously, in decisions you make when gambling (that's where the term originates). For example, if you are betting on horses, you may take the bet with the worst odds, but with the highest returns if you win. One horse, Josephine, has odds of 27-1, so if you put down $100 on her and she wins, you will get $2,700 in return. Another horse, Rawhide, the one who is largely favored to win, has odds of 2-1. This means that if you put down $100 on him and he wins, you will get $200 in return. What are you going to do? You want the $2,700, but you don't want to lose your $100. So you decide to hedge your bet. You put $100 on Josephine in hopes of winning big, but just in case, you also put $100 on Rawhide. If Rawhide wins, you lose the $100 you bet on Josephine, but you win your money back because you win $200. If Josephine wins, you lose the $100 you bet on Rawhide, but you still win big.

You may face decisions in your personal life that are similar to this, and you can hedge your bet. Sometimes they are financial decisions, but not always. These types of decisions may also be relationship decisions, career decisions, or decisions at work.

Jamie faced an example similar to that of the gambler, only he wasn't betting on horses. He was hedging his bet on a decision about his career. He really wanted to be an actor in Hollywood and had been acting in plays throughout high school and in his first year of college. He knew, however, that most people who want to act in movies never make it big, and some never make it anywhere. While he was fairly confident that he was a good enough actor to be successful, he didn't want to stake his entire future on it.

So what did Jamie do? He hedged his bet and decided that he would spend a large amount of his time in college taking acting classes, performing in plays, and formally becoming a film major. At the same time, however, he decided that he would also spend time taking business classes and double-major in film and business. This way, in the unlikely event that he didn't make it big as an actor, he would still have a business education.

You likely also face more-routine decisions where you use this decision technique, whether you know you're using it or not. When you go out to dinner with someone else or a group of people, for example, you may hedge your bet on your food. Say you're out with your husband or your wife, and you can't decide whether to get the salmon or the chicken. You like salmon better, but you're not sure if you would like it the way that it's prepared. The chicken is pretty simple, and you're likely to be

When you need to choose between two or more options, try to understand what the costs and/or benefits of each option are.

happy enough with it, but you're really feeling like having salmon tonight.

After talking it over with your dinner-mate, you decide that one of you will order the salmon, and the other will order the chicken. You both have similar tastes, and you decide that by getting both options and sharing them, you will be covered in the event that one of you decides that you don't like one of the options. If both of you like both options, great. You've hedged your bet and come out on top.

But don't fool yourself into thinking that hedging your bet always works. It doesn't. Sometimes you still lose. In the case of the horse racing discussed above, for example, just because you're hedging your bet doesn't mean you're going to win. There are more than two horses in the race, and while chances are most likely that Rawhide will win (that's why his odds are 2-1), there's no guarantee that either of your horses will win. You could end up losing all $200 now instead of the $100 had you bet on only one horse.

So how do you apply this lesson to the decisions that you face, both large and small, in your everyday life? When you approach your decisions, you need to do a cost-benefit analysis of all of the options. If you need to choose between two or more options, whether they are good or bad, try to understand what the costs and/or benefits of each of the options are. Does it make sense to choose the option that you want the most or that you think would have the highest positive returns (or the lowest negative returns), and then spend a little extra (money, time, commitment) to choose a second option in the event that the first one doesn't work out?

What are the costs of choosing a back-up option? How much higher are they than choosing just one option? Are you willing to spend that much extra for the potential increase in the results? If you are, then hedge your bet.

50

Milk or Cream

D o you take milk in your coffee or cream? Or maybe you like it black? If you're a daily coffee drinker like me, you face this question every day. How do you respond? Do you change the way you drink coffee based upon how you're feeling that day? That's pretty unlikely. When you're ordering your coffee at the local coffee shop you face this decision, but you're likely to have already made up your mind before you even walked in the door.

Every day in our lives, we face dozens of decisions such as these that we call routine. You may refine the type of coffee you drink or how you take it over time, but you probably don't change every day. That's why we call them routine — we've already made the decision ahead of time. They are decisions that are just waiting to be repeated.

> **Routine decisions help us to break free from spending too much time on the least important decisions in our lives.**

Routine decisions are good for us. They help us to break free from spending too much time on the least important decisions in our lives and enable us to commit more of our limited decision-making time to the decisions that matter most.

For the coffee you drink, for example, you make conscious decisions about how you want it. Do you want to use sugar? Or how about Sweet'N Low or Splenda? Do you take it with skim milk, regular milk, or cream? Or do you just take it black?

Some people are latte drinkers or cappuccino drinkers. Maybe you want it with skim milk because cream has too much fat, and with Splenda to reduce the amount of carbohydrates you're drinking. Or maybe you take it the old-fashioned way with cream and sugar because it tastes better.

Of course, we face a variety of routine decisions daily, weekly, or otherwise occasionally throughout our lives. Think about all of the routine decisions you typically make on a daily basis. What time am I going to get up? What am I going to wear? What am I going to have for breakfast? What route am I going to take to get to work this morning and back home this evening? What type of music or talk am I going to listen to on the way to work? What gas station am I going to use, and what grade of gas am I going to put into my car? What space am I going to park in at work? What am I going to eat for lunch? What time am I going to leave the office to go home? What time am I going to go to sleep?

In addition to these routine daily decisions, you also make routine decisions that are less frequent. What stores do you shop at? What type of television shows do you watch? How often do you travel and to where? What flights do you take? How long before your flight do you get to the airport?

Some routine decisions are made more difficult for us by those we interact with. Take Starbucks as an example. When I go to a Starbucks and simply want a cup of coffee, they present me with too many choices. According to the company, there are 87,000 different choices of beverages at Starbucks. I used to go into decision overload just to order a cup of coffee. They make things even more difficult by using words on the menu that I don't even understand. Now I just order a small regular coffee and let them figure it out. That's my Starbucks decision routine.

Sometimes you'll find the need to change your routine — either because you're bored with your current habits or out of necessity. One example of this could be in your eating habits. Maybe your favorite food is a hamburger, and you eat them four or five times a week. Eventually, you may say to yourself, I need a change. I don't want to eat any hamburgers this

We face hundreds of decisions every day in our lives, but you shouldn't be overwhelmed by them.

week. When you go to your favorite restaurant, the waiter — who knows you by now — asks you if you want the usual. Even though it's routine for you, you simply say to him, "You know what, bring me a salad today instead."

Occasionally, you get stuck in your routine and find it difficult to break out of it when you decide that it's time for a change. When you start to notice negative results of your routine decisions, and you find yourself unable to change, it's often known as being "stuck in a rut." So sometimes it's good to reevaluate your routine decisions and make a change. The other day I even decided to order something different at Starbucks and enjoyed it.

While most of these are relatively insignificant decisions in terms of the overall quality of our lives, you need to be careful about turning rather important decisions into routine decisions. More important decisions, such as those related to your job, your studies, your relationships, or other important aspects of your life, are more important and shouldn't be routine. Avoid making the important decisions routine.

We face hundreds of decisions every day in our lives, but we shouldn't be overwhelmed by them. Many of them are routine decisions — or decisions that you should make routine. Don't spend too much of your life agonizing over which of the 87,000 drinks to order today. Simplify your life by making your decisions routine, but break out of the routine periodically if you need to or want to. Periodically examine your life and the decisions that you make to determine whether there are decisions that you make that should be routine but are not, and vice versa.

Don't agonize over the routine decisions, because if you do, you will be exhausted by making too many decisions every day. When your routine decisions are truly routine, you can focus on the more important life decisions and make a better life for yourself.

So how will you take your coffee today? I'll take mine with cream — as I always do.

51

The Getaway

When former U.S. President Bill Clinton was forced to explain his indiscretions involving Monica Lewinsky, he ended up offering a disturbing rationale for his decision: "I did it because I could." He didn't decide that it was the right thing to do; in fact, he later admitted it was the wrong thing to do. He decided to do it simply because he could get away with it. What kind of decision process is that? Don't think that Bill Clinton is alone in that decision-making weakness. In fact, it may be the primary rationale for many dishonest decisions. People commit crimes because they think they can get away with them. People tend to steal only when they think they can get away with it.

In the late 1990s, some corporate executives took personal advantage of their companies by diverting money to themselves because they thought they could get away with it. Some companies even inflated their financial results because they thought they could get away with it. Martha Stewart sold $288,000 of stock in ImClone Systems in December 2001 based

Why do people decide to do something they wouldn't normally do because they think nobody's watching?

on inside information, even though she knew it was illegal. She obviously thought she could get away with it.

But those are the wrongdoings that make headlines. People also decide to commit small transgressions in life because they think they can get away with them. For example, they might say things about someone that they would not say to their faces or tell small lies — "white lies" — in order to avoid problems, gain advantage, demonstrate power, or even protect a friend. They might take office supplies home for their own personal use, something that costs industry billions of dollars annually.

Have you ever been tempted to keep the change when you realize the clerk has overpaid you? Or keep something you found in front of a store? Or cut in line at the movie theater?

Bill Clinton has given us something interesting to consider. Why do people decide to do something when they think nobody will know that they would not do if someone were watching them? Frankly, I do not have an answer for this.

It also makes me wonder how many people make decisions because they think they can get away with them. We see similar cases of thieves or corporate executives who eventually get caught after taking advantage of their companies. Are most people caught, or only a few? Is this type of decision-making rampant?

Former President Bill Clinton may have provided all of us with a learning experience, although one that was very costly for him and for the United States. You need to make the following "policy decision" for yourself: Will you decide to do something just because you think you can get away with it — something that you would not do if others knew about it? How will you apply this to the decisions you make in your life?

Oh, by the way, do you ever exceed the speed limit when there are no police around to catch you?

52

Ben Franklin's Letter

On September 19, 1772, Benjamin Franklin posted a letter to a good friend of his, Joseph Priestly, advising him on a major decision that Priestly was having trouble making. The letter provided Priestly with useful advice, not on which decision should be made, but on how he should approach making the decision. It is useful to include the entire text of the letter, as it is fairly short:

> In the affair of so much importance to you, wherein you ask my advice, I cannot, for want of sufficient premises, advise you what to determine, but if you please I will tell you how. When those difficult cases occur, they are difficult, chiefly because while we have them under consideration, all the reasons pro and con are not present to the mind at the same time: but sometimes one set present themselves, and at other times another, the first being out of sight. Hence the various purposes or inclinations that alternatively prevail, and the uncertainty that perplexes us.
>
> To get over this, my way is to divide half a sheet of paper by a line into two columns; writing over the one Pro, and over the other Con. Then, during the three or four days consideration, I

put down under the different heads short hints of the different motives, that at different times occur to me, for or against the measure. When I have thus got them all together in one view, I endeavor to estimate their respective weights; and where I find two, one on each side, that seem equal, I strike them both out. If I find a reason pro equal to some two reasons con, I strike out the three. If I judge some two reasons con, equal to three reasons pro, I strike out the five; and thus proceeding I find at length where the balance lies; and if, after a day or two of further consideration, nothing new that is of importance occurs on either side, I come to a determination accordingly.

And, though the weight of reasons cannot be taken with the precision of algebraic quantities, yet when each is thus considered, separately and comparatively, and the whole lies before me, I think I can judge better, and am less liable to make a rash step, and in fact I have found great advantage from this kind of equation, in what may be called moral or prudential algebra.

Wishing sincerely that you may determine for the best, I am ever, my dear friend, yours affectionately, B. Franklin.

What Benjamin Franklin came up with here was essentially one of the first uses of the pros and cons list, a method of helping to approach a decision where you have to choose between selecting one of two options. While a great number of useful lessons can be drawn from this letter that Franklin wrote to his friend Priestly — who is most notably known for his discovery of oxygen — I want to emphasize one in particular. It is the importance of writing down the implications of a decision.

Franklin states that all the reasons, pro and con, cannot be present in the mind at the same time. Sometimes you think of a particular set of reasons and lean toward one alternative, but other times you think of a different set of reasons and lean another way. What causes you to go back and forth is the different set of reasons in your mind at a particular time. To correct this problem, you should write down all of the reasons, pro and con, and then you'll see them all at the same time. Once you see them all together, you can better weigh one set against the other. Many times the preferred alternative will be clear as soon as you see them all, but sometimes you will need to weigh the factors more closely.

There are many types of decisions where writing down your thoughts proves very useful, and I use it frequently when facing major life decisions. Should I take

> **Weighing the pros and cons of a decision in your head can often lead to mistakes.**

the new job I was offered or stay in my current position that has room for advancement? Should I go on vacation in May or in June? Should I have surgery? I wouldn't recommend doing this for all of the small decisions, such as deciding where to go for dinner, because it would simply take too much time. I do, however, recommend using it for the major decisions that you encounter in your life, including career decisions, major purchase decisions, medical decisions, and relationship decisions.

I have found Benjamin Franklin's way of writing a pros and cons list very useful on a number of occasions. Taking it at its simplest, Franklin's decision-making pros and cons list works in the following way: Draw a line down the center of a piece of paper, labeling the top of one side "pros" and the top of the other "cons." Then proceed to place the factors you would feel as beneficial on the pros side of the sheet; and place the factors you feel would be detrimental on the cons side of the sheet. Then compare all of the factors and make your decision.

While this is the simplistic way of looking at this method, there are some more complicated and, perhaps, more accurate methods based on this method. This includes how to assign a value or a weight to each of your pros and cons — something that will be discussed in the chapter Weighing Your Options.

Fred, an old high school friend of mine and a professor at a local community college, was offered a great new job as a professor at a prominent liberal arts college. The new position would be much more prestigious than his current one, but it would require him to leave his colleagues and enter a new academic community. The salary, while similar, had greater potential to grow if he received tenure at the new school, although it was certainly not something that was guaranteed. He was on track to be tenured at his existing job, but he thought he would prefer to teach at the school that offered him the new position. He really agonized over his decision. Sometimes when he thought about it, he convinced himself he should stay where he was. At other times, he convinced himself to take the new opportunity. Fred began to think of himself as wishy-washy.

One day, when I was speaking with him about it, I told him that it sounded as though he just didn't have a clear understanding of all of the factors at the same time, and I advised him to write down all of the factors that were important to him. By having them all in front of him at the same time, he would be better able to visualize the decision. The correct choice would come to him more easily and he could make his decision clearly, based on all of the considerations. This followed the advice of Benjamin Franklin.

> There are many types of decisions where writing down your thoughts proves to be very useful.

Perhaps just as important is that Franklin also noted the need to do this process over a period of time. You will not have all of "the various purposes and inclinations" present in your mind all at once. (After all, if you could think of all of the pros and cons at the same time, you wouldn't have to write them down.)

Fred followed this advice and spent a week brainstorming. Later he commented that the first time he wrote down the factors that came to mind, he thought that he captured them all. But then later he thought of others and added them to the list. It took Fred about eight revisions before he had a complete list. When he was done, much to Fred's surprise the decision was clear: He should take the new opportunity. Even though some of the reasons against taking the new position were emotional, when he looked at all of the advantages, they were overwhelming. Today Fred is so happy that he made this decision.

When I personally reflect on some of my bad decisions, I realize that I failed to consider what turned out to be an important factor when I made the decision. It wasn't that I hadn't considered that factor prior to making the decision; I did. The problem was that I didn't bring that factor sufficiently into my mind when making the decision. If only I had written everything down, I may have avoided making a bad decision.

Weighing the pros and cons of a decision in your head can often lead to mistakes. Follow the advice of one of the smartest people in history, Benjamin Franklin, and take the time and care to write them down. This can make all of the difference and lead to better results in your decisions.

!53

Here's How

'm often asked how to go about making major decisions. Is there a useful process or template that can be applied to many different decisions? Fortunately, for many types of decisions, there is. To help you work on making more successful decisions, I created a worksheet that is useful in situations where you need to decide among several competing alternatives. (You may find it helpful to look at the decision worksheet, which is available on our website.)

This method of making decisions works best when you are deciding among several alternatives. It can, for example, work well for making a decision about which of three job offers to take, or whether or not you're going to move to another state. It can be useful in business decisions, especially those made by a team.

To better understand how this approach to decision-making works, let's use the following illustration. There's a small advertising company with four full-time associates and three administrative staff members. The company needs to move because its space is currently too small for its expansion. They have searched various office spaces and found three viable alternatives. In an effort to make the best decision, the company gets all of its staff members involved. The head of the company tells them that they all have a say in the process, although he will make the final decision. He also tells them that he wants them to follow a structured, disciplined process for making this decision.

Approaching your decisions in a disciplined way requires six steps and should be done in writing. The first step is to define the decision you want to make. I know this may sound simple, but if you don't have a clear understanding of what it is that you're trying to decide, you're going to have difficulties in approaching the decision. Write out the decision clearly. "Should I move from Missouri to New York?" "Should I take the job at company A, company B, or company C?" In terms of our small advertising company, the decision would be: Which of the three office space alternatives are we going to take? The employees of the advertising company also talked about whether this was a long-term or short-term decision and how long they expected the new office would fit. In the end they decided to simply make it a decision among the three alternatives, since each of the lease timeframes was roughly the same. Define your decision in the simplest terms you can, so you don't overcomplicate it.

> Sometimes decision-making can be fun and exciting, but quite often you will benefit from a more structured and disciplined approach.

The first step should also include setting a deadline for making the decision. You can either choose to select a single deadline for when the decision should be completely made, or choose to select a timeline for when you should have each portion of the larger decision process completed. (For example, when do you want to have step three completed, when do you want to have step four completed, and when do you want to make your decision.) The advertising firm set a deadline of four days for step three, another three days for step four, and a total of 10 days from the time they began the process to come to a final decision.

Step two is to determine the objectives of your decision. Where do you want to be at the outcome of the decision? What do you want to accomplish? Think about this a little, as the outcomes are different from the decision that needs to be made. You may be saying: I already said the objective is to choose a job. But the objective is a little more specific than that. Perhaps you are looking for the perfect job? Maybe you are looking for a job in a new industry? Or is your objective to get into a company with growth opportunities or to make the most money in a short period of time?

In our example, the company thought the objective was clear — until they started talking about it. Was it the lowest cost? The nicest office? The most convenient location? The most flexibility for growth? And how do they prioritize these objectives? What were the most important? It took the group several hours over two days to agree on the objectives, but they later found that this was perhaps the most important step in making a good decision. They agreed on three objectives in the following priority order: 1. It had to be affordable (this objective was different from lowest cost but recognized the importance of cost); 2. It should have sufficient expansion space; and, 3. The new location shouldn't add a major inconvenience to any of the current employees (which was different from a location preferred by one employee over another). Before they went any further, they reviewed the objectives with the head of the company, and he was quite impressed by the quality of the objectives.

The third step in the process is to define the alternatives. In our example, the three alternative locations were determined. In other cases, more work may be required to define the alternatives, and some alternatives may be variations of the others. You want to be careful defining alternatives, since you limit your decision at this point to the ones you selected. Generally, it's best to limit the alternatives to a manageable number, and if you need to, you can create a longer list and then narrow it down. The decision worksheet I created provides for the analysis of two alternatives; if you have more, simply use another sheet. In terms of the advertising agency, the alternatives were already selected — the three office space options.

Step four is to determine the pros and cons of each alternative. Take some time to think about these, as you most likely won't be able to think of all of them at the same time. I usually spend a few days thinking about the pros and cons, and as you think of more, add them to your decision worksheet. The head of the advertising company posted three pieces of paper on the wall, one for each of the three new office alternatives, with columns for pros and cons on each sheet of paper. All of the employees were expected to think of the things they believed were beneficial and those they thought were detrimental in each alternative. He gave them four days, and by the end of the fourth day, the papers would be removed from the wall and no more entries would be allowed on them.

Some of the pros and cons that the employees listed included: the new commute time; the amount of office space available for expansion; the number of window offices; the price per square foot of the space; the proximity of good restaurants for lunch; and, a few additional factors, both positive and negative.

In addition to writing down the pros and cons in this step, you should also consider what risks are involved in each of the options and write these down as well. In our case study, the employees got together over lunch on the fourth day and reviewed the pros and cons. They found that some were similar, so they were able to combine them. They also agreed that some others weren't very important and crossed them out.

Step five in the process is to carefully evaluate the pros and cons and the risks involved in each of the alternatives. This step also requires spending some good quality time to fully understand all of these factors. The advertising firm gave themselves three days to evaluate all of the pros and cons in their decision on office space. They sat down on the first day and began a discussion of all of the factors they wrote down on their three sheets of paper. How important is the new commute time to each person? How about the length of the lease and the overall cost of the space? How about the ability for expansion? They agreed to think about each of these factors for two more days.

After evaluating and weighing all of the factors of each option, the final step in this process is to come to a decision and accept the outcome. The advertising company reconvened and discussed each person's thoughts on the alternatives. The head of the business was surprised that the decision was clear to him and to everyone. While two people had a personal preference for another alternative, they understood why this was the best decision for the company.

This disciplined approach to decision-making works great for groups who are attempting to make a decision among multiple alternatives. It also works well for individuals when making important decisions in their own lives. Think about the decisions you make and use this approach when you think it would work. Sometimes decision-making can be fun and exciting, but quite often you will benefit from a more structured and disciplined approach. It could make the difference between a good decision and a great decision, or maybe even a bad decision and a great decision.

54

Clear Objectives

According to an ancient Chinese proverb, "If you don't know where you are going, then any road will lead you there." You need to know where you want to go before choosing the right road to get there. Similarly, if you aren't clear on what you're trying to achieve from your decisions, how are you going to be able make the right choice?

Without clearly understanding your objectives (where you're going), any decision you make (how to get there) will be fundamentally flawed. So it's important to spend the necessary time to clarify your objectives, particularly when you're dealing with the most important decisions in your life.

Objectives are the foundation of how you generate and evaluate your alternatives. What are objectives when it comes to decisions? Quite simply, they are your goals — what you're trying to accomplish. If you don't have clearly constructed objectives, you won't be able to generate and evaluate your best alternatives. You won't be able to make the best decision about which alternative to select. And then you won't be able to implement your decision successfully.

If you're faced with a decision to go on a vacation, for example, you should define what your objectives are for this trip.

Are you looking for a vacation where you can relax? Or one that is more cultural or historical? Would you be happiest if you went on a family vacation and your kids enjoyed it? Or a romantic vacation? Do you want to get some sun? Or be in the mountains? While this is a fairly simple example, it illustrates the point that you can't simply approach a decision such as where you're going to go on vacation by saying "I need to decide where I'm going to go for vacation." You need to define exactly what your objectives are: What are you hoping to take away from your decision? If you don't define your objectives clearly enough, you may end up camping in the Everglades when you really wanted to be on the beach in Miami.

Defining your objectives clearly will help you right from the beginning of your decision process, by helping you to understand how important the decision is to you. If you define your objectives and determine that the outcome of your decision is life-changing, then you will know that you need to assign an appropriate amount of time and energy. If you determine that the objectives are not as important, then you can spend less time.

Clarifying your objectives sets the stage for the rest of the decision-making process.

Having clear and accurate objectives will help you in the subsequent steps of your decision, too, including defining the best alternatives to consider. Clear objectives open up new and better alternatives that you may have missed or passed over. When trying to determine what vacation to take, for example, if you say that you want to take a family vacation in the sun, you may be able to find other options to consider that you hadn't thought of before. Maybe you now would consider going to Disney World, taking a family cruise, or going on a beach vacation?

In the next step of the decision-making process, your objectives will help you to balance the things that are truly important to your decision as you evaluate your alternatives. When you have defined that you want to take a family vacation in the sun, you will know that the happiness of your children and spouse with the trip will be very important, whereas the travel time to get to your destination, for example, may be less important.

Once you've clarified your objectives, defined your alternatives, evaluated these alternatives, and made your decision, clear objectives can help you even further. By knowing why you set your objectives the way you did, you will be in a better position to implement your decision by knowing that you made the correct decision.

When you set about defining your objectives, there are a number of guidelines to follow. First, as with many of the other steps discussed in this book, writing down your objectives enables you to be as clear as possible. Once you have them written, you will be able to refine and revise what you've come up with more easily and more successfully.

You don't want to be too brief or simple in your definition. You want to be comprehensive, but clear. Saying "I'm going to choose a good major to study in college" isn't useful. What does a "good major" entail? You need to be much more comprehensive, but again, make sure that you're still being clear.

In the previous chapter, we looked at an advertising agency that was trying to make a decision on a new office. The location was important to all of the employees, but they wanted to clarify this particular objective. They agreed that "the location shouldn't add a major inconvenience for any current employee" as the specific, clear objective for location. This clarified that it would be no worse for anyone in particular, as opposed to being much better for some people and much worse for others. It also placed more importance on current employees than how good the location would be for recruiting future employees.

The advertising agency team clarified another objective as an affordable space, which was different from the space with the lowest cost. They were willing to pay more for the office space, within reason, for other benefits.

In most cases, you will have several objectives for a single decision, but try to keep them to a reasonable number. In the advertising agency example, they defined three primary objectives. You may also find that once you start to evaluate your alternatives, you may want to add another objective. That's OK; it's part of the learning process.

When you have multiple objectives for a decision, you need to prioritize them, especially if you have more than a few. An example: Charlene knew that someday she would make a decision on a spouse. In fact, she was ready to start "developing alternatives," as she told her friends. So she started by defining the objectives of what she wanted in a husband and generated a list she jokingly called "the 28 objectives I want in a husband." While this entertained her girlfriends, it also made Charlene realize that she most likely would not find a man who fulfilled all of the objectives. She worked on prioritizing her list.

> Take the necessary time and energy to make sure that you have clear objectives before proceeding with your decision.

Charlene found this to be a very important exercise. For example, when she started her list of objectives, she put "good looking" as her first objective, but when she prioritized them later, this objective slipped to number 10. Other objectives, such as being financially stable and being intelligent, were more important objectives for her.

When defining your objectives, you also have to be sure that you correctly separate the ends from the means. Don't confuse objectives with alternatives and benefits. Going back to the example of choosing a major in college, if you said, "I want to major in biology because I want to go to medical school," you're not separating the ends from the means. To correctly define your objectives in this case, you would say, "I want to choose a major that will help me to go to medical school."

Be careful not to ignore your long-term objectives in favor of the short-term ones. I know that sometimes when I'm setting my objectives, I think only about what I'm trying to achieve in the short-term. Then I step back and realize that I've completely forgotten to consider what I'm trying to accomplish in the long-term. That's when I go back and revise my objectives to more properly fit what I'm trying to get out of the decision.

Be careful not to ignore qualitative objectives in favor of quantitative ones. It's far easier to set objectives that are quantitative (I want to make a million dollars, I want to spend less than $20,000 for my new car, I want to finish the project in three months) than qualitative (I want to live a rich life with my family, I want to buy the car that is right for me, I want to finish the project completely and correctly). Frequently, qualitative objectives are more important than quantitative ones, even if they are more difficult to measure.

Another important way to ensure you set clear objectives is to determine what it is that you want to avoid in the outcomes of your decisions. In other words, rather than considering only the positive results of your decisions (a great vacation, etc.), you should also consider the negative results that you want to avoid (spending more than $5,000 for the vacation).

If you're making a group decision, defining the objectives clearly can be even more important. One thing you can do is to have everyone in the group go through the process of defining the objectives on their own, then come back as a group and work toward a group consensus on the objectives. It's much easier to get a group consensus on the objectives before you make the decision than to get consensus on the decision if you didn't have consensus on the objectives.

Clarifying your objectives sets the stage for the rest of the decision-making process. Without clearly defined objectives, your entire decision could be flawed. Do yourself a favor and take the necessary time and energy to be certain that you have clear objectives before proceeding to the next steps in making your decision.

55

Generating Alternatives

One of the most important steps in making successful decisions is to define all of your alternatives, since you limit yourself to those options. If you define only options A, B, and C, you will be able to select from only those three alternatives, and your outcome can be only as good as the best of those three options. If you add D, E, and F, the best outcome can now be the best of any of the six total choices you now have.

Identifying the best alternatives for your decision will help you to get the best outcome.

When people tell me about their bad decisions, I ask them what a better decision would have been. Surprisingly, in many cases, the better decision was an alternative they failed to consider.

Identifying the best alternatives for your decision will help you to reach the best outcome. Some alternatives may be very obvious in many of the decisions we face, but quite often, not all of the options are so easily apparent. Some alternatives have to be actively sought out. Assuming you have some time to spend on making the best decision, you should be sure to dedicate the appropriate amount of your time and effort to generating these alternatives.

Let's look at one approach that I've found to be very useful. I'll illustrate this with the following example: Richard was a chef who had always wanted to own a restaurant. One night at a family function, he was talking with his uncle, who told Richard that he would give him a deal on a great space he owned in one of the historic areas of town, since the building had been empty for a while. The only caveat was that, being from the Italian side of Richard's family, his uncle wanted an authentic Italian restaurant.

Later that night, Richard discussed this with his wife and told her that he needed to make a decision on this offer soon. He had two alternatives to choose from: Take his uncle's offer, or not.

You can use the experiences of others who have been in a similar situation as you're in now.

Richard's wife was very supportive of the idea but suggested that if he was going to open a restaurant, he should consider other alternatives in addition to his uncle's offer. Richard realized that this was good advice. Sometimes when we have to choose between two alternatives — alternative A and alternative B — the best choice is alternative C. Don't limit yourself to just your two starting alternatives. This is step one: Identify all potential alternatives. Don't leave anything out.

So Richard looked around town the next week and found another possible location on the other side of town near the college, which had more flexibility in terms of setting up the restaurant, but it was more expensive. In addition to considering opening an Italian restaurant, he also was considering opening an Irish pub with traditional Irish food, as well as a more generic sports bar with American food. He now had some more alternatives, but he wasn't sure he had all of the alternatives he needed to make the best possible decision. Opening his own restaurant was a big move in his life.

There are a number of things that you should do when defining your alternatives. One thing I like to do to help me generate options is to start writing them down right away, beginning with the most obvious ones. Having your alternatives down on paper will not only help you to generate the best options, but it will also help you later when it comes to finally making your decision.

When putting together your list of alternatives, don't discount anything. Sometimes, we discount some of our options because we think they're not possible or because we think they're too difficult to do. You can always eliminate them in a later step when you're narrowing down your list of alternatives. Using Richard's example, his uncle said he would not let him open an Irish pub at his location for a variety of reasons. One of them probably was that the other side of Richard's family was Irish. But Richard thought he might be able to approach his uncle about an American restaurant at that location, if it made the most sense.

In step two, you should open up your thinking to an even broader set of alternatives. Be creative. Think outside of the box. Don't just make small changes to the options that you've already defined. Think in bold terms. Set high goals for yourself. Richard needs to be creative about both the type of restaurant he will consider and the location. Just because his uncle is offering his location and there's a great location near the college doesn't mean there aren't other options. The same holds true about his choice of restaurant types.

Richard came up with two very different alternatives. He and his family had always vacationed at a seaside resort, and he knew the owner of their favorite seafood restaurant, who last summer told him that he was thinking of selling. Richard decided to call him and consider this as a different alternative. It would require relocation, but it could be exciting and profitable. He also thought he might talk with his good friend, Al, who was also in the restaurant business and might consider a partnership.

At this point, you may need to structure your alternatives a little, which is step three. Each alternative needs to be clearly defined and not intertwined with other alternatives. Moreover, there may be several similar options, but you need to separate them and include them on your list as distinct, individual options. For example, alternative A could have sub-alternatives 1, 2, and 3. You should therefore include A-1, A-2, and A-3 as three distinct options on your list. This would mean that each type of restaurant on Richard's alternatives list should be paired with each location on his list as distinct alternatives. One alternative was to do nothing.

Once you've done your brainstorming, and you think you've exhausted all of your ideas, it now may be time to bring in someone else. This is step four. Some decisions you want to consider and make yourself, without anyone else's input. On other decisions, however, you may benefit from discussing them with others.

You can use the experiences of others who have been in a similar situation as you are in now. Look at what choices they made, and it may help you in thinking about more options. Richard should certainly do this. He should reach out to others who have started restaurants to find out what options they considered. Since Richard was already in the restaurant business as a chef, he talked with some of the people he knew who had opened their own restaurants. Several told him that they wished they had considered more alternatives, because in hindsight they thought they had been too impulsive. In addition, a friend who was in real estate came up with six other potential locations for his restaurant. At this step, you are still generating as many alternatives as possible, so let the people you talk to know that you're not yet evaluating alternatives, but merely generating as many new ones as possible.

> Generating alternatives when making a major decision may not be fun, but it is crucial to making the best decision possible.

At some point, you will inevitably have to stop generating alternatives and begin to evaluate them. So when you are comfortable that you have a complete set of options, start the next step, step five, to clarify and simplify your alternatives. Rewrite them to make sure they are clear. You may need to get more specific here. What type of Italian restaurant would work in that location? How many months of the year would the seaside seafood restaurant be open?

You also may need to cut down your options to a reasonable number. If you have more than five or six, it begins to get unworkable. Richard reduced his alternatives to five, plus the alternative of doing nothing. He cut out many locations that didn't seem to be as good and decided against the partnership with his friend because he didn't think it could work. There are a few ways to reduce your alternatives to a manageable number. Some alternatives may just not be feasible. Some clearly may not be as attractive as others. You can eliminate these.

Generating alternatives when you're making a major decision may take some work, but it is crucial to making the best decision possible. Unfortunately, major decisions require work, and the more you work on them, the better decisions you will make. Understanding that you need to seek out new and better alternatives will increase the possibility of a significantly better outcome once it comes time to make and implement those decisions.

!56

Evaluating Alternatives

Now that you've clarified your objectives and defined your alternatives, you're ready to make your decision! To do this, you need to evaluate your alternatives against your objectives.

Making the best decision you possibly can when the outcome really matters takes time, energy, and effort.

You can evaluate your alternatives in a number of ways, the most basic of which is to simply compare the advantages and disadvantages (or costs and benefits) of each alternative, also known as the consequences. The alternative with the preferred consequences is the one to choose for your decision. Let's use the following example to help to illustrate how to best evaluate alternatives.

Jackie has been in the same job for about seven years and has determined that now is the time to make a decision about staying or moving to another company. He has defined his objective as taking the best course of action for the success of his professional career. He has decided to seek out his other options and has received two offers from different companies. He now has three options: Stay in his current job (option one); take the job at company A (option two); or, take the job at company B (option three). Now it's time for Jackie to evaluate these alternatives and make a decision.

When evaluating alternatives, the first thing that I do is to write everything down. If you've already begun to write down everything while you generated your alternatives (see previous chapter), you're already on your way.

You need to evaluate each of your alternatives based on the same criteria. Without consistency of evaluation, this exercise is useless. Take selecting a restaurant to go to for dinner as an example. You've already decided that you will choose between the Italian restaurant and the Chinese restaurant. You're not going to compare the costs of one to the quality of the other. You need to compare the costs of both to each other and the quality of both to each other. Be consistent. Compare all of your options along the same criteria.

Going back to Jackie and his decision about employment, he created the table below with his three alternatives listed along the top and each of the criteria listed along the side. In Jackie's case, he decided that the criteria important to making his decision are: salary; health benefits; number of vacation days; time it takes him to commute to work; number of hours he is required to work every week; flexibility to work from home; potential for growth at the company; stability of the position;

Criteria	Current Position	New Job #A:	New Job #B:
Salary	$45,000	$55,000	$50,000
Health Benefits	Health, Dental	Health, Dental	Health, Retirement
Vacation Days	14	10 (up to 15 after 2 years)	15
Commute Time	30 minutes	45 minutes	45 minutes
Work Hours	40 hours/week	50 hours/week	50 hours/week
Flexibility to Work from Home	No	10 hours/week from home	No
Growth Potential	Maybe	Probably	Probably
Stability of Position	Very Stable	Stable	Very Stable
Work Environment	Good	Very Good	Excellent
Reputation of Company	Very Good	Very Good	Excellent
Personal Satisfaction	Satisfied	Somewhat Satisfied	Very Satisfied
Coworkers and Boss	OK	Very Good	Very Good

general work environment; reputation of the company; his personal satisfaction with the projects he is working on; and, the relationship with his coworkers and his boss. These criteria will be different for each person, but Jackie identified them as being the most important to him.

As you can see from the chart, he has completed it with the information he gathered about each of the alternatives. It's important to note as you look over the chart that you need to be as precise as possible when evaluating alternatives. Whenever you can quantify something using numbers, you should. Many criteria are objective, such as the salary — he was able to write down the actual amount he will make with each of the jobs. This number is not based upon his feelings or understanding of each alternative. The same goes for the number of vacation days, the commute time, the work hours, and the flexibility to work from home. These are absolute numbers.

Other criteria on Jackie's list are not so easy to quantify. It's not a problem when you can't use numbers for one or more of your criteria when evaluating alternatives, but you do need to be sure to be as careful and as thorough as possible. Many of the criteria on Jackie's chart, for example, are subjective and are based upon his view of the three options. Take the reputation of the company as an example. He determined whether the reputation was "very good" or "excellent" (or "terrible," "decent," or "good") based upon how he believes the company is viewed. The same holds true for several of the other criteria. Does he think he will receive more personal satisfaction with his work at company A or company B, or with the work he is doing at his current job? That's a subjective criterion that he needs to determine for himself.

Many times, though, it can be useful to ask for assistance from your friends, your acquaintances, your coworkers, or experts. When determining the reputation of the companies, for example, maybe Jackie will use rankings provided by an outside source such as a magazine. When trying to predict how much he will like his coworkers and boss, maybe he has friends at the two other companies and can ask them their opinions of these coworkers and bosses. The important thing is not to be arbitrary. Do your research. Don't simply look at the criteria and make a guess. If you need to guess, at least be sure that it's an educated guess. Gather all of the necessary information that you can find to make your assessment of the criteria for each of your alternatives.

Once you complete the evaluation, then it's time to compare the options. There are various ways of doing this. Jackie circled the items where one alternative had an advantage over another. This may work OK in some cases, but it doesn't measure the magnitude of the differences or the importance of each criterion. For example, if one new job paid only $30,000, then Jackie would have discarded the entire alternative instead of offsetting this with criteria where that alternative was favorable.

Here are suggestions for evaluating alternatives:

❶ Highlight and note your evaluation. If some factors are equivalent, such as benefits in this example, then you can ignore them.

❶ Eliminate any alternative where the disadvantage is so great on something important that you can't even consider it to be comparable. Then conduct your evaluation on those that remain.

❶ Look at the comparison, and if one alternative stands out as superior on enough important factors, then choose it.

❶ If it is still a close comparison, see which one has the most advantages. If an advantage is really small or if the criterion isn't that important, then ignore it. Focus on the differences in the comparisons, weigh them in your mind, and then choose.

In Jackie's case, he evaluated his options and the consequences of each, and then made his decision to leave his current position and take the job at company B. He used the following logic to derive that decision. Both of the new job opportunities were superior to his current job, so he turned his attention to which new job he should choose. Company A paid a salary $5,000 higher than Company B, but B had an extra week of vacation. He made that trade-off in his mind, realizing that a week's vacation was worth about $1,000. So Company A still had a $4,000 net salary advantage. Two of the criteria were the same, so he ignored them. Working at home didn't really matter much to him, so he took it out of the evaluation. It then came down to the four qualitative advantages of B. Were they worth the $4,000 net salary advantage? He thought they were worth the difference, so he chose Company B.

Making the best decision you possibly can when the outcome really matters takes time, energy, and effort. Properly evaluating each alternative you have available is one of the most crucial components of this process. If you do it correctly, it will all be worth it.

57

Weighing Your Options

In the previous chapter, we looked at a simple approach to evaluating your options. While this works effectively in many decisions, it doesn't always work in more complex decisions where some criteria are more important than others. When this is the case, you can use weighting factors to quantitatively measure the importance of different criteria. This is a powerful evaluation technique that can help you to make better decisions, but it's also risky and can guide you to make an incorrect decision if you weight the criteria improperly.

Let's consider the following example to help to understand how to best weight criteria when making an important decision: selecting a college to attend once you've been admitted. I've advised a number of students in this area. After having gone through the grueling process of visiting schools, interviewing, selecting several to apply to, taking the required exams, writing the essays, completing the applications, and waiting for their replies, the real decision needs to be made. Which one are you going to choose? Which school will you spend the next four years of your life at? How are you going to make this decision?

There is a wide range of criteria you need to consider when making your decision about what school to attend, but you shouldn't consider all of them equal. Some criteria are more important than others. For example, should you consider a good cafeteria to be as important as academic reputation? Probably not. I've developed a worksheet that I use whenever I'm trying to help someone make this college decision. (A link to the full worksheet is provided at the end of this chapter.) For the purposes of this chapter, however, it makes sense to provide a shorter version of the worksheet to illustrate the forces involved in weighing how important various criteria are.

In terms of the college decision, for example, I have found that one should consider approximately 30 to 40 criteria, each of which falls into one of five different categories. The criteria will vary based on each individual situation, and there may be additional categories, but these categories work pretty well. They are:

- ❶ Location (close to home; close to friends; climate; urban/rural);
- ❶ Academics (availability of major; availability of second-choice major; quality and prestige of professors; general academic environment; curriculum; level of academic pressure; average class size; use of technology in education; quality of academic facilities);
- ❶ General Characteristics (prestige of school; size of school; public vs. private institution; disability-friendly; demographics; any religious affiliation of school; quality of housing; beauty of campus; your "feel" of the school);
- ❶ Costs (net tuition costs; financial loan availability; work-study availability; room and board costs; travel costs); and,
- ❶ Social Life (Greek life availability; extracurricular activities; overall social environment; housing options; great sports to watch; ability to play on sports teams).

So for a decision like this that includes so many criteria,

how do you weigh them accurately? One approach would be to assign a weight to the criteria relative to each other. While this is workable, the problem comes when you may have more criteria in one category than another. For example, if you listed a lot of criteria to evaluate social life, but only one for cost, you could end up putting more value on social life without recognizing it. So I recommend that you not only assign a weight to each individual criterion, but also assign a weight to each of the categories.

Criteria	Category Weight:	Criteria Weight:	College 1	College 2	College 3	College 4	College 5
Location	10%						
Close to Home		2	3	3	4	5	2
Close to Friends		0	5	5	5	5	5
In Climate You Want		1	3	3	4	3	2
In Urban/Rural Location		3	5	5	4	5	5
Academics	40%						
Has Your 1st Choice Major		2	4	4	3	4	5
Has Your 2nd Choice Major		1	4	5	5	5	5
Has Professors You Admire		3	5	5	3	4	4
Gen. Academic Environment		3	5	4	3	4	4
Curriculum		2	4	5	4	5	4
Level of Academic Pressure		1	3	5	5	5	5
Average Class Size		2	4	4	4	5	3
Use of Technology in Education		2	5	3	5	3	3
Quality of Academic Facilities		2	5	4	5	3	5

    Begin your weighting by focusing on each category of criteria. How important is cost to your decision? Is it twice as important to you as the location of the school? Is it half as important to you as the academics of the school? I find it useful to distribute 100% across the categories in order to easily get a relative value for them. Only after determining the weighting of your five categories, as in this college decision example, should you move on to determining the weight of each individual criterion contained within each of the categories. The chart included in this chapter provides a sample of the breakdown of how you can weight and value the alternatives in the college decision. As you can see, for the two of the five categories that are listed in our sample chart, location and academics, our sample student has decided that the location is worth 10% of his decision, whereas academics is worth 40%. (The remaining three categories — general characteristics, costs, and social life — combined are worth the remaining 50%.)

When it comes to weighting the criteria within each category, this sample provides for the ability to assign a number from 0 to 3 to each of the criteria. Once the weights are assigned, the student assigns a value, in this case from 1 to 5, based upon how well each of the schools meets his needs in each area.

While the college example is one of the more complicated decisions, this same theory of weighting the importance of your criteria can be applied to all of the decisions in which you balance the costs and benefits of different alternatives. For example, you can apply this weighting when you're deciding on buying a new car. You may have narrowed it down to three similar models of cars and you need to choose from among them. You should make your list, with columns for each of the three cars, writing the criteria that are important to you on the left-hand side. These may include, among other criteria, the cost of the car, fuel economy, safety ratings, comfort, cargo space, acceleration, reliability, resale value, your personal attachment to the car, and drivability. While you believe it's important to include all of these factors when making the decision, you may not think acceleration is as important as the cost of the car.

> Not all criteria are created equal, so you shouldn't consider them to be equally important in your decision-making.

To solve this problem with making your car buying decision, you should assign a weight to each of the criteria. There are a few ways you can do this. The simplest way would be to list your criteria in the order of how important they are to you and to assign a reducing value to each criterion as you go down your list. For example, if you have 10 criteria listed in order from most to least important, you would assign 10 points for the first one on your list, reducing down to 1 point for the last criterion on your list. Whichever car gets the best rating for each criterion will get the points for that criterion. Add them all up at the end and the car with the highest number of points would likely suit your needs the best.

While that method may be simple, it's certainly not the most accurate. A second way for doing this could be to reflect the method discussed in the college decision example. Using this method, you would assign a point value to each criterion — maybe from 1-5, with 1 being least important and 5 being most important — and then evaluate how well each of your alternatives achieves your needs with regards to each criterion. If option A meets your needs best for one criterion, with a value of 4, and option B meets your needs best for two criteria, each with a value of 2, you can consider that these two will cancel each other out.

Not all criteria are created equal, so why would you consider them all to be of equal weight when you make a decision? You shouldn't. To make the most accurate decision when considering several different options, you need to assign a varying weight to each of your criteria. Only then will your decision be accurate with the best outcome.

(To access the full college decision worksheet, please visit the DecideBetter! website at www.DecideBetter.com/college.html)

58

Stick to It

When you make a decision, stick to it. Don't start questioning yourself right away and begin doubting your decision. This will only make you indecisive and hesitant to implement your decisions.

This axiom is particularly true for group decisions. Once a group reaches a decision, then everyone in the group must commit to following it. I've seen lack of this commitment undermine group decision-making too often, particularly in business situations. For example, a CEO and his management team met regularly to discuss their opinions and reach the decisions they needed to make, and everyone had the opportunity to present and discuss his or her views on the decision. There were always different viewpoints from representatives of different departments. The perspective of the Vice President of Marketing was different from that of the Vice President of Manufacturing, and they were both different from the perspective of the Chief Financial Officer. The sharing of opinions was an important element of the decision-making process in this company because many decisions were difficult ones that required a broad understanding.

However, the process broke down after the decision-making meeting ended and the managers went their own ways. Some of the participants would openly complain about the decision in hallways and at lunch with others, particularly those who reported directly to them. This only served to undermine the decisions that the company made as a team, and it often prevented them from being successfully implemented.

A group decision-making process doesn't end when the decision is reached. It continues with unanimity of support behind the decision while it's being implemented. The price you pay for having a voice in a group decision-making process is a commitment to support the decision reached by the group. If you want to be involved in the process, you are responsible for the decision — like it or not. If you have reservations about the decision that's being made, then you need to raise these issues during the discussion, not after it's over.

In this example, the lack of support for decisions eventually undermined the company's CEO, and he had to be replaced. The new CEO set down his rules very clearly for his management team. "I want to hear your opinions on all major decisions, and I'd like to get a reasonable consensus whenever possible. If not, then I'll make the final decision. But once we make the decision, we all support it. I don't want any of you complaining about the decision, telling others you don't support it, or being critical of it. We need to be unified in implementing the decisions we make — and especially the difficult ones. Now if you can't play by these rules, let me know now and I'll replace you." This clarification worked. Interestingly enough, other managers and employees felt like the new CEO made better decisions than the former one. In reality, however, he just made sure everyone understood the process and was committed to it before he began.

> The price you pay for having a voice in a group decision-making process is a commitment to support the decision reached by the group.

This commitment of sticking to decisions as a group applies to families as well as businesses. A husband and wife can disagree about a major decision, but once they come to a decision, they both need to support it. For the husband to say to the children, "This is what your mother wanted to do, but I don't agree with her," undermines parental authority. Both parents are part of the decision-making process, and while they may disagree about some of the factors of the decision — or even about which decision they should make — they still need to make a decision. Once it's made, there's no turning back, and they need to move full-steam ahead to implement it. This unified commitment to a decision also applies to divorced parents, but unfortunately it is even more difficult in these situations.

While sticking to your decisions is critical to the successful implementation of group decisions, it also applies to the decisions you make as an individual. You often are uncertain about what decisions you should make. Should you take the new job or not? Should you move to another city or not? These are important decisions, and you need to recognize them as such. I discuss strategies for how to approach these decisions in other chapters, but once they're made, there's no turning back. Do everything you can to implement your decision. Don't regret what you've decided and don't second-guess yourself. The decision has been made, and now you must work to achieve the best possible outcome. You can always look back and tell yourself that maybe another decision would have been better, but you will never really know.

Whether making a decision with a group of people or as an individual, perhaps the most important thing to do after the decision has been made is to follow through and not question whether it was right or wrong. Make the best of the decision by sticking to it.

!59

Decision Autopsy

An autopsy, also known as a post-mortem examination, is a medical procedure to examine a corpse in an effort to determine the cause and manner of death and to evaluate any disease or injury that may have been present. The term is used more broadly, as well, to describe an assessment of a process. In many cases, the purpose of an autopsy is to learn how to avoid making mistakes again. A "decision autopsy" can be very useful to help you learn from your mistakes, so you can make better decisions the next time around. Decision-making is a process that we need to work at to keep improving, and we need to learn from our previous decisions — good and bad — to do this.

We need to periodically review our decisions and determine if a particular decision was a good one, or if we could have made a better one at the time. Identify what we did right and what we did wrong, and turn these into lessons for ourselves and apply them to improve how we make similar decisions the next time. This review can work well with a wide variety of decisions, including relationship, career, purchase, and vacation decisions, as well as everyday decisions such as what to order at restaurants, what movies to see, etc.

When you buy a car, for example, you go through a process that will result in choosing the car you're going to purchase. After going through this process and getting your new car, either you begin to enjoy it and are happy with it, or you regret your decision. Now is a good time to look back at the process you used when you bought the car to learn from your decision. How did you finally settle on a particular model or brand of car? Did you meticulously research your options online beforehand? Did you speak with your friends and family and ask for their advice? Or did you just pick a car company at random and go to the dealership, unsure of what you were looking for, walking out a few hours later having bought a new car? Whether you think you made a good decision or a bad one, now is a good time to review the process you used.

Here's a checklist that you can use to perform your own decision autopsy.

- ❶ Was this a good or a bad decision? Most likely you will be more eager to learn from your bad decisions because you will be motivated to correct them.
- ❶ What would have been a better decision? With hindsight, you will probably have an opinion of what you should have decided.
- ❶ Why would this have been a better decision? This will lead you to understand what you should have considered or tried to find out before making the decision.
- ❶ Did you know this other option at the time of your decision? Maybe you could have considered it but didn't, or maybe it was a complete unknown.
- ❶ What should you have done differently? The essence of the decision autopsy is identifying what you can do differently the next time around.
- ❶ How can you use this experience to make a better decision next time?

Once the decision has been made, it may very well be too late to change your mind, but you can certainly learn from the process. You shouldn't dwell on bad decisions — or good decisions, for that matter — but you should learn lessons about how to make similar decisions when you face them again in the future.

Relationship decisions can be improved with experience, as April learned. She met Philip and quickly became enchanted by him. He was witty, fun, and not bad looking. Their relationship became serious and intimate right away. In hindsight, she made that decision too impulsively. Later, she learned more about Philip and found out that he had a serious drinking problem and was financially irresponsible. It wasn't too long before he started to abuse her when he was drunk and borrow money from her.

When April broke up with Philip, it was messy. She regretted her impulsive decision and did a decision autopsy using the checklist. She knew it was a bad decision, and she shouldn't have gone as far in her relationship as she did. She concluded that she should have learned more about him first, in this case his financial and drinking problems, although she realized that there could be different problems with other guys she could date. She determined that she should be more careful the next time, go more slowly and find out more about the man before she decides to get involved. This decision autopsy served April well, helping her to avoid potentially bad relationships in the future.

> **Once a decision has been made, you can certainly learn from the process.**

One of the problems in judging decisions, however, is that short-term results weigh much more heavily than long-term results. It's human nature to be short-term oriented, but a decision judged to be good in the short-term may not be as good in the long-term. For example, a person may be faced with a decision on accepting a new job opportunity that requires moving his family to another part of the country. This is typically a difficult decision that has both short-term and long-term consequences and needs to be evaluated in the light of both. If the person decides to take the new job and move his family, the short-term consequences will most likely be unfavorable, particularly when children are involved. They have to leave their school and their friends, and when they get to the new city, they don't like their new school, and they don't have any friends. Maybe the new neighborhood is very different from the one they moved from, or the house is designed differently, and it has problems different from those of their old house. If judged in the short-term, this will almost always be perceived as a bad decision.

However, over the long-term, it could be a great decision for everyone. The new job may offer potential opportunities that weren't available at the old. The children could make new friends who become a key part of their futures. They could end up loving their new school after a few months there and be very happy they moved. The spouse could find new career opportunities. They could end up liking the new neighborhood and fitting in better in the new house. It could also be a failure over the long-term, but decisions like this can't be evaluated in the short-term alone. They have to be evaluated when all of the consequences are realized.

An abbreviated version of the decision autopsy can also work for routine decisions. After I went to see a terrible movie, I thought through how I made my decision and realized that I picked the movie by simply relying on the title and the actors in it. So I changed my decision process, and now I won't go to see a movie unless someone with similar taste recommends it or if I read the movie reviews from the Internet.

Once you have made a decision about something in your life it's not over. Learn from these decisions, and you will be sure to improve them when you make similar decisions in the future. Don't let your decision be realized without performing a decision autopsy.

!60

The Dog Ate My Homework

"**T**he dog ate my homework." "I would love to hear about your recent vacation to the desert." "Oh, you called me last night? I didn't get the message." "Please, tell me more about your grandchildren."

Have you ever lied so that you wouldn't hurt someone's feelings? Chances are you have — maybe a small lie, maybe a big one. A lie about something that doesn't have major negative consequences is often known as a "little white lie."

Many people think of a lie as an action. In reality, however, it's a decision. Lying is not something you just do. You need to make a conscious decision to lie and carry it out by telling it to someone. Even though you may do it quickly without knowing it, you weigh your options and then decide whether you're going to tell the truth or whether you're not. I'm not going to pass judgment on whether or not it's acceptable for you to lie — inevitably it may sometimes be the best option. But you need to make a decision on whether you are going to lie based upon the ramifications of that lie — both positive and negative.

When a lie is called little and white, it usually refers to one of two types of lies:

1. A lie told either to avoid hurting, or to create benefit for, someone else; or,
2. A lie told either to avoid hurting, or to benefit, yourself, but by telling it you are not significantly hurting anyone else.

This first type of lie is seen in the following example. One of your good friends has just bought a new pair of glasses, and when you see her later that day, she asks you about them. She decided that she was tired with her old style of glasses and bought a completely new type of frame. When she sees you she says, "I love these new frames I just bought — what do you think about them?" You may think that they are the most hideous frames you've ever seen, but you don't want to hurt your friend's feelings. So you tell her, "I think they look fabulous on you." You've lied to your friend, but you did it for her own benefit. No harm done and you retain your friendship with her.

I was watching the reality TV show "American Idol" recently and the judges were giving feedback to a young man who was truly awful — he sang completely out of key and should never have been singing in public. They asked him why he decided to sing on the show and if he had ever sung for anyone before. The contestant said that he had sung only for his family and for some of his good friends. When asked what they told him about his singing, the contestant said that they loved his voice, and when he asked them if he should try out for "American Idol," they said absolutely. Listening to his singing, however, it was very clear that he was a terrible singer, and his family and friends were all lying to him in order to not hurt his feelings. They told him a little white lie so that he wouldn't be hurt. In fact, in the show that I watched, almost half of the contestants were so bad that I had to believe that their friends and

> The problem with telling lies, including small ones, is that it is very difficult to accurately predict all of the short-term and long-term consequences.

family were lying to them about their talents — or lack thereof.

The second type of lie considered little and white is also fairly common. You may have heard the all-too-frequent expression that "the dog ate my homework." In this common lie, a student who neglected to do his homework for one reason or another pretends that he actually did do the homework, but when it was finished, his dog chewed it up, and it couldn't be completed again. Rather than having to admit that he never did the lesson he was assigned, he blamed it on someone else, in this case his dog, who of course doesn't care. Nobody is harmed by his lie (besides possibly himself in the long run), and he can benefit from it by not facing the wrath of the teacher. In fact, this lie is so common that it can't even be used by anyone whose dog actually did eat their homework. (If your dog really does eat your homework, now you need to make up another lie that is more believable than the truth.)

This type of lie, however, is not only a decision to lie. It's actually two decisions: first, a decision to do something wrong (in this case, to not do your homework), and then a second decision to lie about what you've done wrong. Skipping class in college and saying you were sick, for example, requires the first decision to skip the class and then the second decision to lie about why you were unable to be at class. You benefit in the short-term, since you don't have to go to class, and nobody is harmed. The only harm done is to yourself because you will have to cram the night before the exam to learn the material that you missed by skipping the class.

There are many occasions when you may think telling a little white lie is preferable to telling the truth, either because it will benefit someone you care about or because it will benefit yourself. The problem with telling lies, of course, including small ones, is that it is very difficult to accurately predict all of the short-term and long-term consequences of your statements.

Returning to your friend with the new eyeglass frames that she absolutely loves, it's possible that you could cause harm to her by telling her how much you loved her glasses when you actually hated them. After being reassured by you, her best friend, that she had made a good choice with the new glasses, she went on a date, full of confidence. She had a nice time at dinner and was hoping it would lead to a second date, but when the dinner was wrapping up, he told her that he didn't think it was going to work. Bewildered, she inquired as to why. He replied: "I think our styles are just too different from each other." Was it the glasses? Had you told her that you didn't like the glasses in the first place, would she have returned them for something more traditional? Would she have gotten the second date she wanted?

The same may hold true for the contestant on "American Idol." Had his family and friends told him the truth about his terrible singing, he might have avoided the larger embarrassment of people laughing at him in millions of living rooms throughout the country.

When telling a little white lie for the benefit of someone you love, make sure you accurately assess the potential for both good and bad. Sometimes little white lies are necessary and beneficial to you or others. But sometimes they backfire and end up hurting the one you were trying to protect even more than if you had told the truth to begin with. Don't let the dog come back and bite you in the behind after he eats your homework.

!61

The Decider

resident George Bush, in a speech he gave about the war in Iraq, brought up a useful point about decision-making. He stated that, while almost everyone seemed to have opinions on the withdrawal of troops from Iraq, he, as President, was the Decider. In other words, he was the one empowered to make the final decision, not anyone else. Over the long run, of course, the American people can change who the Decider is through the voting booths, or Congress can change the decision alternatives through legislation.

The concept of the Decider can be a useful one in situations where multiple people are involved in the process of making a decision. By understanding who is the Decider, you clarify who is authorized to make the decision. In some cases, it may be obvious who the Decider is. Organizational authority, such as the articles of incorporation for a company or the bylaws of a board of directors, may define the CEO or the chairman of the board, for example, as being the person responsible for making certain types of decisions. Authority may also be specified less formally by tradition or by the election of

> In group dynamics, it's best to discuss who will be the Decider up front.

a person to serve as the chair of a committee for a specified amount of time.

In some cases, the Decider needs to be clarified to avoid confusion when it isn't known who is responsible for making the ultimate decision. In other cases, the authority of the Decider may be delegated to someone else by the person who would have been responsible for the decision.

In a wide variety of group interactions, from families to corporate board rooms, it may not be clear who gets to make the final decision. For example, if a parent supporting the family has a job offer that requires the family to move to a different state, does that parent get the final say in the decision? Or do both parents make the decision together? What about the children in the family? Do they get a say in whether to move or not, making it a majority vote?

When a child is making a decision about going to college or attending a new school, a decision that typically has financial implications for the parents, who is the Decider? The child or the parents? Or does it require a consensus? Families all operate in different ways, and some would fall in the category of consensus, some in the category of the parents being the Deciders, and still others in the category of the child being the Decider.

Similarly, who makes the decision on where a family goes on vacation or where they live? Typically, everyone's opinion is considered, but in the end if there's disagreement, who makes the decision? If the group comes to a point where they can't agree, what happens? Most group decisions cannot simply be ignored, so how do you proceed when there is no agreement?

In group dynamics, it's best to discuss who will be the Decider ahead of time. The Decider shouldn't wait until consensus agreement doesn't arise and only then jump in and override the opinions of the others. It may also be useful to establish boundaries to the decision. A group may want to establish the parameters in which the decision must take place before delegating the authority to the Decider to make the final decision. Maybe the group wants to lay out the specific options from which the Decider must choose.

Here is an excellent framework one family gave to their son when making his college decision. "John, we want you to go to the college of your choice, so the final decision is yours. It's your life, not ours. So in this decision, you are the Decider. Please take our input into consideration in your decision. We may have different views on things like whether you should choose a college because your friends are going there. We would like to have some input on how far from home you go. We also have certain limits on how much financial support we can provide you, which we will discuss during the decision process."

> Be sure the parameters in which you, the Decider, must operate are clearly defined before the decision process begins.

As an executive, I've found that it's sometimes useful to delegate the Decider role for a specific decision or category of decisions. Maybe I do this because I know that someone else has the experience to make a better decision than I do, or to develop decision-making skills in others. (After all, what good is a management team with inferior decision-making skills?) Other times I do it because the person given the Decider role is also charged with implementing the decision. In this case, their commitment to implementing the decision is perhaps more critical than the decision itself. If the person doesn't have ownership of the decision when implementing it, they may not put as much effort into ensuring it's successful.

Delegating the Decider role also can be important in families and relationships. It's a great way to empower your children to make responsible decisions. By formally delegating the decision to them up front, you show them that you trust them, and in most cases they will act more responsibly.

Delegating the Decider role to your kids is much better than arguing over the decision, then saying in anger, "OK, fine, if you don't agree with me then you can do whatever you want.

Just don't come crying to me when it doesn't work out." That would be a much less productive way to encourage your kids to make responsible decisions. Give them ownership over these decisions, but do it before the decision process begins.

A key element of delegating the Decider role is that you cannot later blame the person who made the decision. Unfortunately, you see this sometimes in office politics. A boss says, "I'll let you make the decision," but then when the decision is bad, he says, "You made a bad decision," and you receive the full blame for the mistake. The decision made by the original Decider to delegate the Decider role is itself the decision, and the outcome is ultimately the responsibility of the person who delegated the role to someone else.

When I would delegate a decision to someone on my management team, I would tell them that if it was a good decision, they would get the full credit for it, but if it turned out to be a bad decision, I would take the responsibility and not blame them.

In many situations, it's helpful up front to determine who the Decider is. And don't overlook opportunities to delegate the Decider role. Understand the parameters in which you, as the Decider, must operate, and be sure these parameters are clearly defined before the decision process begins. It could make all of the difference in achieving a successful and accepted outcome.

62

The Lady or the Tiger?

ave you ever heard of the story of "The Lady or the Tiger"? It's a short story written by Frank Stockton in 1882 that takes place in a fictional ancient civilization run by a cruel — but just — king. When the king comes across someone who deserves punishment, he puts the offender in an arena with two doors and tells him he has to go through one of them. One door contains a ravenously hungry tiger. If the offender picks that door, the offender is proclaimed guilty of his crimes, and the tiger will tear him apart in seconds. The other door contains a beautiful woman who has been handpicked by the king. If the offender chooses that door, he is proclaimed innocent. Regardless of his current marital situation, he is forced to marry the beautiful woman and spend the rest of his life with her. The man has no idea which door holds which fate, so his decision is based completely on luck.

> When we are forced to make major decisions that have good and bad consequences for multiple people, there are often several underlying powers, motives, and emotions involved.

One day, the king's daughter falls in love with a suitor whom the king determines is too far below her social status, so he sends the suitor into the arena. When it came time for him to select a door to go through, he looked to the princess for guidance. The princess knew which door held the tiger and which one held the beautiful maiden. If she steered her love to the one with the tiger, he would be killed instantly, and she would never see him again. If she steered him to the door with the beautiful maiden, she would be devastated because he would marry the other woman instead of her. She pointed him to a door and he opened it. The author then asks, "Did the tiger come out of that door, or did the lady?" Did the princess send her true love to the tiger to protect herself from the pain of seeing him spend the rest of his life with another woman? Or would she protect her true love and let him live by sending him to the beautiful maiden? The story ends there, and we never find out the fate of the suitor.

This story is designed to rouse emotions in its readers and can provide us good insight into decision-making. When we are forced to make major decisions that have good and bad consequences for multiple people, there are often several underlying powers, motives, and emotions involved in the process of coming to the decision.

In the decisions that we make involving our relationships, for example, whose interests are being considered as more important? If you are making a decision for your husband or wife, are you considering their interests or your own?

Sometimes, there are hidden agendas and individual behaviors at work, not just rational thinking. What motives are driving each of the players in the decision? How do we each weigh our own self-interest against the interests of others, especially those we love? Do we put our interests over theirs, or the other way around? What are our motives in our decisions? Why do we do the things we do? Why do we make the decisions we make?

In our story, many different motives come into play. The king is clearly motivated by a twisted sense of justice and doesn't care about his daughter's wishes or the suitor she loves. The suitor was originally motivated to make his decision to stay with the princess because of love, but he has likely changed that motivation now to one of survival. The tiger simply is motivated by hunger. But what about the princess? By what is she motivated?

There are also many emotions involved in this story. These include the emotions that cause the princess to decide whether to send her true love to death or to a life of pleasure, as well as the emotions involved in the suitor's decision of whether to trust the advice of the princess. How much does the suitor love the princess, and how much does he think she loves him in return? How should the suitor proceed based on his evaluation of her emotions and interests?

So when your true love is facing death by a tiger or a life of pleasure with another woman, what fate will you choose for them?

!63

Catch-22

Have you ever heard of a Catch-22? It's an impossible situation that you're put in when you need to do one thing to achieve another, but you need to do the other thing first to achieve the first thing. As defined by the Oxford English Dictionary, a Catch-22 is "a set of circumstances in which one requirement . . . is dependent upon another, which in turn is dependent on the first."

The term Catch-22 originates from the book of the same name by Joseph Heller, set in World War II, which focuses on a B-52 bombardier. In the book, everything consists of bureaucratic and illogical reasoning that is so prevalent that they started assigning numbers to each bureaucratic operation. Catch-22 was the name assigned to the attempt to avoid doing any more bombing runs, which were extremely dangerous and often resulted in the deaths of the crew. The only way to get out of continuing to do more bombing runs was if you were insane. But if you claimed you were crazy and, therefore, that you couldn't do the bombing runs, you had to be sane. Only a sane person would try to stay out of danger and not do the runs. If you claimed that you wanted to do more bombing runs, however, you must be insane and had to be grounded. Hence the Catch-22.

We sometimes find that there are Catch-22s in our lives that involve this type of circular logic. A number of times I've heard of people who are turned down for car or health insurance on the basis that they didn't have prior insurance coverage. If they did previously have insurance, the company would have offered them a new policy. If they've never had insurance in the past, however, the company would not offer them a policy.

A more well-known phrase that also sums up the Catch-22 dilemma is that "you need money to make money." The theory here is that it is difficult to make money if you don't already have money to invest and make more money. Another such dilemma can occur when you try to purchase your first car or house. When you try to get a loan for these items, the bank will likely turn you down if you don't have any credit history. But how can you get credit history without getting credit?

Students who graduate from high school or college and go out to get a job sometimes encounter a Catch-22. They are told that they need work experience to get the job, but they can't get work experience without a job.

Another Catch-22 is one that existed in the early elections of the United States, but is no longer in effect (although it is arguable that perhaps it should be). During these early elections, it was considered a very poor personality and leadership trait to tout your own virtues, and this included people who were interested in being the President. Candidates who went around talking about how great a President they would be were often thought of as being poor choices for the Presidency, since they lacked the sense of humility people believed the position required. Essentially, this meant that if someone decided that they wanted to be considered a candidate for the Presidency, they would be discounted as a responsible choice. If someone decided that they absolutely did not want to be considered as a candidate, all of a sudden they became one of the front runners. Hence the Catch-22 in the Presidential election system at the time of the founding of the American government. Candidates nowadays hold no such pretenses that they shouldn't be shameless self-promoters in the pursuit of the nation's highest office.

So what can you do if you find yourself stuck in a Catch-22? What decisions can you make to get yourself out of or around the situation you're in? In the novel *Catch-22*, the main character finally finds a way out of the situation he's in. After not returning to base one day, he is arrested and threatened with a court martial. The only thing he can do to avoid the court martial is to publicly approve of a plan that would require each pilot in his unit to fly 80 missions, which would significantly increase their risk of death. If he does this, he will be honorably discharged and can go home a free man. To protect his fellow soldiers, he refuses. He then escapes custody and flees to neutral Sweden, where he can't be prosecuted for desertion.

Obviously, when you're in a Catch-22 situation, you have limited options. You have intentionally been placed in a decision framework by someone who is trying to force your hand. What I suggest doing is to work very hard to break free from this framework and redefine your options. The main character in the book deserted the army and fled to Sweden, something more extreme than you're likely to be able to do, but he did successfully reframe his options.

If you've just graduated from college and can't find a job, for example, think about other options. Perhaps you can become an intern somewhere for a few months, or maybe you should consider volunteering at a local nonprofit organization to show your abilities. While this isn't quite work experience, potential employers may see your dedication and use this experience as proof of your abilities.

The next time you're in a Catch-22 decision situation, will you decide to claim you are insane and fly another bombing run, or will you claim you want to fly another run and be grounded? Or will you abandon both of the options and flee the situation completely?

!64

Double Black Diamond

W hen I go skiing, I rarely make a decision to ski down a trail that is designated as a "double black diamond." The designation "black diamond" is reserved for the most challenging terrains, and two diamonds indicate a trail with the most difficult terrain you can encounter on the mountain.

My two sons, however, love to ski double black diamonds, perhaps to prove to themselves that they can, and perhaps be-cause they actually like skiing terrain with very steep slopes and large mo-guls (challenging bumps of snow on the mountain). For some reason, they always seem to ski these trails, while I can be found skiing on the "blue square" trails, which indicate a trail that is moderate in difficulty. I simply find it more enjoyable and rewarding than the difficulty on my body that results from skiing the more challenging terrains.

> A balanced decision portfolio includes green circles, blue squares, and even double black diamonds.

The codification of ski trails is a very useful analogy for the codification of decisions that we face in our lives. Green circles are the easy trails/decisions; blue squares are the intermediate trails/decisions; and, black diamonds are the difficult trails/decisions. As for double black diamonds, well, those are the most difficult trails/decisions that we can possibly face in our lives. Just as you would prepare yourself mentally and physically for each trail type that you are going to ski, you should prepare yourself adequately for the various types of decisions you face.

When skiing, we make decisions largely by calculating the potential risk factors and the possible rewards. Each level of difficulty entails a similar level of risk and potential reward. Should I ski the difficult slope and risk falling and possibly hurting myself? What if I end up skiing it successfully and get to the bottom with a sense of satisfaction with myself for having completed it without getting hurt? How should I balance the risks and rewards of my decisions in skiing? How should I balance the risks and rewards of my decisions in life?

I find that I'm continually weighing the risks and rewards of investing in various types of stocks and bonds. Sometimes I'll find a very "hot" new company that is just going public, and I'll study how likely the stock is to increase in value quickly. I need to make a decision as to whether I think the potential rewards are worth the risk and what I'm likely to gain or lose based upon whether the stock goes up or down in value. Sometimes, though, I make a decision to invest in a risky stock because I want to prove to myself that I'm good at predicting which companies will succeed and which ones will fail. I'm willing to accept the risks for the potential returns. While I'm not always right, I do relish the times when I've predicted the success of a high-risk investment.

An investment portfolio that is considered "balanced" will include a wide range of risks and rewards, from the least risky bonds that also carry the least returns, to the most risky stocks that have the potential for the greatest returns (or greatest losses).

Likewise, a balanced decision portfolio includes green circles, blue squares, and even double black diamonds. Unfortunately, we don't always get to choose what difficulty levels we have in our decision portfolio, but we are able to classify them and treat them appropriately. The decision on what you're going to wear to work today is a green circle. The decision on whether you're going to pursue a second date with a woman you really like is a blue square. The decision on which house you are going to buy is a black diamond. The decision on what career you're going to pursue is probably a double black diamond.

The codification you give to your decisions should be determined by the amount of importance you place on each decision and the level of risks and rewards involved in those decisions. That codification, in turn, should determine the amount of time and energy that you spend on these decisions. Black diamonds and double black diamonds should entail an appropriate amount of time and effort, while green circles and blue squares should require less.

Many relationship decisions also involve a decision based upon calculating the risks and rewards involved. When you meet someone who you really like, you need to continually assess the risks and rewards. You need to understand whether each decision in the continual cycle of decisions in your relationship is a green circle or a black diamond. And you'll need to then determine the amount of time and energy you're going to spend on it. While a decision on your first or second date may be a green circle, the decisions become more risky, but more rewarding, as the relationship progresses. Making a decision on whether to move in with your significant other is more like a blue square. Getting married and having children? Well, those are certainly double black diamonds. They're very risky, but very rewarding if they work out.

> The codification you give to your decisions should be determined by the amount of importance you place on each decision and the level of risks and rewards involved in those decisions.

Relationships themselves vary in risk/reward. Some can be blue squares with moderate risk and moderate reward. Others can be black diamonds with big risk and big reward. You can see two women sitting in a bar, looking at a guy and saying, "I'm not going to even look at him; he's a double-black-diamond guy and I'm a blue-square girl." The other responds, "I like to try a double black diamond once in a while. Then after I get hurt, I go back to green circles for a while."

How and why do you decide when to take a risk? Will you ski down the double black diamond or stay on the bunny slope? I think I'll balance my skiing portfolio just as I'll balance my decision portfolio. And I'll expend the appropriate amount of time and energy on each.

65

The Chicken or the Egg

Which came first, the chicken or the egg? This theoretical and philosophical saying is designed to help us ponder how there could possibly be a chicken if there hadn't been an egg to hatch it, and conversely, how there could be an egg without a chicken to have laid the egg. It was theorized by influential philosophers as early as Aristotle and Plutarch as a method of trying to understand the origin of life, and it provides a line of circular reasoning that is nearly impossible to break.

It's also a useful tool for understanding certain types of situations in which we find ourselves and for understanding how we should go about approaching and making decisions under these circumstances. Sometimes this is referred to as circular cause and effect, where one thing causes another, which in turn causes the first thing over again, leading us back to the other.

When I graduated from college, I was determined to pursue an MBA almost immediately, something that was generally unheard of at that time. Most MBA candidates worked for several years before they entered graduate programs. I didn't want to wait, so I applied to get my degree before beginning my professional career. One of the schools I hoped to get into was Harvard Business School, the most competitive business school in the country. After applying, I was asked to interview with one of the admissions officers from the school. After discussing various topics, the interviewer told me that I was one of the youngest applicants. He told me that he thought I should get three years of experience before going to the school, because I would get more out of my time in the program with prior experience. I replied to him that I would get more out of my three years of experience if I already had an MBA degree. Which should come first, the chicken (experience) or the egg (MBA program)?

Many times, when you're in a chicken-or-egg situation, the decision you have to make is not which of the options can or cannot be done without the other one being done first. The decision, rather, is which one of the two things you should do first in order to make the second option better. Going back to my interview with the admissions officer from Harvard, I guess my logic prevailed. The admissions officer told me that I would not get accepted, but "if we make a mistake and send you an acceptance letter, I don't want you to tell me that you want to get three years of experience first." I received my acceptance letter three days later and graduated with my MBA from Harvard at 23.

> **Many times in a chicken-or-egg situation, you need to decide which of the two things you should do first to make the second one better.**

Some people I know find themselves in chicken-or-egg situations in their relationships as well. One person who wrote to me on the DecideBetter! website looking for advice on her relationship was in this type of situation. This woman, Alexis, told me that her longtime boyfriend was ready to get married, but he had one caveat. He wanted Alexis to pay off her credit card debt before they committed to getting married. He wanted to enter their new lives together with a clean financial slate. Alexis would be keen to agree, but she was having difficulty paying down her debt. She knew that she would easily be able to do so if they got married, however, since her living expenses would reduce substantially. So she could not get married without paying off her debt, but she couldn't pay off her debt without getting married. She had to figure out which one to do first. I advised her that the best approach to this chicken-or-egg scenario was to come up with a very specific plan to pay down her debt in coordination with her boyfriend. They needed to decide together that they should pay down half of the debt before getting married and have a payment schedule for how to pay down the second half after getting married. In other words, sometimes the best decision is a little of the chicken and a little of the egg, even though the analogy breaks down in this case.

An example of a chicken-or-egg decision that our society recently faced was related to digital (high-definition) television, usually referred to as HDTV. In the early 1990s, TV broadcasters and TV manufacturers both wanted to take advantage of this new technology to produce a higher quality of television. The government was also interested in freeing up the traditional analog airwaves for use by emergency personnel.

> **Sometimes the best decision is a little of the chicken and a little of the egg.**

While everybody seemed to want digital TV, nobody wanted to take the first move to do so. The TV manufacturers didn't want to make new TVs that would be more expensive if there were no digital TV programs for consumers to watch with them. On the other side, TV broadcasters didn't want to spend the additional money to broadcast digitally if consumers didn't own TVs that could view them. It was a classic chicken-or-egg scenario. It finally took an act by the U.S. Congress to solve the problem by passing a law in 1996 requiring broadcasters to begin sending digital broadcasts simultaneously with analog ones, while providing some incentives to do so. It also set a deadline of February 17, 2009, for all television to be broadcast digitally and for the broadcasters to cease using analog signals altogether. If an outside entity (the U.S.

government) hadn't intervened, the broadcasters and TV manufacturers would probably still be caught up trying to figure out which one would be the chicken and which one would be the egg.

So the question is: How do you break free from the chicken-or-egg situation when you are faced with one? What decisions can you make to move forward and not be stuck within the vicious circle in which you find yourself? While there is no one solution, the best thing to do is to step back and reframe the decision as it's being presented to you. You need to assess the two decision options you're faced with and make a logical and rational decision about whether you're going to choose the chicken or the egg.

!66

It's Personal, Not Rational

I f you were in a situation where you could save the lives of a dozen people on the condition that one other person would be killed, would you decide to have that person sacrificed to save the others? Most people would agree that the loss of one person in order to save 12 would be a worthy decision. What if you were the one who had to personally kill that person? Would you still do it and be the savior of 12 people? Do you have what it takes to kill someone in the effort to save others? Now, if the person who had to be sacrificed was the person you loved most in the entire world — your wife or husband, your son or daughter — would you still be able to kill that person to save 12 other strangers? Can you save 12 strangers at the cost of personally having to kill your loved one?

DecideBetter! conducted a poll of more than 900 people, asking them this series of questions, and the results were very interesting. The first question was whether they would agree to sacrifice one person in order to save 12 others. A large percentage of the respondents, 73%, said they would agree to that scenario. The decision was easy and rational — the value of 12 people's lives is much higher than the value of one person's life.

As terrible as it is to have to sacrifice one person, this option is really the only rational one.

When the respondents were asked whether they would kill that one person themselves, however, the number who would do so precipitously dropped to 40%. That's just a little more than half of those who would have allowed the one person to be killed when they weren't required to commit the act themselves. It's much more personal when you think that you're going to have to look someone in the eye and tell them their life is not important enough for you to save. While you would be saving 12 people, and you may feel justified morally, the intentional act of murdering someone is something that 60% of the survey respondents simply can't do.

When asked the final question in the series — if they would be willing to kill the person they loved most in the world in order to save the 12 people — the numbers dropped even more dramatically to a tiny fraction of respondents, with only 16% saying they could do it. With this question, your emotions completely take over your decision-making. While you should be rationally drawn to kill your loved one in order to save the others, only 3 in 20 people would do so. The other 17 would allow everyone to die, rather than having to look their loved ones in the eyes and tell them they were going to die at their hands.

> As emotions begin to seep into our decision-making process, our rationality begins to seep out.

This series of questions is designed to make people uncomfortable in their approach to decisions, and the range of situations shows how we approach and make decisions differently when we become more personally involved. When the parameters of the decision change, you can see how the emotions become more prominent and the decisions become less rational.

Emotions play a very important role in the decisions that we make. I've found that as emotions begin to seep into our decision-making process, our rationality begins to seep out.

Our relationships are full of emotions. Many of the decisions that we face involving our relationships are affected by our emotions. If we were to make these decisions rationally, on many occasions we would have made a different decision than we would once our emotions come into play. Ellen, who e-mailed me for decision-making advice through the Decide-Better! website, was caught up in her emotions in a major decision she was facing. She was in a bad relationship with her boyfriend of five years, and while they had many problems and constantly fought, she really loved him and didn't want to hurt him. All of her friends kept telling her to break up with him and that he was bad for her. Her friends were looking at the decision rationally — if the relationship was bad, get out of it. Her decision, though, was clouded by her emotions. She found it difficult to hurt him and consequently stayed with him.

Ellen would have given the same rational advice to any one of her friends. But when it came to being the one to break up, she couldn't bring herself to do it; just like the majority of people who couldn't personally kill one person to save 12.

> **Much too often, we let emotions cloud our rational judgment in decision-making.**

Not only do emotions come into play when talking about negative situations such as death, but they are also involved in positive decisions that we face when it involves the people we love. We often favor people we love when we wouldn't do the same thing for people we don't love. A good example of this is when parents are dealing with their children. People are constantly telling others not to spoil their children. Spoiling your children leads to problems in the long run, and while we know we shouldn't do it, we do it anyway. Rationally, we shouldn't spoil our kids, but because we care about them, we still do it.

Much too often, we let our emotions cloud our rational judgment in decision-making. Dealing with people we love can skew how we would normally approach many of the decisions that we face in our lives. Sometimes allowing our emotions to become involved is a good thing, because we need to foster the relationships we have with our loved ones, even if it comes at the expense of the most efficient outcomes of our decisions. Other times, though, allowing our emotions to take over can simply lead to bad outcomes for all those involved.

My advice for how you should approach decisions when your loved ones are involved is a three-step process. First, step back and realize that your emotions may be clouding your rational judgment. Second, assess how you want to make the decision based upon your emotions and how you believe you would make your decision based upon being rational. Finally, compare the two different outcomes (emotional vs. rational) and make your decision. You can then better understand which decision is best for you, your loved ones, and everyone else affected by the outcome of the decisions you make.

67

Once in a Blue Moon

"That will happen only once in a blue moon." You've probably heard someone tell you that before. What they're trying to say is that it's not going to happen very often. But what does it really mean? A blue moon is technically defined as the second full moon to occur in a single calendar month, something that happens approximately once every two and a half years.

The saying has become part of our everyday language because it helps us to realize that we sometimes have unique opportunities that come into our lives. When we do have a blue-moon opportunity, we need to decide whether to take advantage of it. Usually we're not prepared for it, so the normal decision is to pass on it and hope that we may have the opportunity again.

Something that happened to Ben provides a great example of this. One day, he received in the mail an invitation to a wedding from one of his childhood friends. Having been to dozens of weddings in the past three years, this was nothing new. But it wasn't a wedding in a familiar place. This one was in Istanbul. This type of opportunity happened just once in a blue moon. And while he hadn't had plans to go to Istanbul previously, now he knew that he had to seize this opportunity because it would never happen again. While he had other things he knew he probably should have spent his money on and other things that he knew he probably should have been doing with that time, he was willing to make sacrifices to take advantage of this blue-moon opportunity. He went to Istanbul with his girlfriend, and the two of them had the time of their lives. It was an experience they would never forget.

Travel is a great example of blue-moon opportunities that should be seized. Many college students have the chance to study abroad for a semester or an entire year. They likely will never have the opportunity again to do this, because once they graduate they will have to move on to a professional career and be saddled with other responsibilities, having missed this opportunity.

I once had a blue-moon opportunity to spend a couple of days at sea on the aircraft carrier, Nimitz, something I always wanted to do, but it was difficult to change my plans. I labeled this as a blue-moon opportunity and decided to make the changes I needed to make to go on this trip. It was one of the best experiences in my life.

When my company opened its first offices in the United Kingdom, I decided that it would make sense for me to go there and spend about six months getting everything set up and meeting with new clients. I decided, however, that this could also prove to be a blue-moon opportunity for my kids, and I decided to take them with me, enrolling them in elementary school in the town we stayed in just outside of Glasgow, Scotland. It was an amazing opportunity for them that they tell me to this day they will never forget.

> **We sometimes have unique opportunities that come into our lives when we're not anticipating them.**

Career opportunities that we just can't pass up can also arise once in a blue moon, and we need to determine if we're going to jump on them or not. Shortly after James received the promotion he had wanted for many years, he was offered an unexpected opportunity to join his former boss at a new company. He needed to decide on it quickly, so he decided to pass it up, thinking he would have similar opportunities. The new company went on to be tremendously successful, and James would have become a multimillionaire with the stock options he was offered. His decision to pass up this blue-moon opportunity bothered him forever.

I think most people tend to be like James, and they decide not to take advantage of blue-moon opportunities. They're unprepared for them and uncomfortable about making changes to accommodate them. Later they regret their decisions.

It's typical to struggle with blue-moon decisions. My son Chris had a blue-moon opportunity to work for

> **Blue-moon decisions are one of those things that make life exciting.**

several months in Ramallah, in the Middle East, and after struggling with the decision, he turned it down for many valid reasons. Later that night, he felt he shouldn't have passed up that blue-moon opportunity and called me at 3 a.m. to discuss it. He changed his mind and accepted it, and he had the experience of a lifetime.

Blue-moon decisions can present themselves in many forms. Entertainment opportunities can come as blue-moon experiences. I've had opportunities to go to a baseball all-star game, golf's Ryder Cup, and others that came up as opportunities. I needed to change other plans to take advantage of these, but I did it.

There can even be blue-moon relationship opportunities. Perhaps you have the opportunity to ask out someone that you never thought you would even meet, or your friends may invite you to go with them on a special trip where you will get to know them better.

Sometimes, investment opportunities appear to be blue-moon opportunities. Be careful here, though, for more often than not when they appear to be too good to be true, they are.

Investments are a different kind of blue-moon decision. These involve a major financial commitment, and you need to make a more rational decision rather than an emotional one. Most blue-moon investment opportunities leave you feeling blue if you do them.

In general, blue-moon opportunities are one of those things that make life exciting. We all have them arise in our lifetimes, but there are several things you can do to have more and make the most of them. The more active your life, the more blue-moon opportunities you will have — like my trip to the aircraft carrier, which came about from an organization I had done volunteer work for. You need to be ready to jump on blue-moon opportunities. This means that you need to be ready to decide to expend the time, energy, and financial resources. Going to Istanbul for a wedding can be expensive, so you need to be sure you save your money and your vacation days from your job for just these types of activities.

I have some friends — a couple who I have known for many years — who actually created a "blue-moon fund" for themselves. They had already paid to put their children through college, and they had a retirement fund set up for the time when they got to that point in their lives, but they decided that they wanted to be sure they were able to take advantage of opportunities that they would never forget for their entire lives. They put $100 a month into the fund to enable them to do these things when they arose.

You should label a blue-moon opportunity as such and treat it as special. Realize that it happens rarely, and you may never see it again. Given a blue-moon opportunity, what will you do? If you're prepared and know what decisions you'll need to make, maybe you'll have the experience of a lifetime.

!68

Rube Goldberg Decisions

've found that on several occasions throughout my life, I've overcomplicated my decisions, causing them to be much more difficult to make, if not impossible. Yet when I eventually thought more about them, quite often I was able to make these decisions much simpler. I think there is a tendency to overcomplicate decisions, but when you realize that you're doing it, you can avoid it.

There was a noted cartoonist, author, and engineer named Rube Goldberg who was well-known for intentionally over-complicating things. He created extremely complex machines to perform simple operations that could have been accomplished in a much quicker and simpler manner. These machines came to be known as Rube Goldberg machines. In fact, his name has been defined as a noun in Webster's dictionary as "a comically involved complicated invention, laboriously contrived to perform a simple operation."

Rube Goldberg was of the theory that there are two ways of doing

Rube Goldberg would overcomplicate things for amusement, but when it comes to decisions, overcomplicating things is not advisable.

things: the easy way and the hard way. He marveled at the fact that many people unnecessarily choose to do things the hard way when they could do them the easy way.

When I think of Rube Goldberg, I think of overly complex decisions. Sometimes we overcomplicate our decisions unnecessarily, and we need to step back and simplify them. We opt for making decisions the hard way rather than the easy way. The vast majority of decisions that we make in our lives are difficult enough without making them more complex and agonizing over them. It's not only a waste of your time and energy, but it's also a detriment to the success of the decisions.

One example comes from Maria, who wrote to me for help with a decision she was facing. She needed to decide on a new apartment, since her lease was ending. While the one she liked was near where she went to school, she would be graduating in a year and thought that she might move to a different part of the city to work when she graduated. She also thought that she might be able to afford a better apartment once she started working. She was thinking of getting a dog and wouldn't be able to have one in this particular apartment or the others she looked at. She also had a new boyfriend and was hoping that if their relationship progressed, they might try living together in a few months. This had her feeling pressured to decide if he was serious about her and whether she was in love with him. So she spent a lot of time wrestling with her feelings about him.

When she discussed her dilemma about her apartment with her parents, they told her she should move back home, but she didn't want to do this. Her best friend suggested that they both move into an apartment together in six months when her friend's lease was up. All of this had Maria struggling with a complex set of what she viewed as intertwined decisions. Should she get this new apartment? Should she get serious about her new boyfriend? What does she tell her parents? What about the dog? Where should she live for the potential job she hasn't been offered yet? Should she move in with her friend in a few months and should she get a larger apartment now in anticipation of that?

I pointed out to her that she essentially had only one decision to make and that she was making it overly complex. One way or another, she needed to sign a one-year lease on an apartment, and her only decision was between the one she had and the new alternative. Since she wasn't moving in with her boyfriend right now, she needed to lease an apartment without him. Where she took a job in a year didn't matter be-

> Sometimes we overcomplicate our decisions unnecessarily and we need to step back and simplify them.

cause she could move in a year in any case. She didn't have an alternative of an apartment that would permit dogs, so she could ignore that for now, and she could always get a dog in a year or two. She could ask her friend to start paying rent now for a larger apartment, rather than in six months, but she already knew that her friend couldn't afford to do this. She just needed to thank her parents for their gesture and tell them she wasn't going to move in with them.

Like Rube Goldberg, Maria had made her decision unnecessarily complex, and this drove her emotionally to the point where she was overwhelmed. The more she thought about it, the more she made it increasingly complex. With a few simplifying assumptions, she was able to reduce the complexity and focus on the real fundamental decision she needed to address. Maria decided to move to the new apartment and sign a one-year lease. She was relieved and happy that she made the decision and was able to put off the other decisions until they needed to be made.

Of course, it's easier to help others simplify decisions than it is to simplify our own. Everyone tends to lump more and more decisions together because our lives are complex. When you make another decision interrelated to the one you're currently facing, this in turn makes you think of still another decision that is related, and then another and another. All of a sudden, you have multiple decisions that you incorrectly perceive as one single decision.

When you face a complex decision, ask yourself how you can simplify it. Can one or more of the related decisions be deferred? Are they truly dependent on the primary decision? If you make your primary decision, are you in fact making the other decisions or just influencing them in some way? All decisions indirectly affect other decisions you make in your life, but they don't make them interdependent. Instead, consider them as a pro or a con in the decision — they are one single factor among many others in the overall decision. You should also look for simplifying assumptions, just as Maria did by realizing that she needed a place to live and needed to sign a one-year lease in any case.

Rube Goldberg would overcomplicate things for amusement, but when it comes to decisions, overcomplicating things is not advisable. Try to simplify your decisions as much as possible. Don't make a Rube Goldberg out of your decisions.

!69

Matters of Principle

You have a lawsuit against you that you believe has absolutely no basis. You did nothing wrong, but someone is using this legal action to extort money from you. Your attorney tells you that you will likely prevail, but that you will incur $30,000 to $50,000 in legal fees defending the suit, and it's unlikely that you would get your legal fees reimbursed even if you prevail. The other party has made a settlement offer to drop the lawsuit in return for $20,000, and your attorney recommends that you take the settlement and most likely save money. What do you decide?

You are on the board of trustees of a local hospital, and you're presented with a questionable scheme. The other hospitals in the state and the state government have come up with a scheme to pretend to tax the hospitals, submit the money for matching federal Medicaid funds, and then give more money back to the hospitals. You believe this scheme is unethical, even though it may be marginally legal based on a loophole in the regulations, but your hospital will get a much needed $1 million from the scheme. What do you decide?

These are both real-world examples where you need to make a decision between a matter of principle — doing what you believe is right — and making or saving money. Money or principle, which do you want? In this case, a principle is a rule of action or conduct or a guiding sense of the requirements and obligations of right conduct. A matter of principle is not just doing what's legal; it's doing what you believe is right, even if it hurts.

Here's another example. I once agreed to sell a piece of land, and I asked the buyer if he had a pen so that I could sign the sales contract. While he was looking for a pen, my phone rang. It was someone else offering $25,000 more for the land. After I hung up, I told the expectant buyer about the new offer and that I would have signed before the call if he had a pen readily available. After I let him squirm for a few moments, I told him we had agreed to a deal and I would sell it to him at the price we had agreed to. It was a decision of principle over money.

> If you live your life based on the principles you hold to be true, no matter what the consequences of following these principles, you will be satisfied with the outcome of your decisions.

I believe that in decisions between principle and personal or organizational gain, the right decision is always to follow your principles, no matter what the cost. In the end, the right thing is to do what is right. Don't settle the lawsuit if you really believe that you did nothing wrong or illegal. Don't support the scheme that would bring additional money to your hospital because it's unethical. You do what you think is right.

Making decisions based on your principles is much simpler when absolutely applied. It doesn't depend on the amount of money involved. You don't have a price that is sufficient to compromise your principles. You simply follow your principles and do what is right no matter what the cost. Principles can't be bought. This is easier in circumstances when there is one clear option that follows your principles and one that doesn't.

You easily and quickly select the one that is in line with your principles.

If you live your life based on the principles you hold to be true, no matter what the consequences, you will be satisfied with the outcome of your decisions. You may face decisions throughout your life that will challenge you to either stick by your principles or accept some type of gain by compromising them. While you may wish that you could take the option that would provide you with the gain, you will be happier with yourself in the long run that you stuck by your beliefs. It's just a matter of principle.

> **You will be happier with yourself in the long run if you stick by your beliefs. It's just a matter of principle.**

!70

The Butterfly Effect

I n chaos theory, there's something known as the butterfly effect. This is the propensity of a system to be sensitive to a single condition, giving rise to the notion of a butterfly flapping its wings in one area of the world, which causes a tornado to occur in another area of the world. Think of it this way. The atmosphere, including the weather, will vary according to a number of conditions, including wind speed. If a butterfly decides to fly to the left, it will create some minimal effect on wind speed and therefore upon the overall atmosphere. Now what would happen if the butterfly decides to fly to the right? The change would affect the overall condition of the atmosphere in a different way.

The butterfly effect, first described by Edward Lorenz at the December 1972 meeting of the American Association for the Advancement of Science in Washington, D.C., vividly illustrates an essential idea of chaos theory. In a 1963 paper for the New York Academy of Sciences, Lorenz had quoted the assertion of an unnamed meteorologist that, if chaos theory were true, a single flap of a single seagull's wings would be enough to change the course of all future weather systems on the earth. By the time of the 1972 meeting, Lorenz had examined and refined that idea for his talk, "Predictability: Does the Flap of a Butterfly's Wings in Brazil Set off a Tornado in Texas?" The example of such a small thing as a butterfly being responsible for creating such a large and distant system as a tornado in Texas illustrates the impossibility of making predictions for complex systems.

The same theory can be applied to some of our decisions. Many of our decisions — even what we think are small ones — have an effect that we cannot possibly anticipate. Are you going to drive to work on the highway or on the side roads today? Will you stop to get coffee today or just get some when you get to work? If you do indeed decide to stop at the coffee shop on your way to work,

> **The small decisions we make today can shape the decisions we will face in the future.**

you could run into an old high school sweetheart whom you hadn't seen in years. You could decide to ask her out. A year later, you make a decision to ask her to marry you. This major, life-changing decision about getting married was directly affected by your extremely minor decision about where to get your coffee.

If you hadn't stopped for coffee that day, you wouldn't have bumped into your future wife; just like if the butterfly had not flapped its wings at just the right point in space and time, the tornado wouldn't have happened.

The main precept behind this theory is the underlying notion of small occurrences significantly affecting the outcomes of seemingly unrelated events. The small decisions we make today can shape the decisions we're going to face in the future. Where we will be and what we will do in the future, therefore, can often be random and depend upon such minor decisions that we previously made.

The decisions we make affect not only ourselves but others in ways we can't anticipate. For example, as the CEO of several companies, I've personally hired hundreds of people and indirectly hired thousands, many for the most critical jobs of their careers. For most of them this determined where they would live, what their lifestyle would be like, and who some of their new friends would be. For some, it may have even triggered meeting a future spouse. In most of these cases, the job determined where they lived and, therefore, where their children went to school and, by extension, their children's friends and many of their children's futures. It's actually scary to think about how many thousands of lives I've changed through these hires. I hope, overall, it was for the better.

Your decisions are a continuing demonstration of the butterfly effect. So what should you do about it? The butterfly effect of your decisions should not make you shy away from making decisions. Even though some of your decisions — even the seemingly small ones — will shape your life in major ways you can't possibly anticipate. Even though some of your decisions will shape the lives of others in major ways that they can't even anticipate. There really isn't much you can do about it.

> **Many of our decisions, even what we think are small ones, have an effect that we cannot possibly anticipate.**

There is no way to predict the major decisions that will result from some of your minor decisions, so anxiety about this is only harmful to your present decisions. Simply live your life and make your decisions as you will. Some of the major decisions you face in the future will appear to come at you randomly, even though they may have been triggered by some small decision you made in the past. So go ahead and flap your wings.

71

Achilles' Heel

According to mythology, the only weakness of the famed invincible character Achilles, that which led to his fatal downfall, was his heel. As is written about the myths from the Trojan War, the warrior Achilles was finally brought down by a poisoned arrow, fired by Paris and guided by Apollo, landing in his heel.

The source of his invincibility and the related weakness in his heel stemmed from when he was a baby. As the story goes, Achilles' mother, Thetis, held her son by the foot and dipped his entire body into the river Styx, creating an invincible person everywhere that the boy was immersed in the water. Forgetting to dip him a second time by holding her son in a different spot, of course, left the boy with a vulnerable spot — where Thetis was holding Achilles by the heel, between her thumb and fore-finger. Hence, Achilles' heel.

The story of Achilles' heel is frequently used as an expression for an area of weakness or vulnerability, sometimes physi-cal and sometimes emotional or mental. In fact, while the term Achilles heel is usually meant to imply a physical weakness in Achilles, notably in his foot, in some versions of the story, the actual weakness of Achilles was his pride, not his heel.

In our decision-making as individuals, we all have our own decision Achilles heels. Sometimes, our decision Achilles heel is related to the types of decisions we make. For example, we could make bad career decisions or relationship decisions. Or maybe we make bad financial decisions or health decisions. There are just certain types of decisions that we make poorly. Often, our decision Achilles heel is caused by a breakdown or general problem with the process of our decision-making, whether in general or related to specific types of decisions that we face.

In business, I have often found managers who simply make bad hiring decisions. They pore over résumés and interview all of the candidates for a particular position, and then they inevitably decide on someone who is not right for the job. Perhaps they really liked that person or thought they would fit in well with the other employees, but in the end, the new hire simply didn't have the experience or skills that were needed to be successful. If these managers worked for me or for a company I consulted for, I would insulate them from the hiring process. Their Achilles heel was hiring decisions. It doesn't mean that all of the decisions they make professionally are bad, and they often have very strong managerial skills in other areas. They just can't make good hiring decisions. By realizing this, a company can solve the problem by not depending on them for hiring decisions in the future.

In our personal lives, we may make bad purchasing decisions or bad decisions about alcohol. Some people are what can be called "shopaholics," and they simply can't bring themselves to decide not to buy things they generally can't afford. Their decision process breaks down. Instead of rationally making a decision whether to buy something based upon whether they can afford it, they generally make the decision without considering their financial situation. Rather than paying in cash for the item, they will put it on their credit card and end up with too much credit card debt. The solution to this problem? Well, it certainly starts with not spending all of your time at the mall.

Another strategy may be to change the parameters of how you approach shopping. If you don't have enough cash to pay for the item, for example, decide not to buy it. As for alcoholics, a good way to prevent being put into a situation where you can't make a good decision to not drink in excess is to not spend time in a bar or other location where alcohol is available.

We also find societies, governments, structures, and organizations affected by a decision Achilles heel. Noted political theorist and historian Alexis de Tocqueville surmised that the Achilles heel of American democracy was its foreign policy. He believed that a representative democracy such as that of the United States could never muster the necessary resolve to make a decision on, and implement, a strong foreign policy.

When it comes to decision Achilles heels, there are differences between your own Achilles heel and someone else's.

When you recognize your own Achilles heel, then you need to protect yourself from the consequences of your decision mistakes due to this weakness. Don't let anyone exploit it, and decide that you will work to decrease the effect of the weakness. If you can avoid putting yourself in the situation where you have to make the type of decisions that you know you make poorly, then you won't have to make these decisions.

If the decision Achilles heel is someone else's, what will you do with that information? If it's someone you are close with, you can approach them and explain the problem. If they don't know their weakness, they may appreciate you looking out for them. If it's someone you are trying to get something from, you could exploit their weakness.

There are three things that you can do to try to counter the effects of your decision Achilles heel. The first strategy is to solve the fundamental problem within the decision-making process itself. For the manager who makes bad hiring decisions, for example, this could mean taking a course on how to make these decisions better. The second thing you can do is to compensate for your weaknesses in some way. For the shopaholic, for example, this may mean paying only in cash and no longer using credit cards. This way, you would be forced to make an assessment of your ability to buy something based upon your current resources. The third thing you can do is to avoid these decisions at all costs. For the manager this could mean no longer being in charge of hiring or, for the alcoholic, no longer going to the bar.

I sometimes make poor decisions when it comes to eating dessert. I know that I shouldn't have dessert when eating out, but it is my Achilles heel. If I see a dessert menu — or worse, a dessert cart — nine times out of 10 I decide to have dessert, regardless of whether I'm hungry for it or not. If I refuse to take or look at the dessert menu, however, I never order dessert. The weakness in my decision-making process when it comes to dessert is seeing the menu or seeing the dessert. I understand my dessert Achilles heel and can respond to it accordingly — by not looking at the menu.

Do you have an Achilles heel in your decision-making process? Most of us do. Do you know what it is? What are you going to do about it? Will you protect yourself against it being exploited by someone else? Maybe you can protect yourself from the same arrow that took down Achilles.

72

Strategic Decisions

I've seen so many companies and individuals struggle with strategic decisions. It's not just about making the decisions, which is difficult enough; it's also about knowing when to make them. People get hung up in strategic planning, envisioning the future while losing sight of the strategic decisions they need to make today to get there.

Strategic decisions are those that we need to make today to achieve something we want in the future. One of the unique characteristics of strategic decisions is knowing when to make them. Make the decision prematurely, and you may make the wrong decision; but make it too late, and you will miss your goal.

So what is strategic planning and strategic decision-making? Peter Drucker simplifies this, as usual, with his clear thinking: "Strategic planning does not deal with future decisions. It deals with the futurity of present decisions. Decisions only exist in the present. The question that faces the strategic decision-maker is not what his organization should do tomorrow. It is: 'what do we have to do today to be ready for tomorrow?'"

In other words, strategic planning focuses on the decisions you need to make today to achieve what you want in the future.

Don't worry yet about the decisions you need to make in the future.

Companies would frequently ask me, as a strategy consultant, what their planning horizon should be: three years, five years, 10 years? The answer depended on how long it took for decisions they make today to affect the future they wanted to achieve. In some companies, such as technology companies, the planning horizon could be short, while in others it needs to be longer. If a company wants to develop new products over the next three years to leverage its technology and grow rapidly, then it needs to make decisions today on products it would sell in three years. If it has to develop an entirely new technology, it needs to make decisions now that would affect it five to 10 years out.

The failure of strategic planning is that companies — and individuals — don't identify the decisions they need to make until they are already too far within their planning horizon. They can't decide today to develop a new product that will take three years to develop and expect that it will increase sales next year. It seems that they just didn't think to make that decision two years ago.

A successful high-technology company had an annual planning process where it assembled its entire executive team for three days. They discussed how they envisioned the future and put together the company's annual plan for the next year. One year the executive team realized that they needed an entirely new technology to replace the one they used in most of their products, because competitors were introducing better products using a new technology.

We can make decisions today to help us reach our goals tomorrow.

When they confronted this, they found that while they could do it, three to five years would be necessary to complete the new technology. Sales would plummet in the meantime. The shock for them was that they realized they should have — and could have — made this decision two to three years ago, but they just didn't think about it at the time. They neglected to identify a critical strategic decision when it needed to be made. The board of directors terminated the CEO for this failure, and the company was forced to make an extremely expensive acquisition of a competitor who already had this technology. The stock price of the company dropped by half and didn't recover for four years. If only they had thought of the strategic decisions they needed to make ahead of time, it would have been a lot different.

Just like companies we, too, as individuals, can make decisions today to help us reach our goals tomorrow. What decisions do we need to make and what steps do we need to take to be where we want to be? We need to plan for ourselves and our families far enough ahead so that we know what decisions we need to make today. Of course, we don't need to worry about the decisions we need to make in three years or in three weeks, for that matter. But what is important is that we address what decisions need to be made today. If we miss the opportunity to make these decisions, or if we ignore them until it's too late, we won't achieve our goals in the future.

Tom, for example, was entering his mid-40s and started to dream of his retirement. Would he buy a home in the South and play golf, or maybe retire by the ocean? By the time he reached his mid-50s, he thought he should start making decisions about this retirement goal. But now, Tom realized it was too late. Even if he started saving as much as he possibly could, he would not be able to save enough to retire as he dreamed. The time to make the strategic decision for his retirement was 10 years earlier. Tom missed his strategic decision for retirement. He ended up working until his late-60s and then retiring in the same place he lived, able to travel only a few weeks a year. If only someone had told him when he needed to make that strategic retirement decision.

Here are some practical tips for knowing when to make strategic decisions in your life. First, think ahead. Dream a little. What do you want to achieve in your life or in your company? Think about everything. If you want to be healthy and fit, what will that require? If you want to have a particular career, what do you need to do? If you want to have your own business, how do you get it? If you have retirement plans, what are they?

Then determine the decisions you need to make now to achieve these goals. The timing of some of these decisions may be clear, such as when you need to decide about applying to college. The timing of others may not be as clear. When do you need to make decisions about retirement? Do you need to make decisions today about your long-term health, or can you wait a couple of years? If you eventually want to own your own business, what do you need to decide today to make this happen?

> **One of the unique characteristics of strategic decisions is knowing when to make them.**

Companies must have a planning process that identifies when they need to make strategic decisions. The difficult part of doing this is that not all strategic decisions fall in the same timeframe. Some need to be made a year in advance, others three years, and some five or more years.

You can also identify strategic decisions through budgeting — for everything from next month to 20 years from now. Maybe you want to go on a really nice vacation with your family next spring, and again, you will need to save up for it. You need to decide today that you are going to cut back on your expenses and save enough money to make the vacation great next year. Maybe you want to be able to retire from your job at 55 years old with enough money to live as well as you do now. Is this your dream? Well, you better decide today how you're going to achieve that goal and how you're going to save and invest enough money to make that dream a reality.

Just as Peter Drucker says, all decisions are made in the present, not the future. What do you have to decide as an individual today to be where you want to be tomorrow? Don't miss your opportunity by thinking that you can make these decisions tomorrow, or even worse, neglecting to even think about the strategic decisions you need to make.

73

The White Elephant

White elephants are truly rare, but they may be more trouble than they're worth. In Burmese culture, a white (or albino) elephant is considered sacred. If you own one, you are not allowed to put it to work and must spend untold amounts of money and time providing the absolute best care for it.

It has been said that when the King of Siam wanted to punish someone without inflicting physical harm, he would give them a white elephant. He knew that the person would then be ruined financially because of the amount they would have to spend on the upkeep of it. Since the elephant was believed to be sacred, and it was considered a high honor to receive this gift from the King, the person who was given the elephant wasn't able to give it away or sell it. They had to keep it and care for it.

In contemporary life, the term white elephant has come to be synonymous with a project or item that requires more trouble for the owner or person responsible for it than it's worth. We have all encountered times in our lives when we stop and realize that we're dealing with a white elephant, but we don't always know what we should do about it. Do we stop the project? Do we sell the item? Do we try to dispose of it by whatever means necessary?

The business world is rife with white elephants. A company may know that it is the proud owner of a white elephant (a new product, an employee, a board member) and may try to get rid of it by selling it to someone else (firing the employee or buying out the shareholder). It may sell it at a significant loss or even be willing to give it away.

Governments often do the same thing. The Social Security system in the United States provides us with an example of a white elephant. The system is struggling to provide services and financial resources to its beneficiaries. Originally created as a social safety net for retired people, it was designed when there were far more active workers than there were people collecting benefits. In 1940, there were 159.4 workers for each beneficiary. Over time, however, the ratio of workers to beneficiary has changed dramatically, with the past three decades holding almost steady at 3.3 workers for each beneficiary. Within a few decades, the ratio will drop to roughly 2 workers per beneficiary, at which point the system will be unable to pay the full benefits it has promised to those who have paid into the system. Caring for this white elephant will require more resources than the system can create.

Another example of a government realizing it had a white elephant is the famous London Bridge, actually called the New London Bridge. In 1831, as the previous London Bridge had been deemed unsafe, the New London Bridge was opened to much fanfare. Designed by John Rennie, the bridge was 928 feet long and 49 feet wide. In 1902, however, the bridge was widened to accommodate the increase in traffic. The widening proved too much for the bridge to handle, and it began to fall down in 1962 (hence the nursery rhyme). The city decided that, while the bridge held immense historical value, it would simply cost too much to keep it operational. They realized that they had a white elephant. So they made a decision — sell it.

American entrepreneur Robert McCulloch bought the bridge

in 1968 for $2,460,000 and transported it to Lake Havasu City, Arizona (at an additional cost of $7 million). The city of London had realized it had a white elephant and made the best possible decision — sell it and use the money to replace it.

While the problem of a white elephant occurs less often in our personal lives than in the business world, it does occur. Jody and her husband, Fred, faced a white elephant when they inherited a small summer cottage on Cape Cod in Massachusetts. The cottage had been in Jody's family for more than 100 years, having been built by her great-grandfather. While they were upset that Jody's father had passed away, they were thrilled that he had decided to leave them the cottage.

It had been several years since they had been there, and a few months after Jody inherited it, she and Fred went to the cottage to check it out. They noticed that it had been in disrepair since they had last seen it, and it needed a number of minor upgrades. They hired someone to fix it up for them, and when he was making the upgrades to the house, he noticed that the roof needed to be completely replaced and that the outside of the house was in dire need of refinishing. Jody and Fred couldn't afford to make these upgrades, but they decided that they really had no choice, so they secured a loan to cover the costs. The following fall, after all of the upgrades were finally completed, there was a major storm and the cottage received significant water damage to its foundation. They quickly realized that their homeowner's insurance wouldn't cover the damage, and they would have to pay to fix it themselves. Once again, they took out a loan for repairs, mortgaging their primary residence in Boston to do so. A few months later, the house got termites and many of the floorboards had to be replaced.

At this point, Jody and Fred finally realized that they had a white elephant. They understood that they were now taking care of a second home that they would probably use for less than three weeks every year and were forced to sink tens of thousands of dollars into it for repairs. While they knew they would have no problem selling it, Jody couldn't bring herself to get rid of the house that her great-grandfather had built and where some of her best childhood memories were made. In the end, they decided that they would keep the house and most likely spend a huge amount of money to do so. They knew they had a white elephant, but because of the sentimental value of the house, the emotional costs of selling it were much higher than the financial costs of repairing it.

The concept of a white elephant can be applied to other areas of our lives. For example, some people have white-elephant relationships. These require a lot more care and feeding than the relationship is worth. They seem to keep putting more and more into the relationship, but they still get little back from it.

The first thing you need to do with a white elephant is to realize that you are, in fact, dealing with a white elephant. It's not always easy to come to this understanding, especially if it's something that has been a long time coming. Once you realize this, a period of relief is often experienced because you know what you need to do next and you can stop worrying about the small, often incremental, costs you face from your white elephant. You now have two choices — get rid of the white elephant (by selling it, trading it, giving it away, destroying it, or using whatever other possible ways you have for getting it off of your hands), or keep it and understand that you will face continued costs in money, effort, time, and other resources.

If you find yourself burdened by something you own or are involved in, will you realize if it's a white elephant? What will you do? Will you spend the resources to keep it? Will you do whatever it takes to get rid of it? That is your white-elephant decision.

74

Don't Push Me

We face pressure in all aspects of our lives, including pressure from others trying to push us to make decisions. People we know press us to make certain decisions. Even people we don't know pressure us to make decisions. So how do you cope with these pressures? Do you give in? Do you reject the pressure outright and make the opposite decision from the one you've been pushed to make? Or do you decide whether you will give in to the pressure or not depending upon who it is that's pressuring you?

One of the most common places we see decision pressure is in relationships, such as between parents and their children. Parents are constantly pressuring their children to make certain decisions throughout their entire lives. They push them to make everything from their smallest decisions to their major life decisions. "What courses are you going to take in high school? I think you should take French and Physics." "What are you planning on doing this summer? I think you should work at the local donut shop rather than spending another year at summer camp."

There are many motives involved when people pressure you to make the decision they want you to make. These motives generally fall into two categories. The first category involves people who pressure you for their own benefit. They really try to get you to make your decision in a way that would benefit them, although this is not always because they are bad people. In some of these cases, they deserve a decision from you because it affects them. The second category involves purely honest motivations. People who pressure you under this type of motive do it because they believe that if you make the decision the way they're asking you to, you will benefit.

Usually, the decision pressure caused by parents on their children is driven by the parents' desire for the children's best interests. They believe that their child may not yet be experienced enough to make the best decision, so they're anxious to help.

Other times, however, you may be pressured to make a certain decision, but the benefit is not clearly in your best interest alone. This is a hybrid of the two categories of pressure. Again turning to a relationship example, one person in a relationship may be ready to get married or move on, while the other isn't. In this case, that person may pressure the other for a decision on marriage before the other is ready. It's not necessarily bad or good for one party or the other. It's just that it's time for the two people to get their relationships aligned — one way or another.

Many times, friends pressure one another to make a decision. Anna, a high school senior, provides us with an example of this. One Friday, as school was ending for the week, Anna was talking with her friends about their plans for the weekend. There was a party on Saturday night, and she needed to decide if she was going to go to it or go to the movies with her younger cousin, something they had been doing on the first Saturday of most months for the past several years. Her friends are pushing her to go to the party, and she wants to go, but she also wants to keep her

> **When you're under decision pressure, step back and recognize the pressure you're facing.**

promise to her cousin to go to the movies. Now she must decide — give in to the pressure being put on her by her friends, or honor her longstanding commitment and go to the movies.

In some cases, people we don't even know pressure us to make a decision. This happens often when you're considering buying anything expensive, like a house or car, where the salesperson is getting a commission on your decision. Sometimes, companies pressure employees into making decisions that are for the benefit of the employees. One trend that's becoming more popular is for companies to automatically enroll its employees in their 401k plan, and then allow employees to opt out. This is a different method than not having them enrolled and allowing them to opt in. By gently pushing the employees to save for their retirement in this way, they're pressuring them for their own benefit. In these cases, companies find that twice as many employees enroll in the 401k plan.

When you're under decision pressure, there are several things that you can do to handle the pressure. First, step back and recognize the pressure you're facing. It's usually pretty easy to tell when you're being pressured. This helps you to get beyond feeling that you just don't like being pushed to make a decision, so you can start to work on your decision more productively.

Second, analyze the motives lying beneath the pressure that's being placed on you. Is the person who's pushing you looking out for your best interests, or are they pushing you for their own gain? And if they are pressuring you for their own benefit, do they have a legitimate reason for doing so? Understanding these motives can have important effects on your decision.

Third, after understanding where the pressure is coming from and the motivations behind this pressure, you need to put the pressure aside and look at the decision that you're facing. Try to identify what you think the best decision would be based purely upon the facts of the situation. Without being pressured, how would you make your decision?

Finally, you should reintroduce the pressure to your situation. There may be valid reasons why you should consider mak-

276 · Don't Push Me

ing your decision as you are being pressured to. You may have determined that without being pressured, you would decide to do option A, but after considering the pressure being placed upon you, you decide that you're actually going to choose option B. You may decide, for example, that it would be better to defer to the opinion of the person pressuring you. The child in our example may realize that his parents are right. You may decide that it's to the benefit of your relationship with the person pressuring you to appease them. The person in the example who is pressured to make the decision on marriage may realize that he or she loves the other person too much to lose him or her. You may also simply give in to the pressure for no reason other than that you're torn between one decision and the other, so you just do what you're being pushed to do. Sometimes, you can even be pushed to make a decision in a way that you don't want to because someone has done something nice for you and you want to return his kindness.

When under pressure, analyze the motives lying beneath the pressure that's being placed on you.

The next time you find yourself being pushed to make a decision, take a few moments to understand the reason for the pressure and then either resist it or go with it. Then make your decision with full appreciation of the pressures involved.

Provoke Decisions

Making sure that important decisions get made is an essential leadership characteristic. If you look at successful senior executives, particularly CEOs, they don't so much make all of the decisions as they provoke decisions. Of course, they make many decisions themselves, but the majority of the decisions need to be made by someone else. The CEO has to be sure that the most important issues are addressed and that the decisions are made at the right time by the right people.

Decisiveness is not a common trait. Not all businesses or individuals act decisively and opportunely, so this is something that needs to be worked on. Pushing people to make decisions is an important leadership trait — perhaps even more important than making decisions yourself. I talk about the need to push yourself to make decisions in other chapters. The important lesson here is that it is often necessary to push others to make decisions that they either are hesitant to make or don't know they should make. This is quite common in the business world, but it's also something that happens often in other group dynamics, such as families. It sometimes even happens with individuals.

There are several ways to provoke decisions. You can encourage someone to make a decision, or you can force someone to make a decision. Some companies, as well as society in general, have processes that force decisions to be made. These are generally good, orderly ways to provoke decisions. Here we are generally not dealing with getting others to make a decision one way or the other, but simply getting them to make the decision.

All too often, decisions can be delayed or go unmade because of confusion over who should make them and when they should be made. A major electronics company identified an exciting new market opportunity and launched a team to develop a product to take advantage of this opportunity. Soon after the project started, however, it began to drift. Several important design alternatives were identified, but a decision was needed to select one and go forward. Precious months slipped by with no decision. Later, another delay of several months occurred when a decision could not be made regarding initial functionality of the first product release. In the end, the actual decisions were unimportant since the delay in making them proved to be fatal to the project's chances of success. A competitor beat the company to the market opportunity, so the company never released its product. If someone had just pushed them to make the decisions, they could have increased their profits significantly. Instead, someone who worked for their competitor was successful in provoking the decisions that ultimately led to the competitor reaping all of the profits.

Pushing people to make the decisions that need to be made is an essential leadership trait.

Many companies have solved this problem by using management processes to trigger important decisions such as these. Over the past five to ten years, for example, most companies have implemented a phase-based decision-making process to force "go" or "no go" decisions at clearly defined phases of product development. The process identifies who is responsible for making these decisions and when they need to be made. Simply correcting this decision-making deficiency can take a third of the time out of a company's development cycle! It also creates a new respect for senior management: "They sure know how to make the difficult decisions!"

Companies have also instituted processes to trigger more routine decisions. A material-requirements planning system alerts a purchasing manager, for instance, when a decision needs to be made on reordering a component. A performance-appraisal process and schedule is designed to force managers to make decisions on salary increases for their employees.

In a similar way, the annual planning process forces decisions. For most companies, however, the focus of annual planning is on budgeting, not strategy. This is where companies are most vulnerable to overlooking or deferring strategic decisions that should be made. They are not focused on the proper decision — and are not pushed to make these decisions when they should. Often, when there is no event triggering a decision, there is no decision.

Making sure decisions get made is an important responsibility of a company's senior management. Sometimes, they do this by implementing formal management processes that define who needs to make what decisions and when they need to be made. Sometimes, they may simply challenge individuals: "Decide what you think we should do about this problem and let me know by the end of next week what you decide." In other cases, they may make the decisions themselves. In the best companies,

> Successful companies and successful families are decisive. While they may not always make perfect decisions, they know when decisions need to be made and they make them.

decisiveness becomes part of its culture. It becomes something that is prevalent among everyone from the CEO to the lowest man on the totem pole.

Just as with companies, oftentimes parents also need to provoke decision-making in their children. Many kids don't know when they need to make decisions, and their parents need to push them so they're made. This instills in kids a sense of good decision-making and good judgment.

Successful companies and successful families are decisive. While they might not always make perfect decisions, they know when decisions need to be made, and they make them. They do this by provoking decisions.

76

Size Matters

When it comes to decisions, size matters. Success in business and in your personal life comes from getting the big decisions right and not dwelling on the small ones. If you make better decisions about your career, your family, your education, your job, etc., than you do about where you shop or what clothes you wear, you'll be on the right track to having a better life.

While this may sound obvious, I am continually amazed at how many people tend to spend more time on the little decisions in their lives than they do on the big ones. I see people agonizing over decisions on something they purchased or someone they dated, while they may accept as fate a decision about their career.

It's true that we face many more small decisions than major decisions in our everyday lives, but this doesn't mean that we need to put more energy into small decisions than we put into ones that truly affect the quality of our lives.

One example relates to Becky, who continually worried about how she looked, spending most of her time reading fashion magazines, buying new clothes, and deciding what to wear. She made many more fashion decisions than most people. In fact, it consumed a lot of her time and energy. I don't want to imply that looking good is not important, and social acceptance was extremely important to Becky, but she spent too much of her decision-making time on it. At the same time, she spent almost no time at all on decisions regarding her career.

Given an opportunity by her company to take a training course that would further her career, Becky thought about it for a minute or two and then decided not to do it. Later that day, she spent close to two hours trying to decide on the right shoes to buy for a weekend date. She also ignored or spent little time on decisions regarding her own health, relationships, and family, believing that she really couldn't affect the outcomes of these decisions.

Eventually, all of this caught up with Becky. She never progressed in her job. She didn't get married. While she dressed great, she wasn't very interesting. And her health declined. She made excellent decisions on things that mattered little because she invested a lot of time, but in the end she made poor decisions on the things that truly mattered most because she invested very little time.

> **Allocate time every day to sit down and mull over your major decisions.**

The ability to concentrate on the most important decisions is a characteristic of successful leaders. Throughout history, some American Presidents have been noted for their ability to focus on the big decisions, while others tended to dilute their time with too many minor decisions. For example, some presidential historians feel that Ronald Reagan focused on big decisions while Bill Clinton seemed to get involved in many smaller decisions. Clinton liked to delve into the details of every project as a micromanager, which is sometimes considered a positive trait. He had an endless curiosity and a tendency to be drawn in too many directions at once. When it affects your ability to spend an adequate amount of time on the largest decisions, however, this can be an impediment to being a successful leader. Delegating smaller decisions is important when you, as a leader, face so many big decisions that demand a large portion of your time.

As is evidenced by his achievements and his writings, Reagan identified the major decisions of his administration and worked on them. Unlike Clinton, Reagan delegated the less important decisions.

I think there are several reasons some people spend too much time on small decisions and too little time on big ones, and I have suggestions for avoiding this trap. First and foremost, the little decisions are thrust continually in front of us. Every day you must decide what to wear, what to eat, where to go, etc. So you figure you should spend the time to make these decisions as best as possible. You have to make them immediately since they can't wait. In contrast, the bigger decisions in life can usually wait — at least a little while. They are not as immediate; you can work on them when you get around to it. To avoid this trap, you should try to keep your major decisions front and center. Allocate a certain amount of time every day to sit down and really mull over the major decisions you face. To balance this, give yourself a break on the smaller decisions. It really won't matter much in your life if you wear a blue or tan shirt today.

> **Keep focused on the big decisions in your life — the ones that will shape your life and truly define who you are.**

You should keep telling yourself that the big decisions deserve more time. Becky's decision about the training program was more important than her decision about the new shoes. She should have spent two hours deciding on the training program and 15 minutes deciding on the new shoes, rather than the other way around. If a big decision is 100 times more important than a smaller decision, doesn't it stand to reason that you should spend 100 times more time on it?

Second, big decisions are harder than smaller ones to get right. It's not fun deciding about your career and the training you might take, but it's a lot of fun deciding on new shoes (at least for some people). We all have a tendency to be more interested in what's fun, but sometimes we need to realize that the most important things, the most important decisions in this case, require work. But with hard work comes large rewards. You will be much better off if you take the time to think about your big decisions instead of making them on impulse or emotion.

Finally, you also tend to get quicker feedback on the smaller decisions. Becky got a lot of compliments on her new shoes, but nobody commented about the training. When you decide on what to eat, for example, you get a quick self-evaluation of your decision — did you like what you ordered or not?

In contrast, you don't see the results of the bigger decisions until further in the future. Recognize that bigger decisions have delayed gratification compared to smaller ones. But also recognize that good decisions on the bigger ones also have more gratification when the outcomes are realized. You shouldn't worry about the smaller decisions, and you shouldn't evaluate yourself on them.

Keep focused on the big decisions in your life; these are most likely the ones that will shape your life and truly define who you are. In the case of decisions, therefore, size matters.

77

Flying by the Seat of Your Pants

U sually, you want to avoid making a hasty decision, but it's not always possible. Sometimes you just need to wing it, otherwise known as flying by the seat of your pants.

The origin of this phrase comes from early pilots who were required to have a feel for the airplane before navigational and flight control equipment was widely available. They had to understand what the plane was doing in order to make decisions on how to fly it. Essentially, they could feel the movements of the airplane and decide what they needed to do to turn the plane, increase altitude, or decrease altitude. The place for contact between the airplane and pilot with the best connection and transmission of feeling was in the seat of the pilot's pants.

In our lives, we can't always predict how things are going to happen and what decisions we need to make in reaction. Sometimes we need to start moving in a particular direction with a goal in sight, and then fly by the seat of our pants while working to reach that goal. Once you decide on a goal, you need to interpret the data that continually comes in to you and make a decision about how to proceed. A seat-of-your-pants decision is one that requires you to interpret the (often imperfect and always unpredictable) information you have available in any given situation and make a decision on which way to proceed to reach that goal.

Even in situations where you thought you've sufficiently planned ahead, sometimes you'll experience something you didn't anticipate that will send you in a completely different direction. What do you do then? You interpret how you've been set off course and you determine what you need to do to get back on track. You need to make a series of decisions by interpreting your rapidly changing situation. You need to make decisions "on the fly."

In the decisions that you make on a daily basis, you'll inevitably encounter situations when you'll need to fly by the seat of your pants, and you had better be prepared for them. You may wonder how to prepare to fly by the seat of your pants. By practicing, just as pilots practice flying without instruments, in the off chance that the instruments fail unexpectedly during flight. By training for the unexpected, you can be sure that you have the right skills to make decisions on the fly. You can never be fully prepared for all of the decisions that will come at you, so you need to use experience, preparation, and your best judgment to make them.

> **By training for the unexpected, you can be sure that you will make good decisions on the fly.**

Just as pilots have instruments to help them fly, we too have instruments to help us decide. The instrument we use most to navigate our decisions is our minds. We need to take in all of the background information available to enable us to understand a particular scenario we are in. What are the potential consequences of what we are experiencing? What is the desired outcome? What are our alternative actions? What do we need to do to reach that outcome? What are the risks of one decision over another?

There are four basic things that you should know about seat-of-your-pants decisions and how you should approach them. First, you need to understand the characteristics of these decisions: They must be made rapidly, and they're based largely on the actions of other people or on influences otherwise outside of your control. Second, you should recognize a decision that you need to make by the seat of your pants. Third, when you know you are going to have to fly by the seat of your pants, you can prepare in advance. Finally, just as you need to recognize when to fly by the seat of your pants, you also need to understand when you need to avoid doing so. Sometimes it's just too risky and foolish.

Have you ever played blackjack or any other card game, or any board game, for that matter? If you have, then you understand that you need to make decisions based on rapidly changing and variable situations. In blackjack, for example, you need to make a decision on whether you are going to "hit" and take another card or whether you are going to "stand" and keep what you have. Based on the underlying rules of the game (to get as close to 21 points without going over that number) and your previous experience playing it, you make your determination.

> We occasionally find ourselves facing decisions that require us to make the best possible decision based upon the frequently limited information that we can acquire.

You have no idea what cards the dealer has and whether or not the next card in the deck is going to help you get to 21 points or if it's going to make you exceed 21 points and "bust," losing automatically. So how do you decide whether you are going to hit or stand? You fly by the seat of your pants and rely on previous experience and your preparation, using the foundation of the rules of the game (such as, the dealer must hit if he or she has 16 or fewer points).

I lived in Boston for several years, and if you've ever been there, you know that it has terrible traffic. I found that whenever I was driving in the city, especially during rush hour, it was a constant challenge to select the best route to take to get home (or wherever I was trying to go). At first, I would take route 93, the primary highway that cuts through the center of the city. Usually, however, it was backed up completely. I could see the onramp before getting onto the highway, and if it was severely backed up, I would turn around and take an alternate route through downtown and onto Storrow Drive. On my way over there, I would suddenly hear the radio traffic report tell me that it was gridlock on Storrow, and I would decide to take another route to get over the river and on my way home. Due to the rapidly changing and unpredictable traffic patterns, I found myself flying by the seat of my pants every single day on the way to work and then turning around and doing it once again on the way back home.

In our everyday lives, we also find ourselves required to fly by the seat of our pants when it comes to more important decisions. We need to do this for a whole range of decisions — from career and professional decisions to relationship and other personal decisions.

Quite often, decisions involving our personal and work relationships require us to fly by the seat of our pants. We can never accurately predict what other people are going to say or do, so we cannot always predetermine what we will do in response to their actions. Whenever dealing with situations that require us to make a decision based at least in part on someone else's actions, we are required to fly by the seat of our pants.

One place where we make decisions by the seat of our pants is during job interviews. We've all likely faced this situation. You've been given the opportunity to be interviewed for a great job. You know that you're qualified for it, but you also know that there are other good candidates being interviewed. You've had interviews before, so you know what to expect. They will ask you about your current job, why you feel you want to change to the new position, why you feel you are qualified, and other standard questions. But you obviously can't predict all of the questions they will ask. While you know you will need to fly by the seat of your pants during your interview, you can still prepare for it. You should prepare for the questions that they may or may not ask in the chance that they are asked. By doing this, you can be sure to achieve your best results when flying by the seat of your pants.

You also need to make seat-of-your-pants decisions in relationships. How do you respond when asked out on a date? How do you respond to a question concerning what you want to do with your life? In some ways, a date can be similar to a job interview. How will you answer the questions that are asked during the date? How will you react to romantic advances? You can be better prepared for these decisions if you anticipate the potential situations and consider your options in advance.

Just as some pilots are better than others at flying by the seat of their pants, some people are better than others at seat-of-your-pants decisions. They go into situations knowing they'll need to fly by the seat of their pants, they prepare for what may come, and they anticipate how to react. So when your decision navigational instruments go out, how are you going to respond? Are you prepared to fly by the seat of your pants?

!78

Step by Step

"Let's take things one step at a time." This phrase is typically associated with new romance, and in that context, it's a good suggestion for how to proceed in a relationship.

After all, the path from first date to wedlock is a sequence of escalating emotional decisions. First date, second date, third date, getting serious, getting engaged, getting married. At any step along the way, the relationship investment may be stopped: "I want to end it." "I like you, but not enough to get serious about you." "It's not you, it's me." As the couple gets to know each other better, they have a progressively better sense of whether to ratchet-up the relationship investment, slow it down, or end it and go their separate ways.

This step-by-step decision-making process applies much more broadly than to just relationships, though. More than 25 years ago, I applied it to a new decision process in the field of high-tech product development. The management decision process is critical to innovation, and it wasn't working well in most companies. At the time, most executives thought that R&D investment decisions were a matter of gut instinct. In other words, these decision-makers in the most empirically driven sector of the economy were telling me that if this were a relationship, it would be similar to the following decision-making process: You are a single man and met a woman you found attractive. On your first date, you need to decide how to proceed, choosing from the following three options:

1. Propose to her on the spot and hand her your credit cards as an engagement present;
2. Tell her to get lost because you don't like the way she's done her hair; or,
3. Get her phone number and then agonize for five years over whether to call her.

This makes just as little sense in a relationship as it does in the business world or in your everyday life, but that's the way things often were for R&D investment decisions.

My consulting firm changed that with a rational and systematic approach to managing the product-development process. We called it PACE (Product And Cycle-time Excellence), and it has saved companies millions of dollars, collectively saving billions and getting the most successful products to market in half the time. Today, it's become the standard practice in the global technology sector. A key element of PACE is making investment decisions in phases or steps, starting out small and then increasing the investments as success becomes clearer. This strategy is also applicable to how you make hard decisions in your life.

Investments in new technologies, new relationships, and other "projects" in your life can be expensive in different ways. Since there is a high level of uncertainty about whether the project will succeed or fail in the end, it's best to make the decision progressively.

At the end of each phase (of your relationship, project, etc.), you should ask yourself a set of predetermined questions that screen out undesirable or low-priority projects as early as possible.

In product development, the first phase (typically called Phase 0) is a rough screening phase: Does this opportunity have the potential to succeed? Do we have the resources to do it? Does it fit our strategy?

The next phase (Phase 1) is a planning phase where the project really starts, but no development investments are made until the questions of this planning phase are answered satisfactorily: Is the projected return on investment sufficient? Is it technically feasible? Do we have the resources available to do the project?

Development then occurs in subsequent phases with specific milestone hurdles at each phase. The key to this decision-making process is defining the right questions that need to be answered at each phase to weed out poor projects or redefine project opportunities as soon as possible and for the lowest investment.

I found that this phase-based decision process applies in many other decisions as well — particularly those that tend to unfold or develop over time. Career decisions, relationship decisions, home construction decisions, etc., are good examples.

These life projects lend themselves to this type of approach because at the end of each decision phase they offer a decision milestone or Go/No-Go point. For example, in the "phase-based" relationship process, after the first date you inevitably reach a decision milestone. The date is over, and you need to decide how to proceed. Generally, you have three options:

1. Make another date and invest more time and money in the relationship;
2. Meet for another cup of coffee (repeat the first step) and then make a decision; or,
3. Say goodbye forever (cancel the relationship).

The key to using this decision process successfully is that you need to set up specific criteria for each phase of the relationship and ask yourself the right questions about whether the person meets those criteria sufficiently to continue to the next phase. In other words, based on how the last date went, do you want another date?

A very important point about phase-based decision-making is that there is no stigma attached to a decision. At any point in the process, you can cut your losses and walk away. The commitment is continually contingent on your progressively increasing expectations being met by the end of each phase. The demands and expectations don't diminish, but rather they grow as the investment grows. As you become serious about someone, you expect more and more from the relationship if you're going to continue to invest in it.

For those who say that love is blind, I say that there needs to be a method to our madness. Magnetic attraction doesn't make stable marriages any more than cool ideas make profitable technology companies. In business and in our relationships, rational and orderly ways of exploring these risky opportunities can end up being more successful.

79

Chain Reaction

J ust like a chain reaction, every time you make a decision, more decisions follow. You rarely can make a decision by itself and not have it lead to additional decisions.

Just think about it. Even the most mundane decisions, such as deciding where you're going to go out to dinner with your husband or wife, will lead to other decisions, albeit other mundane decisions. Once you've decided where to go, you now need to decide when you're going to go, how you're going to get there, where you're going to park, what you're going to order to eat and to drink, etc. You know ahead of time that your initial decision will set off this chain reaction. You just don't know yet how you're going to make those follow-up decisions.

We continually face this chain reaction of decisions not only in our mundane, daily decisions, but also in our more important ones. Every time we make an important, life-changing decision, it sets into motion a series of decisions that will follow. In fact, your entire life consists of a series of chain reaction decisions. When you're faced with a major decision and need to choose between option A and option B, for example, choosing the first option will lead you to one path that you will take, and choosing the second option will lead you to a completely separate path. By making one decision, you're setting up the decisions that will follow and, inevitably, the choices that will be available to you.

Just like a chain reaction, while you may be able to anticipate many of the decisions you'll need to make, you don't necessarily know how you're going to make them. When a teenager makes a decision to hang out with a rowdy group of friends, for example, he or she should anticipate that they'll have to make decisions about whether they're going to do things like drink, take drugs, steal, etc. While teenagers should reasonably be able to predict that they're going to face these decisions as a result of the initial decision to hang out with these kids, they may not stop to think about it. Similarly, if you go on a date with someone, you may anticipate that you're going to have to make a decision about whether you're going to spend the night with him or not at the end of the date. You should be prepared to make this decision.

> **Many decisions start a chain reaction. Once you know that, you can work with it.**

When I think about chain reaction decisions, I look at them as being of one of three distinct types of decision chains: the normal decision chain; the good decision chain; and, the bad decision chain. In the normal chain, when you make your first decision, the chain reaction decisions that follow are neither positive nor negative. The good decision chain is begun by a very good decision that is followed by a chain of decisions, each with their own positive ramifications. The bad decision chain, on the other hand, is one that's set in motion by one bad decision, and the chain that follows is a series of decisions that sets you down the bad decision path. This type of decision chain is discussed in the chapter "Creating a Mess."

Nearly all decisions, especially the major ones we make in our lives, are chain reactions. They put into motion a series of decisions that we have to make in the next few hours, days, weeks, or even years. Very rarely are our decisions so cut-and-dried that we're required to make just one single decision, and then it's over. Every decision sets up another decision and, depending upon what option you choose with that decision, it will set up another decision — good or bad. Be aware that this will happen, anticipate the consequences, and embrace the decisions that follow as part of the chain — or don't make the decision.

Many decisions start a chain reaction. Once you know that, you can work with it.

!80

Intuition

When I interview someone for a job, I make a decision on them in five minutes or less. It's all intuition. I can tell right away whether they're the right person for the job. I skim their résumé, take a look at them, ask a few questions, and make an intuitive decision. I'm almost always right — not all of the time, but more than 99% of the time. Of course, I still do make mistakes one out of every 100 times. It's efficient, and to finish the interview makes me feel like I'm wasting my time.

When you make an intuitive decision, you have little idea of why you're making the decision the way you are. You instinctively know what to decide without reasoning. When it comes to certain types of decisions, I'm good at making them intuitively. With others, I'm not so good. But over the years, I've been able to calibrate my intuitive decisions to understand how well I should trust my intuition. How are you at making intuitive decisions?

How do we make intuitive decisions? Some people believe that intuition is a spiritual, mystical, or psychic source within us that guides us to make a decision without any thought or logic. Since there are no logical or rational explanations for how these decisions are made, these people believe that there must be some greater force at work that's imparting the decision.

I believe that we make intuitive decisions when our minds rapidly process a great deal of information, mostly small, unrelated bits of information, to arrive at a decision. It all happens so quickly that we don't know how we got there. The brain rapidly draws on past experiences and external cues and then processes this information at a subconscious level, so we're not aware of any rational thought process taking place. All we're aware of is a feeling that our decision is either right or wrong.

Intuitive decisions can be made based on rules of thumb or pattern recognition. Skill in making intuitive decisions can be refined over time through successes and mistakes. Though it's a powerful decision technique, relying too heavily on intuition has its perils.

Intuitive decisions can be wrong. Sometimes it may be difficult to discern between a gut feeling and a guess. You might just be guessing when you think that you have some great intuition about a decision. Sometimes intuition is just an excuse for sloppy decision-making. You don't want to do the hard work to make a decision correctly, so you just leave it up to intuition. I do this when I make intuitive investment decisions. I see one characteristic such as a great new product, popular interest in the company, a new management team, or a hot market, and then I make an intuitive decision based on that. Later, I find out that there was a lot more that I should have known before I made the decision. Most of the time when making an intuitive investment decision, I'm wrong — I'd say about 75% of the time.

> **Intuitive decisions can be powerful; they happen quickly and easily.**

Some people continually make poor intuitive decisions. Samantha tended to make relationship decisions intuitively, deciding quickly if she wanted to date a man or not. Usually her first impression was based on looks or the way he approached her. But her instinctive decisions were always bad, and she ended up dating losers most of the time. After many years, her friends eventually convinced her that she had poor instincts when it came to men and that she needed to follow a more rational approach when selecting whom to date.

Some physicians make intuitive decisions when they diagnose their patients' problems. Clinical intuition is a skill that's created and refined over many years through experience with thousands of patients. The physician processes information on the patient's problems from medical history, physical examination, diagnostics, blood tests, and many other factors. Intuitively these form a pattern, which the physician may recognize to form a diagnostic decision. This can occur quickly, without any conscious analysis or step-by-step determination.

There have been many cases where physicians decide on a correct diagnosis, but don't have a good idea about why they made that particular diagnosis. In some cases, these intuitive decisions are life-saving. However, physicians also make bad intuitive diagnostic decisions. They may jump to a decision prematurely without collecting all of the necessary information. Their instinctive decision may be unduly influenced by recent cases that were somewhat similar. They may apply some mental templates or rules of thumb and fail to consider other possibilities.

I've learned that if I've made a rational decision, but it doesn't seem right intuitively for some reason that I can't explain, then my intuition is usually right. I review my rational decision to see if there was something missing, and usually there was.

Intuitive decisions can be powerful; they happen quickly and relatively easily. They usually leave you with a sense of confidence that you made a good decision. You don't know how you got there, but you like your decision. They can also be wrong and give you a false sense of confidence. The challenge is being able to tell the difference. I believe that you should try to calibrate your intuitive decision-making by category, just as

I've done in making good intuitive hiring decisions and bad intuitive investment decisions, and just as Samantha did when she realized she made poor intuitive relationship decisions. Know yourself and learn when to trust your intuition and when not to.

81

The Duel

Early on the summer morning of July 11, 1804, Vice President of the United States, Aaron Burr and former Secretary of the Treasury, Alexander Hamilton boarded separate boats in the Hudson River and rowed from Manhattan toward the Heights of Weehawken in New Jersey. At 6:30 in the morning, Burr arrived at the site and cleared it of all brush, preparing it for the day's activities. About 20 minutes later, Hamilton arrived.

A few minutes later, Burr and Hamilton each took a loaded pistol in their hands, stood back-to-back, and began to walk. At 10 paces, they both turned. Hamilton fired his pistol first, in a manner to intentionally miss his enemy. The bullet became lodged in a tree behind and above Burr. Upon hearing the bullet whiz by his head, Burr returned the fire, directing his shot straight at Hamilton. The bullet entered Hamilton in the lower abdomen, just above the right hip. Hamilton was mortally wounded and died the next day.

The duel between Alexander Hamilton and Aaron Burr has become the most famous duel in the history of the United States, but what caused these two men of distinction to decide to take this senseless action? In short, they both made the decision to shoot each other based on pride. Pride clouded their judgment and led them both to make a decision that they likely would not have made if they had thought about it rationally. Hamilton and Burr were, well, mortal enemies. They had been insulting one another for years in writings and in speeches. Shortly before the duel, things came to a head, and Burr challenged Hamilton to a duel. Hamilton quickly accepted.

We all have pride, and that's not always a bad thing. We are proud of our identity, whether that is being proud to be American, proud to be Irish (especially on St. Patrick's Day), proud to be African-American, proud to be Hispanic, etc. Pride is an important emotion for identity and is good in many cases. It's only when pride gets in the way of making a good decision that it becomes a problem. If a major decision is made incorrectly or is hindered by your pride, you need to examine whether it's getting in your way or whether you're happy with being proud and making decisions that may not have the best outcomes.

Pride, however, is not always a hindrance to making good decisions. In fact, pride is quite often a very legitimate factor to consider when making a decision. Sometimes it could even be the most important factor to consider.

Would you rather be broke and proud? Or would you rather have money and swallow your pride? For most people, it usually depends upon the situation.

I'm a very proud person myself, and I know that I've made a number of decisions over the course of my lifetime based largely on this pride. Some of them were good decisions, and some of them were bad decisions. I like to tell myself that if I had to make the same decisions over again, I would consider pride as just one of several factors in these decisions. But in reality, I would most likely still let my pride take over, and that's not a good thing.

Many times, when people make mistakes, they are too proud to admit them. Instead of deciding that they will say, "You know, I made a mistake, and I'm going to fix it," they refuse to admit it. This is usually a bad decision too, and it can lead to serious consequences. As we've seen in other chapters, when you make a mistake, you should acknowledge it and see if there's any way to reverse it and make a better decision the second time. Pride can prevent this from happening.

Steve provides a good example of pride getting in the way of making a good decision. He made a series of mistakes at work that cost his company a large amount of money. One day, he was brought into the office by his boss and pretty severely rebuked for his mistakes. His boss told him he was going to suspend him from his position for one month, and then when he returned, he would be in a probationary position for the next month. Once he proved himself again, he would be returned to his previous position.

If your pride inhibits good decisions, do yourself a favor and get over it.

Steve tried to blame each of the mistakes on some other factor involved, even though he knew that he was responsible. After about 10 minutes of the conversation, Steve knew that he wouldn't be able to face his coworkers when he returned for a probationary period. He had been there longer than many of the others and couldn't face being inferior to them. He decided he would quit on the spot. His pride was the largest factor in his decision, and it ended with him losing his job. A few months later, however, he still hadn't found another position and regretted his decision. He wished that he had simply swallowed his pride and returned to the job that he loved and that paid well. His pride interfered with making the best decision he could in that situation.

So if you're someone who has a lot of senseless pride that hampers good judgment, do yourself a favor and get over it. Don't challenge someone to a duel over something that is not worth it. At the very least, if you can't avoid it, agree on the rules ahead of time, or shoot to kill. Don't let your pride be your downfall.

!82

Somebody's Got to Do Something

Recently, when I went to see a movie, we were about 20 minutes into the film and all of a sudden, the movie just turned all black and stopped. Clearly, there was a problem with the projector, and I presumed that they were working to fix it. All of us in the theater waited for about 10 minutes for the movie to be fixed, but nothing happened. We all assumed someone was fixing it.

I finally decided that I wasn't going to wait any longer, and so I went to find out what was wrong. I found the manager outside having a cigarette and told him that the reel had broken. He said, "Oh, the operator is right here having a cigarette with me." He went back inside, and I returned to the theater. After a few minutes, the movie turned back on, and everyone clapped. I wonder, though, if I hadn't decided to find the reel operator, would we all have just sat there waiting forever? Nobody did anything until I decided to do something.

This brings up an interesting phenomenon that happens occasionally in group settings, particularly in circumstances where you're with a group of people you don't know. A situation may arise where someone needs to act to fix a problem or address some issue that has occurred. Everyone thinks someone else is going to do it, so nobody decides to do anything. Too many people decide not to act because they think someone else will. But who is this mysterious "someone" we're always relying on to act? It could be you. It could be me. It should be all of us.

We've all encountered situations similar to the one I encountered in the movie theater, and when we face these situations, we need to make a decision — are we going to act or are we going to assume someone else will?

While we're driving, for example, we may come across a car accident that's just happened. What do we do? If there are a lot of people around, do we just keep driving, all the while assuming someone else is will do something? Or do we call the police while driving away? We could also stop and see if those in the accident are all safe. Whenever I see an

> **Don't wait for someone else to make a decision. Make it for yourself.**

accident on the highway, unless emergency vehicles are there already, I always make it a point to call the police. It's just a good practice. I know I would want that mysterious "somebody" to call on my behalf if I were in an accident.

Of course, with a situation such as a car accident, we're much more likely to make a decision to act, even if that decision is just to call the police. In a situation with less of a ramification or imminent danger to someone, such as the movie theater, people are much less likely to feel a need to do something, so they make a decision to simply sit there and wait for someone else to make the decision to act.

A well-known theory holds that if someone screams in an alley between apartment buildings in a big city, even if many people look out their windows and see a person clearly in trouble, nobody will do anything. Everybody thinks that someone else will call the police, so nobody bothers.

In society in general, we encounter innumerable problems that we tell ourselves someone else is going to address, so we make a conscious decision to do nothing. Who's going to work to solve poverty, hunger, and homelessness? I'm sure someone's doing something about it. Who's going to address the issues of neighborhood safety in your neighborhood? Someone else. Who's going to work on improving the quality of the public school system or the quality of the health care system? I don't need to, because I'm sure someone else has decided to do it. So who is this someone? Is it you?

Whether you're in an ordinary situation or one in which a person's in danger, what will you decide to do? Will you decide that someone else will make the decision to act? Or will you decide that you're not willing to wait to find out and do it yourself? Sometimes making a decision to act can make a big difference — either to being able to resume watching your movie or to ensure that a car accident victim gets the care and attention they need. Don't wait for someone else to make the decision. Make it for yourself. You are "the someone." Decide that now.

!83

Timing Is Everything

Eighteen percent of teenagers make a decision to not attend college before they even go to high school! And as a result of their decision, they don't take courses to prepare for college or put in the work to get the grades they would need to go to college. They receive career and college counseling while they're in their second or third year of high school, but by then it's already too late for these students. According to a study by Vermont Student Assistance Corporation, this number has increased from one in 10 students to closer to one in five students over the last decade. These students are making their decisions too early — before they have the information they need to make a good decision.

Sam and Rebecca decided in January that they would take a family vacation in March for school break. As they started to make their plans, they found that most everything was booked. They couldn't find good accommodations at Disney World. They couldn't get reasonable flights and had to cut the trip short to go on Monday and return on Friday. In the end, it was less convenient, not as good, and more expensive because they made their decision too late.

There is an old saying that "timing is everything." I think that's true in general, and that it applies to decisions. You need to make your decisions at the right time. If you make them too early you risk making a poor decision because you don't have enough information. If you make them too late you risk reducing, or possibly eliminating, all of your choices.

Here are some techniques to help you get the timing of your decisions right. Before you make a decision, pause and ask yourself if there are advantages to waiting. Will you learn more that could help you make a better decision, or do you know enough now to make a sound decision? Might things change if you wait to make the decision? Is it possible that other options may be available if you wait? You need to weigh these advantages against the costs of delaying. Will some of your options be eliminated if you delay? Are there other costs to delaying?

Will was accepted to two graduate school programs, and he and his wife Cathy needed to decide which one he would attend. They lived in Chicago and one of the schools was local, but the other was in Boston. While Will preferred the one in Boston, it was a bigger decision to move there. They would need to sell their home and either buy or rent one in Boston, and Cathy would need to change jobs. Will had to accept by the end of April, but if they had more time they could better evaluate the issues involved with moving to Boston. They could look at the costs of living in Boston and the feasibility of renting or selling their home in Chicago, and Cathy could look for job opportunities in Boston. They needed to make a nonrefundable deposit of $1,000 at each school. Then it occurred to them that they could buy more time for $1,000 if they registered at both schools. That would give them until July to make the decision. So they bought the opportunity to make a better decision for $1,000.

Make the decision when to decide before making the decision what to decide.

Another technique to improve your decision-timing is to plan your decisions in advance, so that you don't make them too late. Think ahead about the decisions you need to make, such as the vacation example, and put it on the calendar. Write down "make March vacation decision" on the calendar in November the year before, so that you will have more options available. You can do this at the beginning of each year or several times throughout the year.

Many business decisions require the right timing. Decide to launch a new product too late and you miss the opportunity, but decide to launch it too early and you may exhaust your investment before the market is ready. Decide to terminate a disappointing employee too quickly and you don't give him enough time to improve, but do it too late and it may cost more time and money. Decide to make a cost reduction too quickly and you may take away business opportunities, but do it too late and you will lose money.

When considering a decision, think through the timing. Identify several alternative timeframes for making it and then evaluate these alternatives. Make the decision when to decide before making the decision what to decide.

Some decision-timing requires assumptions about what may happen in the intervening time if you delay your decision. Stock investment decisions require timing assumptions. Even after deciding on a stock to invest in, you need to decide when to buy it. Will the price go down after you buy it before it goes up again, or will it continue to go up? You need to make an assumption. Sometimes medical treatment decisions require timing, too. Marco's doctor recommended a hip replacement, but he told him it was his decision, and he could do it when he wanted. Marco had to weigh many factors about when to get the replacement. If he waited, the technology would get better and the hip might not need to be replaced again in the future, but he would continue to be in pain for now. If he did it sooner, he wouldn't have the pain, but it was inconvenient and it might need to be replaced again in the future.

Personal relationship decisions frequently require timing. Jane was ready to make a decision on her relationship with

Julio. She was coming to the conclusion that the relationship wouldn't work long-term, but she still wasn't sure. She was uncomfortable going on any longer, but she did enjoy being with him and they had a vacation planned together. Should she make the decision to break up now before the vacation, or use the vacation to give him another chance? She needed to get her timing right. She decided to wait until after their vacation to make the decision. This would give her some quality time to learn more about him and their relationship.

Timing can be everything when it comes to decisions. Too early and you might get it wrong; too late and you might not have the options. It's always a good time to work on your timing.

84

Running with Lemmings

The lemming, a rodent that lives in northern arctic regions, has been noted to have some very odd behaviors — which can be related to the way people sometimes get caught up in making decisions. The population of lemmings fluctuates enormously, and every four years or so, the population becomes so large that its habitation can no longer support it. In response, they begin a massive migration with tens of thousands — or even hundreds of thousands — moving in a single pack through the woods, fields, and even towns. They have no apparent direction when they leave the safety of their homes in search of another habitation, often becoming vulnerable to predators.

When these lemmings encounter a body of water — even an ocean — they simply keep moving. Being able to swim, they jump in and keep going, regardless of the fact that there is no other side to reach. Before too long, if they aren't eaten by birds, seals, or fish, they inevitably drown. Sometimes they just follow each other off of a cliff. This collective fate reduces the enormous population of lemmings, restoring the ability of the remaining lemmings to survive in their original habitats. Four years later, the phenomenon repeats.

Just like the lemming, people sometimes make decisions solely because they follow others, even though they otherwise would have made different decisions based on their own thinking. These actions are called a crowd- or herd- mentality and can include a wide variety of decisions. They could be violent actions, as in the case of a soccer riot. They could be financial, as often happens when people speculate on investing in an inflated market. They could also be social, which occurs every day in schools when kids decide to follow fads or go along with bullies to tease vulnerable students.

One good example of people making bad decisions and blindly following others was the Internet bubble. As stock of Internet companies began to rise significantly in value after going public, an investing frenzy ignited, with an increasing number of investors deciding to get in on the action. The demand for these stocks skyrocketed, and prices jumped to more than the real value of the companies, but investors continued in their frenzy — just like lemmings. Predictably, the bubble burst, and many people lost money. These investors — many of whom had previously invested conservatively based upon detailed research — followed the pack without making their own decisions. They should have examined each of their investments just as carefully as they had in the past, rather than simply following other lemming-investors whom they saw make millions.

This wasn't an isolated historical example. A similar phenomenon occurred in the Netherlands in the early 1630s with tulip bulbs. When the prices of these bulbs became outrageously high, speculators, investors, and average citizens spent untold sums of money to acquire and resell these bulbs. The affair, known as Tulip Mania, was very similar to the Internet bubble. The cost rose as high as 6,000 florins for a single tulip bulb, at a time when the average yearly income in the Netherlands was only

Peer pressure and the crowd mentality are dangerous to successful decision-making.

150 florins. For years, the high price of these tulip bulbs kept rising, with more and more common people investing their life fortunes in the bulb market. And then the bulb bubble burst with the value dropping precipitously. People had blindly followed others who had made a fortune on buying and selling tulip bulbs without stopping to take the time to understand what they were doing.

We face other, non-financial decisions when we need to determine if we're going to make our own choices or follow the other lemmings off of the cliff or into the ocean. We often make decisions to do things that other people are doing for the simple fact that, either we don't want to be left out, or we think that we're supposed to be doing those things. This can often be found when it comes to children and teenagers. We've all undoubtedly heard a parent tell their child, "If your friend jumped off of a bridge, would you, too?" Children and teenagers will frequently decide to go along with others and do things they otherwise wouldn't decide to do on their own. When good kids decide to drink, smoke, do drugs, or bully other kids just because everyone else is doing it, they are acting just like lemmings.

Running-with-lemmings behavior also happens with various beliefs in society. We sometimes make a decision to believe a theory about something that has been presented by a prominent individual or group without taking the time to think about the theory ourselves. Before it was proven that the Earth revolves around the Sun, for example, anyone who didn't profess to believe that the Sun revolved around the Earth was in trouble. It wasn't until Copernicus came along with proof that it was the other way around that people began to support the correct understanding of the relationship between the Earth and the Sun. (Unfortunately for Copernicus, his theory was denounced by many scientists at the time, and he was condemned as a heretic by the Church.)

Peer pressure and the crowd mentality encourage dangerous decisions. If you consciously decide that you want to do something that others are doing, that's fine; but don't blindly follow others without thinking about the ramifications of your decisions. Sometimes, it's extremely difficult to not get caught up in these actions. The human personality is very prone to going along with the crowd, just like a lemming.

When you're caught up in a crowd situation, the most important advice I can give is to be aware of what you're doing. Unlike many other situations you may find yourself in, it's usually fairly easy to recognize when you're acting like a lemming. The first clue is that you're most likely surrounded by hundreds of other people — either literally or figuratively. While this may be true, these situations are also likely to happen without you realizing it. That's why you act in a way that would be against your normal instincts.

The most important lesson to avoid making crowd-mentality decisions is to have the ability to recognize where you are. If you don't know that you're acting like a lemming, you'll never be able to prevent yourself from falling off of the cliff. If you do find yourself in that position, you should step back and understand that you need to make your decision about whether to run with the lemmings or to break free of them based upon the factors of your own situation, without regard to what the others are doing. You have to live with the ramifications of your own decisions. Don't assume others will be looking out for your own good, or that the goals other people are seeking are the same ones you're seeking. Make your own decisions for your own benefit. Don't make the mistake of falling off of the cliff and drowning in the ocean with the lemmings.

85

The Challenger

At 11:59 a.m. on January 28, 1986, 73 seconds after taking off from Kennedy Space Center in Florida, the Space Shuttle Challenger exploded, breaking into millions of pieces over the Atlantic Ocean and killing all seven crew members on board. It was a very dark day for NASA — and the entire country — and one that has had an enormous impact on the space program in the United States.

The cause of the explosion and the loss of the shuttle and its crew was investigated carefully and found to have originated with a failure in the effective functioning of the O-rings on the shuttle's right rocket booster. The O-rings were designed to enable extremely hot gas to pass by the rings and enter the adjacent external tank during the launch, but the investigation ruled that the design of these rings was flawed. Specifically, the flaw was in how the temperature would affect the structural integrity of these O-rings. As the temperature dropped below 53 degrees, the rings began to fail — a structural deficiency that was fully known by both the contractor who produced them as well as the NASA officials charged with overseeing the launch. But the decision was made to launch the Challenger, despite temperatures well below 53 degrees.

The failure to stop the launch has been widely reported as a failure in the decision-making process used to determine whether a launch should proceed or not. As Chapter 5 of the official commission report begins, "The decision to launch the Challenger was flawed. Those who made that decision were unaware . . . of the initial recommendation of the contractor advising against the launch at temperatures below 53 degrees . . . If the decision makers had known all of the facts, it is highly unlikely that they would have decided to launch."

In other words, those responsible for making the ultimate decision on proceeding with the launch either didn't have accurate information or chose to ignore the sound engineering advice given by its experts. At the time, there were several layers of managers between the contractors and engineers who built and maintained the shuttle and the top managers who were responsible for the overall shuttle program and launch. In subsequent studies of the process that ultimately led to the decision to launch the Challenger on that fateful day, two possible explanations for why the information didn't reach those who needed it are postulated. It is clear that the information existed. Evidence has been gathered that engineers and their managers held a series of meetings — often late into the night — about the effect of low temperatures on the O-rings. The managers who participated in those meetings also had safety meetings with their managers, and in turn, those managers held safety meetings with their managers. At some point, the information didn't get passed on to the top-level decision-makers. The reason for this could be that at some level, someone either deemed that the information wasn't relevant or simply decided for one reason or another not to pass it along. Another theory is that there was a large amount of pressure being placed by top-level decision-makers onto lower-level managers to make the launch happen. In an effort to avoid a delay of the launch, the managers could have simply chosen to ignore any information that would prevent it.

Companies, organizations, and other groups of individuals set up decision-making processes in an effort to make the most effective decisions, but these processes sometimes fail. Quite often, these failures are created by communication breakdowns that prevent necessary information from reaching those charged with making the decision. In a typical example, one company had designed a new product that it had high hopes would be a big success. Initial sales were terrific. The new product was a hit with customers. But the company had problems producing it to meet customer demand. It was designed with an advanced electronic component that **Having the necessary information when making an important decision is crucial.** was scarce (probably one of the reasons customers liked it), and it could be produced only in small quantities. Customers eventually became frustrated that they couldn't get the product and turned to a competitor's product that wasn't quite as advanced but was already available. In the end, the new product was a failure, and a post-mortem showed reports and warnings by engineering that the scarcity of the component would severely limit production. Engineering recommended that the new product be sold initially only in low-volume specialty segments of the market. Sales executives chose to ignore or overlook this in their exuberance for big sales. Unfortunately, stories like this are not unique in complex businesses.

Bad decisions caused by overlooking critical information don't happen only in big organizations. In fact, sometimes they happen even to individuals who make decisions without obtaining the information that would enable them to make the best decision. David's decision to join a new biotechnology company provides an example. He had a promising career and was recruited to a higher-level position in this larger company, but in his excitement, he overlooked some crucial information. The company had been sued by a competitor claiming that it copied one of its most successful products. While the information was clearly public, David failed to do background research on the company. He interpreted the drop in the company's stock as an unexplained opportunity, not as a red flag. Less than six months later, the company had to stop selling one of its most successful products. Revenue dropped in half and one-third of the employees were terminated, including David. Had he stopped to gather this important information prior to making his decision, he could have avoided this.

Having the necessary information when making an important decision is crucial. In companies, it's important to ensure that the decision process isn't flawed in some way. Even for individuals, it's important to make sure that you have all of the necessary information prior to making a decision. Remember the flawed decision process that launched the Challenger, bringing seven brave men and women to their death.

!86

Assumptions

In the late fall of 1812, an army of 700,000 men was assembled for the purpose of invading Russia and conquering its army. Napoleon decided to amass this seemingly insurmountable force and invade the Russian countryside, on his way to occupying Moscow and St. Petersburg. Even though he had such an overwhelming force, Napoleon made a number of faulty assumptions in his decision to invade, which ultimately led to his defeat. First, he assumed that his superior force was well able to thrive and fight successfully in the harsh, Russian winter. Second, he assumed that his large force would be able to adequately provide the required food and supplies as his army advanced. Finally, he assumed that his army would be able to advance quickly, regardless of the poor road system and extreme weather. In the end, he was defeated, with the winter invasion of Russia historically seen as the most colossal military error ever.

We all are forced to make assumptions when we make decisions. An assumption is a factor in a decision that is taken for granted as if it were true or a fact, even though we don't have enough information to consider it fact. As opposed to a fact that is known to be true, an assumption is presumed to be true for the convenience of making a decision. For example, if you are deciding to book a trip on a sailboat, you know the price as a fact, but you must make an assumption about the weather.

Many bad decisions are the result of bad assumptions. A common phrase among computer programmers sums up the consequences of faulty assumptions: garbage in, garbage out. In other words, if you're using faulty assumptions in your decisions, you'll get faulty results. Pauline made this mistake. She invested in the stock of a company because she read that it might be acquired by a larger company. This was an assumption, not a fact. She undertook an investment risk with her assumption. When her assumption proved wrong, the value of her investment dropped 20%.

The most common mistake in making assumptions is neglecting to think about them, or just taking them for fact without verifying them. People frequently tell me, "If I only knew that was the case, then I would have made a different decision." I've seen many times in business where a company decides to make an investment, develop a new product, or make an acquisition, and it turns out to be a bad decision because the management failed to consider a major assumption.

One of the most important things to do when you're making a decision is to write out your assumptions. Simply taking things for granted and not accurately recognizing what it is that you're taking for granted can lead to mistakes. This exercise should take place at the beginning of your decision process — before you've started to consider the decision based upon these assumptions. Then you can verify the accuracy and validity of these assumptions and estimate the risk of your assumptions.

Spelling out the assumptions involved in a decision process can be crucial in a group setting. While there are almost always assumptions that can and should be made under these circumstances, all of the participants in the decision process might not know and agree with them. Laying out the assumptions and agreeing to them at a very early stage will ensure that everyone is on the same page when it comes to actually making the decision, and nobody will doubt the basis for the criteria upon which the decision is made.

Not all assumptions are critical to a decision, so it's important to understand which ones are critical when using them as the foundation for an important decision. Sometimes a faulty assumption may actually have little or no bearing on the decision that you're making, and you should not become paranoid about your assumptions. Some assumptions you just don't have control over. You may need to make an assumption about the weather when planning a vacation or an outside event, but you shouldn't let this paralyze you.

But when you make a critical assumption, you need to be very aware of it as you make your decision. One company did 50% of its business with a single customer, which renewed its contract every year. It was a classic case of "putting all of your eggs in one basket." The company made the assumption that the contract would be renewed each year when it made annual planning decisions. One year it found out the contract renewal was going to be competitive. It lost the contract and almost went bankrupt. The company failed to recognize the risk of blindly assuming the contract would be renewed, and even worse, they failed to recognize the increased risk in the assumption when the contract was competitive.

How do we make assumptions? Frequently they are derived from our perceptions and our experiences. In most cases, more perceptive and experienced people make better assumptions, and groups can combine their experience to make even better assumptions. We also make them based upon experiences that we've had with similar situations, and we assume — correctly or incorrectly — that it will be the same in subsequent situations. One instance in which assumptions commonly fail is when you transfer an assumption you've previously used into a new situation without examining whether that assumption should still apply. Quite often, situations change, and the basis for the decisions that we make changes. Not all assumptions are static, having been one way previously and being different now. It's therefore crucial to examine the accuracy and consistency of a critical assumption every time you use it as the foundation for decision-making.

There are some things that you can do to mitigate against risky assumptions. For example, you can make a tentative decision and implement it fully only once you determine that all of the critical assumptions can be proven to be true. This strategy is employed quite often in business and in purchase decisions. When you buy a house, for example, you may be told by the seller that its condition is excellent, and no work needs to be done. From your first look at the house, you assume this statement is true, so you begin the process of purchasing the house. While the process has begun, your actual purchase is dependent upon an inspector viewing the house and giving an opinion about its condition. You've validated your assumption prior to finally implementing the decision to buy the house.

Many bad decisions are the result of bad assumptions.

Businesses do this all of the time, too. When a company is making an acquisition of another company, for example, the acquired company provides information about its sales, contracts, liabilities, etc. With these assumptions, the purchasing company decides to move forward based on due diligence to validate these assumptions. If these things can't be proven, then the acquisition is canceled, or the terms are changed.

You can put additional steps designed to manage your assumptions into the decision-making process itself. An example: A large laptop computer manufacturer was considering production of a highly durable laptop that could survive rugged use. The company had received a lot of feedback from consumers about their need for a computer that could be dropped or have water or other liquids spilled on it. After spending time looking into the possibility of producing these more durable laptops, the top executives became enthusiastic about the project and were hoping to move forward with it. They realized, however, that they didn't want to simply assume that customers would pay the higher price for these laptops. After analyzing the cost increase, they realized it would cost $2,500 more than their existing computers. They decided to validate this assumption by investing $100,000 in doing consumer research. They found that, while people were excited about these new products, few would be willing to pay the higher price for them. Most consumers who were polled said that instead of paying an additional $2,500, they would rather simply buy a second laptop if the one they owned broke as a result of one of these calamities. The project was abandoned by the executives who had decided to validate their assumption, avoiding a $50 million mistake.

Sometimes you can buy a contingency for an assumption. Tony and Brenda did this when they planned an outside wedding on the ocean. They needed to make an assumption about the weather, which of course they couldn't validate in advance. So they paid $2,500 to reserve an indoor facility for use in case the weather was bad.

On other occasions, however, you may encounter situations where you have to implement all or part of your decision based upon an assumption before it can be validated. In these cases, you need to clearly understand the risks involved when making your decision.

Assumptions are a common and necessary component of decision-making, and you should use them accordingly. Good assumptions can help you make good decisions. Bad assumptions can induce you to make bad decisions. Examine the assumptions involved in your decisions by addressing them head-on and attempting to validate them before you implement your full decision. When you can't validate an assumption, then see if you can develop a contingency. If you can't do either of these, then weigh the risks in your assumptions during your decision process. But above all, don't just ignore managing the assumptions in your decision. And don't invade Russia in the winter.

!87

Bold Moves

A fter doing extensive market analysis, Porsche, a car manufacturer who produced almost exclusively fast sports cars, made a bold move by deciding to produce a completely new line of vehicles. This time, instead of a sports car that could achieve speeds of up to 190 miles per hour, it decided to design and manufacture a sport-utility vehicle (SUV). This was certainly a daring move for a company whose cars, for the most part, had no more than two doors. Eventually the SUV model, called the Cayenne, accounted for a full 45% of the company's new car sales. Porsche made a big decision to make a bold move, and it paid off.

Sometimes, in life and in business, you just have to make a bold move. Bold moves are decisions that are highly risky and have the potential for either great returns or great disaster.

People take bold moves when they believe they need or want to seek out a major change in their lives. A bold move is a big, life-changing decision that you initiate based on your own needs, not a decision that you may be presented with by someone else. You actively take the initiative to seek out major change in your life. While they have the potential to achieve wonderful results in one's life, bold moves also have the potential to result in either adequate — or even terrible — outcomes. Bold moves are inherently risky decisions.

What makes people take bold moves in their lives? Many times, people take bold moves when they are frustrated with their current situations and desire significant changes. Sometimes bold moves are made when a person believes they're not achieving as much as they think they could or should. Sometimes bold moves are simply made out of boredom. And sometimes they're brought on by a major negative change in someone's life — a divorce, losing one's job, the death of a close family member, etc. There is no one reason for someone to initiate a bold move in his life, but many of life's best achievements can be realized through actively making the decision to take a bold move.

Helen had lived and worked in Chicago for her entire life, having a great professional career and marrying her high school sweetheart. She thought things were going well, but over the course of several years, she divorced her husband and became disenchanted with her job. She decided that she wanted more — she wanted a change. She decided to make a bold move. She sold her house, quit her job, and moved to San Diego to pursue a new life. She had no job prospects there, no friends, and no family. Soon after she moved to the new city, however, she got a new job that fulfilled her desire to help others, she made new friends who became some of the best friends she had ever had, and she married a wonderful man and had two children. It was a very bold move — and it paid off for Helen in the long run.

George also decided that he needed a change. He had been working for an insurance company for the previous eight years, and he didn't particularly enjoy it or find it very personally rewarding. One day, he simply decided to quit his job and go back to school. He decided that he wanted to be a teacher instead. While nobody had pushed this on him, and he was relatively happy in general,

A bold move is a major life-changing decision that you initiate based on your own needs.

he made this decision in order to be more fulfilled in his life. He completed school and became a teacher a few years later, and he's glad he did.

But bold moves don't always pay off. They are high-risk, high-reward decisions. Just as investing in risky stocks has the potential for you to make a lot of money or lose it all, bold moves in your life have similar risks of paying off big or being big mistakes. Some bold moves are made without the proper thought assigned to them. They can be impulsive.

Alexandra experienced this. She had dated a guy for about six months, at a time when she was feeling particularly vulnerable in her life. She had a young child from a previous relationship and had recently lost her job. She decided that she needed to make a bold move that she hoped would lead to more stability in her life: She asked her boyfriend if he thought they should get married. He said, "What the heck," and they got married two weeks later in Las Vegas. For the first few months, she was happy with her bold move, but then she started to wonder if it had been too impulsive. Her new husband was just not right for her. He had a good job and provided for them, but he seemed to lose interest in her and disliked having her son around all the time. After almost a year, she decided it was time to make another bold move, and she left her husband and moved back in with her parents, getting a job as a waitress to pay for her son's expenses. Her first bold move didn't pan out, but her second one did. Not only did it solve the problems she was trying to fix by making the first bold move, but it also solved the problems caused by that bold move.

Sometimes bold moves have mixed results. Edith made a bold move that completely changed her life, but she experienced results that were positive in some ways and negative in others. When her father passed away just after she turned 18, she was extremely despondent and decided that she "just needed to get away from everything." While she was scheduled to begin college the next fall, she decided that she needed to make a bold move. One day she simply sold all of her belongings — including the house she had grown up in — and bought a one-way ticket to Asia. She traveled throughout the world for the next three and a half years, having some absolutely amazing experiences. When her money finally ran out, she returned to the United States. Once back, she realized that, while she had a wonderful time wandering around the world, she now didn't have anything and would have to start over. The college she had been accepted to wouldn't provide any financial aid, and she was completely broke.

Bold moves are those decisions that require an enormous change in your life. They often involve the most rapid and dramatic changes that you will ever experience. They are high-risk and have the potential to result in either high rewards or high losses — and most of the time you can't predict which you will get.

Making bold moves often makes your life much better, but when considering a bold move, don't do it impulsively. Just like any other decision, you should make it based upon the facts of your situation. Weigh the costs and benefits of your options. Consider how risky each option is, then make your decision accordingly. Impulsive bold moves are unlikely to result in large payoffs. But calculated bold moves can be some of the best decisions you ever make and can significantly improve your life. Just like Porsche did, you can completely redesign your future for the better with one good bold move.

!88

Forest for the Trees

D o you ever feel like you can't make a decision that you're facing because there are too many details involved? Are you ever in a situation where you're so overwhelmed with all of the aspects of something that you're paralyzed and unable to figure out how to proceed? Do you ever have a problem seeing the forest because you're so focused on the trees?

Many of the decisions that we face in our lives are difficult ones. They have many different moving parts and may consist of many different separate, but intertwined, decisions. Moreover, they also have many factors involved and many potential ramifications that will be realized by making and implementing these decisions. When this happens to you, you simply need to focus on the outcome and disregard all of the other aspects, which are less important than the main decision that needs to be made. Focus is sometimes described as the willingness to sacrifice the important for the more important. Some objectives are just more important than others.

There are many useful applications in life for the phrase "You can't see the forest for the trees." In decision-making, the real lesson is to not get caught in what I like to call "information overload." When you're making a major decision, you may be inundated with so much information that you become paralyzed, or worse, that you make your decision after focusing on what could reasonably be considered the less important factors involved.

A good example of this is when you're forced to make difficult medical decisions. Phil had an ongoing cardiac condition that kept him from exercising and leading the life he wanted. He tried several medications and underwent many tests, but still couldn't resolve the problem. Now he needed to decide what to do next.

His cardiologist presented several options, including surgery, other medications, changes in his lifestyle to mitigate the effect, or just living with it. Phil did a lot of research and talked with his friends and family. Soon he was overwhelmed with information and other factors.

He found many opinions on the Internet from others facing the same situation. Few of them agreed with each other. His friends had no end to suggestions he should try, from changing his diet to meditation to unique exercises. His wife was concerned about the cost of surgery, since not all the medical costs were covered. His coworkers

Focus is the willingness to sacrifice the important for the more important.

wanted to know who would do his work while he was out. His family wanted to know how this would change their plans for their summer vacation.

In the end, Phil decided to step back and see the forest for the trees. The big picture and overriding objective was to eliminate the medical problem and not find ways to manage it. He would deal with all of the other issues the best he could, but he viewed them as a result of having the surgery, not part of the decision to have the surgery. So Phil decided to have the surgery and was glad he did.

Information overload can happen in any number of decisions that we face, from major life-changing decisions to more minor decisions. Ben faced information overload when it came to making a decision about what hotel to stay at when he took his family on vacation to Florida. He began to research a hotel that had been recommended by his friends. He viewed a website with testimonials from people who had stayed there, with a wide range of opinions. He got so involved in reading the more than 250 postings on everything from the size of the bathrooms to the quality of the pizza in the hotel restaurant. After spending several hours reading all of the comments — mostly good, but some bad — he finally snapped out of it and realized that he was far too involved in the details. He needed to step back and make his decision based upon the more important factors, such as the hotel's proximity to the attractions they planned to visit, the amenities available at the hotel, and the price compared to similar hotels. He realized he was being blinded by the trees (the details) and couldn't see the forest (the decision).

To overcome this information overload, it's important to first be able to see that you are there. You begin to look at so many factors of your decision — some important and some less important — that you become frustrated and either don't make a decision or make the decision based upon an incorrect understanding of the outcomes of the decision. Don't pay so much attention to the minor details that you make the decision based on the less important criteria. Keep your attention focused on the major outcomes.

Wendy made this mistake when she went to buy a new car soon after graduating from college. She really wanted this one particular model of car, because it was the "hot" car at the time. Her father, who was helping her to buy it, sat down with her and went through all of the features of this particular model and could see that she really didn't examine the important components of the decision. She was intent on buying the car because it was "cool." He asked her if she really needed a convertible, since they lived in the Northeast, where it snowed much of the time. She replied that she really wanted one. He asked her if the car had enough cargo space, since she would likely be moving at least once in the next few years. She didn't care. She really wanted the convertible. Her father recommended she at least consider other models. She refused and bought the car she wanted. Less than six months later, she realized she had focused on the least important factors of the decision, completely ignoring the more important factors. She wished she hadn't done that and ended up spending a lot of money on repairs for the car over the coming years. Three years after buying it, she finally sold the car and was very glad to be rid of it. She won't make that mistake again.

When you're facing decisions — especially the more important decisions — you need to be sure that you don't get caught up in the minor details. They won't matter in the long run. If you can recognize this, you will never lose sight of the forest because the trees get in your way.

!89

Just Do It

Well, you made your decision, but don't think that the process ends there. Now you have to do it. I often find that people agonize over making a decision, and then when they finally make it, they just don't get around to doing what they decided. Avoid this trap. Once you make your decision, just do it! Here are some insights and advice on doing it.

There are several reasons why people fail to execute their decisions. In some cases they may not really be certain they made the right decision, so in the back of their minds, they think that as long as they don't do anything to act on it, they can always change their minds. When this is the case, they really didn't make a decision. They are just pretending to themselves that they did.

To avoid this, you need to realize that you did make your decision. It's done and over with. Now you need to commit yourself to it. One technique for making this commitment is to announce your decision to others, such as your friends and family. They'll bug you about doing what you decided, and you'll feel guilty if you don't get around to doing it.

Justin is an example of this. He decided to quit smoking several times but never got around to actually doing it. Sure, he tried a little, but he kept putting it off. One day a friend told him about this technique of telling others about a decision. So Justin tried it. He decided to stop smoking and told his family and his coworkers. They all congratulated him on his decision, which of course put more pressure on him to actually do it. This pressure forced him to be more serious about it. He made good progress, although he slipped a few times. His family periodically would ask how he was doing, and this would make him feel like he had to keep trying. At work, it was harder for him to go out for a cigarette break, since everyone knew that he was quitting. This also meant that it was more difficult to succumb to the temptation. After six months, Justin successfully accomplished what he decided to do, and he no longer smoked. He realized that he couldn't have done this without the support of others, which he got once he announced his decision.

Many decisions are simple to implement once they're made. You decided to buy car A instead of B. You just go and buy A. You decided what you want to order for dinner, so you just order it. Other decisions, however, require additional steps to achieve what you've decided to do. With these decisions you need to list the steps to implementing your decision and then work on them. But even before you start this list, I suggest that you determine a date to complete what you decided to do. I call this the "do-it date." This is your target date to achieve the end result of your decision.

Kathy decided that she was going to change jobs. She wasn't satisfied with the way her career was progressing, and she didn't like the company she worked for. She set a "do-it date" of six months. She told herself that she would be in a new job by that time. Next, she listed the steps she needed to take: update her résumé, research companies where she might like to work, define her criteria for a next job, start looking at job listings, etc. This process was very successful for Kathy. She worked diligently on these steps and

> With many decisions, making the decision is only the beginning, not the end.

within five months found a great job opportunity. This was the first time that she worked methodically to implement a decision, and she realized that not only had she achieved what she set out to do, she also mastered a new decision skill.

Some complex decisions require still more decisions to implement what you decided. I sometimes call these initial decisions "destination decisions." You decided where you want to go, but now you face more decisions on how to get there. Let's look at an example. Gloria and Terrance had dated for three years, and after talking it through with each other, they decided to get married. This was a destination decision, and now they had many more decisions to make. The first was deciding when to get married. They decided on a tentative date and then had to decide on the location and availability of an appropriate facility and church. They had to decide on the size of the wedding, the wedding party, the wedding arrangements, etc. By the time they got married, they had made more than 100 important decisions. Many times, one decision — particularly a destination decision — triggers many more decisions before you actually do it.

There are instances where you find that you can't do what you had decided to do. Brett found this was the case when he decided to start his own business. He always wanted to own a flower shop, and now that he was approaching 40, he decided it was time to do it. He left his job and started to do it. This was a destination decision, so once he decided what he wanted to do, he had many more decisions to make. He had to decide on a location, how to finance his business, how many employees to hire, how to market his business, etc. He set a do-it date of four months but found that after six months, he was still a long way away from doing it. It was just much more difficult and expensive than he had realized. Brett then decided that he couldn't do what he decided and gave up. Fortunately for Brett, not only was he able to get his old job back, but the owner told him that he would let him get more involved in running the business. Some decisions are like this. You decide to do something, but then find that you can't do it. Don't be discouraged. At least you tried and worked hard to do it.

With many decisions, particularly the important decisions of your life, making the decision is only the beginning, not the end. Once you make the decision, immediately set a do-it date and list the steps and decisions you need to complete. Then work on it. Just do it!

!90

DecideBetter!

By now, we've covered a lot of lessons and gone through many examples. Hopefully, there were several that you found useful as you read this book. I thought it would be helpful to conclude by reviewing some highlights of the lessons.

- When stymied about making a decision, try flipping a coin. See how you react to its "verdict."
- Don't be like a frog in boiling water. Learn to trigger your decisions before it's too late to get out.
- Don't fall for tricks like Nowor Never, Ucant Havit, or being framed to force you to make the decisions others want. You may, however, want to use them to your own advantage.
- Setting decision deadlines for yourself is important to help you not miss your decision windows.
- Learn from your experiences — especially your bad decisions. Making the same bad decision more than one time is paying twice for the same mistake.
- Make sure that you know where you want to be before you make any decisions about how to get there.

- The way people approach decisions varies by their personalities. Know your decision personality and appreciate the differences in others.
- For important decisions, it can often help to take a two-step approach: First determine exactly what the decision that you have to make is and what the alternatives are; then make your decision at a later time.
- Be careful not to make bad decisions simply because you can get away with them. Sometimes you will regret it.
- When facing an important decision, try it on for size before making it.
- Understand the mathematics of your decisions when the outcome can be determined. Don't get caught underestimating the importance of your decisions.
- Team decisions can be better than individual decisions but not always. Sometimes, teams can compromise the success of decisions. Know the difference.
- Understand when a consensus decision works and when it doesn't.
- Recognize the unique dilemma when you are of two minds on a decision. You may favor both options, but you still have to work toward making the final decision.
- Decisions have unintended consequences. Apply the prudent-person criteria to understand if these consequences could have been anticipated or not.
- Don't throw good money after bad. Look at your sunk costs for what they are and consider new investments of time and money on their own merits.
- Emotional decisions can take control over rational decisions when you are confronted by fear or anger. Be aware of this and work to make your decisions based upon rational thought.
- Not all individuals in group decisions should be considered equal. Sometimes, the individuals in a group may have more or less expertise, and should be treated appropriately.

❶ Don't listen to someone's opinion when it is slanted by his own interests.

❶ Don't throw caution to the wind. Always consider your decisions seriously.

❶ Don't get paralyzed by fork-in-the-road decisions. Otherwise, you'll sit there forever. Make your decision and proceed down your chosen road.

❶ Be careful about being too closed-minded or too open-minded in your decisions.

❶ The Internet is a powerful resource for making better decisions. Use it wisely but be careful not to make your decision based on unreliable information.

❶ Be careful about your decisions being distorted because the grass looks greener. Usually, it looks better, but in reality, it is not.

❶ Be careful about decisions that appear to be simple — sometimes they are deceptively simple.

❶ Realize that you will sometimes have buyer's remorse. Don't fret over your decisions — it's unproductive. But be sure to learn from them, so you can make a better decision next time.

❶ There are situations in life that require split-second decisions. Practice ahead for them, and you'll be able to make them better.

❶ Some people start down a bad path and then are faced with increasingly bad choices that make a mess of their lives. When this happens, sometimes it's best to go back and start over.

❶ When it comes to major life decisions, long and hard is the rule, not quick and easy. You need to spend an adequate amount of time and effort to make the best decisions.

❶ Avoid procrastination. If you delay in working on your decisions, you will prevent yourself from maximizing the results of these decisions.

❶ Break free from indecision by employing the appropriate techniques and moving toward decisiveness.

❶ Everybody has a "decision batting average." How well do you do at making decisions and what is your "good decision average"?

❶ We all face conundrum decisions in our lives, but if you approach them appropriately, you can make them well.

❶ Know when to hedge your bet on some decisions. It can sometimes prevent you from losing big, but not always.

❶ Make routine decisions routine. Don't fret over them — it's just a waste of time and effort.

❶ Do you make your decisions in the right decision lane? Remember that you should periodically review the decision lane you're in to see if you need to change lanes.

❶ In group dynamics, it's best to determine up front who will be the decider.

❶ Spend a lot more time on the more important decisions in your life than you spend on the small ones. Some decisions have much larger ramifications, and you should treat them accordingly.

❶ Understand when you have a White Elephant and only then make your decision to either keep it or get rid of it.

❶ Be prepared to take advantage of an opportunity that you've been hoping for when it crosses your path. Usually, the things we want the most present themselves to us at the least opportune times.

❶ Sometimes you need to make decisions while flying by the seat of your pants. But be sure you're prepared for it and only do it when it's appropriate and necessary.

❶ Making decisions one step at a time by using a phase-by-phase process works very well in project or investment decisions and sometimes even in relationship decisions.

❶ Some decisions are like chess: You need to anticipate

the possible reactions to your decisions several moves ahead.

❶ In any complex decision, the pros and cons of different alternatives cannot be present in the mind at the same time, so write them down.

❶ Sometimes you will benefit from a more structured and disciplined approach to your decisions. Following the appropriate structure will help you make your complicated decisions more successful.

❶ Calculate the risks associated with your decisions. You'll better understand the importance of these decisions.

❶ As emotions begin to seep into decisions, rationality begins to seep out. Don't make your decisions irrationally.

❶ Perform a decision autopsy after you've implemented your decisions. It will help you learn from them — both your good and bad decisions.

❶ Stick by your principles when making decisions. If you do that, you will be able to make your decisions easier and more consistently.

❶ Understand when you're good at making decisions based on your intuition and when you're not. Everyone is innately better at making certain decisions intuitively than others.

❶ The price you pay for having a voice in group decisions is a commitment to support the decision reached by the group. Don't undermine a group decision by doubting it after it's been made.

❶ Strategic decisions are those we need to make today in order to achieve something we want in the future. You need to know when to make them, otherwise you will be too late.

❶ Frequently, the best decision is an alternative you hadn't considered, so take the needed time to generate and refine every appropriate alternative.

❶ Be careful when people are pushing you into making

specific decisions. They may have outside motives that are clouding their judgment.

❶ Be sure that your objectives are clear before you make a decision. Succinct and accurate objectives can make the difference between a decent decision and a great decision.

❶ There are several different ways to evaluate your alternatives based on the positive and negative consequences of each option.

❶ Not all of the consequences of your decision are equal, so don't consider them to be. Weigh the more important consequences more heavily in your decision than you weigh the less important ones.

❶ When making major decisions, don't get caught up in the minutia of the details and lose sight of what's truly important.

❶ Keep your eyes open for once-in-a-blue-moon opportunities. They may change your life forever.

❶ Don't run with lemmings, because you could find yourself jumping off of a cliff with them. Make your own decisions.

❶ When you make a decision, just do it. Don't doubt yourself.

❶ Decision processes sometimes fail because critical information is ignored. Don't ignore information because of external or internal pressures or carelessness. It could be disastrous.

❶ Sometimes in life you need to make bold moves that significantly alter the course of your future. Just make sure you don't make bold moves impulsively.

❶ We all use assumptions to make decisions, but flawed assumptions inevitably lead to flawed decision-making. Carefully evaluate the basis for your assumptions and determine whether you will use each as a foundation for making your decision.

❶ Better decision-making skills will inevitably lead to a

better life. By improving how you approach and make your decisions, you will improve the outcomes of these decisions and realize the full potential of all of your actions.

Hopefully, these lessons have been useful to you in working to improve how you make decisions for yourself and those you care about. Better decisions lead to a better life.

Michael E. McGrath
Decide**Better!**
Improve Your Life Through Better Decisions

DecideBetter.com Website and Community

The rapidly growing DecideBetter! website was launched in 2007 as an additional practical resource for anyone who wants to make better decisions. It features a sample of the decision-making lessons found in the first edition of *DecideBetter! for a Better Life*. Some of the other invaluable resources available at DecideBetter.com include:

❶ "Ask Michael," a section that allows users to ask a decision question and get advice;

❶ Quizzes and decision polls that ask DecideBetter.com visitors to test their decision-making skills and compare them to others;

❶ Rapidly expanding collection of tailored decision worksheets that can be downloaded for making and expediting specific decisions;

❶ DecideBetter! America, a promotional program to help American voters make better decisions in the upcoming election; and,

❶ Other on-going valuable resources designed to help individuals improve their decision-making skills.

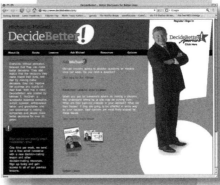

Visitors to DecideBetter.com are asked to register with the site in order to access and download free resources, plus they can also sign-up to receive weekly e-mail newsletters. These updates include featured lessons, selections from the "Ask Michael" section of the website, and information about new features and resources on the site.

For Business

Businesses succeed or fail based on their decisions. Yet most businesses don't focus on decision-making as a core competency because it is complex and subtle. *DecideBetter! for Business* provides a comprehensive and practical guide to all aspects of business decisions, including: the types of decisions, how they should be made, who should make them, techniques and worksheets for making them, the classic business decision-making mistakes, how management processes make decisions, how teams should and shouldn't make decisions, the organizational and political biases of decisions, and many more. This book is an essential reference and guide for anyone who makes decisions in a company and is the best investment a company can make in its success.

For Relationships

Relationship decisions consistently prove to be one of the most challenging, yet critically important, areas of decision-making in our lives. From the moment you wake up, hundreds of decisions are made that will impact the harmony of your relationships and the quality of your life. *DecideBetter! for Relationships* is designed to help improve how you approach and make your relationship decisions, including your personal relationships, your friendships, and your professional relationships. It is also designed to help you achieve the outcomes you desire. These decision-making lessons are provided in short, insightful chapters that will help you quickly understand the various decision pitfalls that we all encounter in our relationships and how to avoid them. Better relationships, through better decisions, are something we can all strive towards, and this book is the ultimate resource for how to accomplish that.

For College

Every year, students leave the comforts of home for college and are thrust into making countless new decisions compounded with academic stresses and social pressures. *DecideBetter! For College* can help students with all aspects of their college experience – from deciding which college to attend to what major to study, right on through to what to do post-graduation. These lessons are presented in short, insightful chapters that are easy and humorous to read. No college student should leave home without it.

For Conferences, Events, Training Seminars, Workshops and Consulting Services

Would you like to take your business, organization, or personal life to the next level of better decision-making? Better decisions are the key to a more successful business organization and the secret to a more successful life. What better way to help your audience or conference attendees benefit from a keynote speech than to help them make better decisions?

This presentation by Michael E. McGrath, founder of DecideBetter!, is a witty, entertaining keynote speech that's fun and useful for any audience. Drawing on the lessons from DecideBetter!, and his vast life experiences, each presentation is custom-fit to cover a wide range of decision-making tips and advice based on each audience. The presentation can also be custom-designed to draw on decision-making skills and goals important to a specific industry or organization. Each audience member will not only find the presentation fun and interesting, but will have learned something that can help them immediately to be more successful.

For information, pricing, and availability about conference or event keynote speeches along with customized Training Seminars, Workshops, and Consulting Services, contact DecideBetter!

Decision-A-Day Calendar — Accomplish Your Three Most Important Decisions Everyday!

DecideBetter! is proud to introduce the Decision-A-Day Calendar, designed to encourage those who want to make better decisions in their everyday lives, beginning immediately. Each day includes an inspirational, humorous, or otherwise instructional quote about decision-making. These daily insights provide a quick lesson on how to make better decisions and the effects of those decisions. Each day features a section to write the three most important decisions of the day. Users of the calendar are encouraged to look ahead to future dates and create decision deadlines. This is an example of one of the many decision-making support resources and add-on tools that are available at DecideBetter.com.

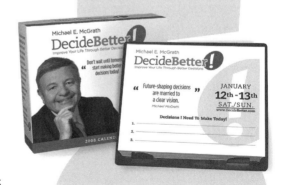

About Michael E. McGrath

Michael E. McGrath is the creator of DecideBetter! and the author of the book *DecideBetter! For a Better Life*. He is an experienced management consultant, business executive and visionary, entrepreneurial leader, author, and family man who has studied and applied decision-making for more than 25 years. Michael is a renowned business consultant and successful turn-around expert, teaching decision-making techniques and processes to top leaders and executives. With DecideBetter!, he now brings that impressive experience to everyone.

He created the PACE™ process for use in making effective decisions in new product development, which today is used by more than 1,000 global companies. He has also applied his decision-making skills as a CEO. He retired as CEO and President of i2 Technologies in July 2007, after leading the turnaround of i2 over the previous two years. In 1976, Michael co-founded Pittiglio Rabin Todd & McGrath (PRTM) and served as managing director until his retirement in July 2004. Under his leadership, PRTM grew to be one of the most successful management-consulting firms in the world. He currently serves as Executive Chairman of the Thomas Group.

Michael has authored five books prior to *DecideBetter! For a Better Life*. In 1994, one of these books, *Product Strategy for High-Technology Companies,* became one of the leading strategy books in the world. It was updated and expanded in 2000, and his books have been translated into several other languages. In addition, Michael has published more than 500 articles and given more than 600 speeches at conferences, industry association meetings, universities, and client seminars. In January of 2007, Michael was featured in Forbes Magazine for his CEO decision-making and turn-around skills.

Michael has established a reputation as a strong, yet personable and witty, decision-maker and credits much of the success in his life to making better decisions. He also studied decision-making principles for more than 25 years and developed practical decision-making techniques that he has shared with friends, family, and business associates. He created DecideBetter! to further develop successful decision techniques and promote these through books and other media to help others make better decisions. Michael currently serves on the board of directors of four corporations and four non-profit organizations. He has a B.S. in computer science from Boston College and an M.B.A. from Harvard Business School.